I AM NO GUIDE
PEARL JAM
SONG BY SONG

BRIAN STIPELMAN AND
BRANDON RECTOR

FONTHILL

For Frank Parisan, dirtyfrank0705, without whom this book would not exist.

'We were but stones. Your light made us stars.'

Fonthill Media Language Policy

Fonthill Media publishes in the international English language market. One language edition is published worldwide. As there are minor differences in spelling and presentation, especially with regard to American English and British English, a policy is necessary to define which form of English to use. The Fonthill Policy is to use the form of English native to the authors. Brian Stipelman and Brandon Rector were born and educated in the United States; therefore American English has been adopted in this publication.

Fonthill Media Limited
Fonthill Media LLC
www.fonthill.media
office@fonthillmedia.com

First published in the United Kingdom and the United States of America 2024

British Library Cataloguing in Publication Data:
A catalogue record for this book is available from the British Library

Copyright © Brian Stipelman and Brandon Rector 2024

ISBN 978-1-78155-908-6

Typeset in 10pt on 13pt Sabon
Printed and bound in England

Foreword

Some Opening Thoughts from Jason Kerepesi

Pearl Jam is community.

The band has underscored that sentence since day one, not only with their ability to understand you to your core by playing music to you, but with their activism as well. In the early days, this community of fans, and its sub-communities, evolved in interesting ways. I use the word evolve because in the early to mid-'90s, you could not easily connect with fans and foster relationships built on Pearl Jam.

To paraphrase Boromir from *The Lord of the Rings*: "One does not simply log on..." At least not until the end of the decade.

Enter the message board forum!

While the official Pearl Jam message boards have existed since before the millennium, for whatever reason I never really engaged with that group. I honestly couldn't tell you why. But in 2001, I stumbled upon a fan site that offered intriguing content I could not find in the usual places. Reviews and song-by-song breakdowns. News buried by other larger publications. It was as if one of those big rock magazines decided to focus only on Pearl Jam (yes, please). That site was (and is) theskyiscrape.com.

I noticed early on this funny little cartoon in the top right corner with the text "Red Mosquito Forum."

"Ok," I thought, "let's give this forum a try."

I was consumed. I lived on those boards. I clicked on every thread and would read and reply for hours. I posted thousands of times. What else was a college kid supposed to do with his free time—party and flirt with girls?

Eventually, I found a happy balance of being a regular college kid and being a Pearl Jam nerd. But the hours I spent getting to know the people behind the usernames, the ones who made me laugh, made me think, and sometimes even made me rage was—no joke—a significant agent of change for me as a human still developing their character.

Talking with the people on those boards and reading the posts on the The Sky I Scrape were a part of my daily routine. When *Riot Act* came out, I was enthralled, engaged, and educated by the song reviews and analysis Stip would post. I hit F5 at least a few times an hour to see if Brandon had posted any updates or new articles relating to the new album. And I deepened the relationships I had made on the Red Mosquito boards as each bootleg dropped in the winter, spring, and summer of 2003.

As the years went on, the time I spent on The Sky I Scrape and Red Mosquito became a little more sporadic. But when there was new Pearl Jam music, or a new tour was closing in on our community, I would always find my way back. Sometimes for communal games like March Madness—where we would all vote on songs deployed into a tournament-style bracket not unlike the college basketball tournament. There were even song contests where one could record a Pearl Jam cover and have it voted on. This eventually turned into covers of other artists. The relationships further deepened as I started collaborating with other users on songs for these friendly tournaments.

For the last four years, my friend, Paul, and I have put everything we know and feel about Pearl Jam and its communities down in ink, so to speak, with our podcast *State of Love & Trust*. I do not remember exactly when the idea came to me, but at some point, I remembered Stip's reviews and how he helped me to understand the songs I loved better, even if I did not understand why I loved them. "Get him on the show," I thought.

Luckily for all of us, he obliged. Stip has been a recurring guest since that first appearance, even joining me in Austin, Texas, in 2023 as a fill-in co-host for a live podcast ahead of Pearl Jam's final concert of that year. The event was hosted by the fan-run nonprofit Wishlist Foundation, which has hosted pre-concert fundraising parties for twenty years. The music and activism of Pearl Jam were coming full circle in my life and in a profound way.

But Stip is just one great example of what the community he and Brandon created over at The Sky I Scrape and Red Mosquito is comprised of. Some of those other usernames became friends in real life, just as Stip has. This kind of relationship building is not unique to their website or forum, mind you. It is happening everywhere around the world, and we have Pearl Jam to thank for igniting the spark that sent us on our journey to find our own sub-community—our own tribe.

This one just happened to be mine, and I am thankful for that.

When Stip told me he and Brandon would be writing a book—a forever, tangible version of what I had been reading on the website for years—I was both unsurprised and ecstatic at the same time. It made all the sense in the world to write a book that could enshrine their analysis of Pearl Jam's music between two hard covers.

Pearl Jam is community, and these two gentlemen have been shepherds of my particular sub-community for over two decades. We all chose ours because, in some ways, we felt lost. Brandon and Stip are no guides, but they are by my side.

And Some Additional Thoughts from Paul Ghiglieri

In the summer of 2010, Pearl Jam was experiencing a renaissance of sorts. They had just released *Backspacer* nine months prior, a critically acclaimed album that would be nominated for a Grammy Award for Best Rock Album the following year. There was a heavily promoted deal with Target to be the exclusive stateside big-box retailer for the album, followed by the end of the European leg of the tour in June that marked the final stretch of a return to prominence for the band with their ninth studio album.

That same summer, Brandon Rector from The Sky I Scrape sought to channel the creative energy of the Red Mosquito forum fan members to inject more life into the site. Serendipitously, Stip had just posted an intro to a song-by-song review of *Binaural*, and the road was paved. What followed was a weekly series taking visitors to the site through Pearl Jam's nine (and future) studio albums, one song at a time. While every new release from the band warrants endless spins on the turntable (or car stereo), extended plays of a new Pearl Jam record invariably led to months of revisiting the entire catalog. Stip's weekly series had become a near requisite accompaniment to every Pearl Jam album.

Each song review opened a portal by which you could almost rediscover Pearl Jam's music for the first time. Stip's reflective meditation on the depth and breadth of every track helped paint a portrait that somehow reimagined each song. He thought he was trying his best to capture the essence of impactful art. I wonder if Stip realized he was making impactful art himself, and Brandon provided the forum for him to do so.

I have long admired Stip and Brandon for always contributing in ways that helped augment the greater Pearl Jam community. While not the architects of that community, they have nonetheless played pivotal roles in building aqueducts to convey even more substance and meaning behind the band's music.

Truthfully, Stip's work helped inspire me to trust my own voice and join Jason in forming the *State of Love and Trust: A Pearl Jam Podcast* during the pandemic in 2020 to channel our dialogue across the fertile valley of the fan community surrounding the band. While discussing the song "River Cross," on episode 165 of our show (7/11/23), I read aloud Stip's eloquent TSIS review of the track in its entirety and had the following to say: "Stip, your review of this song is more moving to me than the song itself."

It has been an honor and a privilege having Stip on the show frequently as a guest. Unsurprisingly, the show is always elevated by his presence.

Shortly after the release of *Dark Matter*, David Hudson from the *State of Amorica: A Black Crowes Podcast* sent a group text to me and Jason. It read simply: "We don't deserve this album." After careful consideration, I may have the audacity to beg to differ, and I will use a few of Stip's words from his TSIS review of "River Cross" to underscore why:

> We are the promise he is singing of. And for every act of horror the world inflicts on us, or we inflict on each other, it is offset by acts of kindness and impossible love. And they always have been. And as long as we don't lose sight of that we can make it. Absent any other touchstone we still have each other.

Enjoy this deep dive into Pearl Jam's music. It is the touchstone of contemplative review that a passionate and dedicated fan base deserves. And if you are new to Pearl Jam's music or only now just returning to it after a long sabbatical, pay no mind to the misleading title of this book.

For you have found in Stip and Brandon the perfect guides.

Jason Kerepesi and Paul Ghiglieri
Hosts of *State of Love and Trust* podcast
Los Angeles, CA, and San Diego, CA
May 2024

Acknowledgments

We are grateful to all the brilliant fans on the Red Mosquito forum who have kept us company for twenty years appreciating, arguing, dissecting, and ranking Pearl Jam. Their influence and insight are present throughout *I Am No Guide*, and those conversations have shaped our love and appreciation for Pearl Jam in countless ways. From the ashes of Mother Love Bone...

Thank you to Jasper Hadman, Josh Greenland, and everyone at Fonthill Media for giving us the chance to write this book, and believing in it enough to delay publication for the inclusion of *Dark Matter*.

After a lifetime of fandom, there are far too many people to name and acknowledge, but Brian is especially grateful to Joseph Clark, Brian Dahlen, Neil Davey, Kevin Davis, Karen Koehler, Carey LaManna, Cory McMillen, Brett Nelson, Jared Stipelman, and Kristi Waters for reading chapters of the manuscript. Thank you to Jason Kerepesi and Paul Ghiglieri at the *State of Love and Trust* podcast for keeping me motivated throughout the writing, and for generally treating *Backspacer* with the respect it deserves.

Eli Triona, for giving me the chance to become a moderator on Red Mosquito, and to Brandon for offering up The Sky I Scrape's main page as a platform for my ramblings—and for suggesting the idea of this book a decade before we wrote it.

My amazing wife, Hilary; my wonderful daughters, Ellie and Mia; and all my friends and family who have indulged my love of this band, especially during the imperial phase of my fandom.

And Pearl Jam, for surviving and thriving, and for being the background soundtrack of my life every step of the way.

Brandon would like to thank his beautiful, supportive wife, Aimee, and his three kids who put up with endless hours of Pearl Jam music and gossip. Chris Phillips, who was enthusiastically behind me throughout the inception of this book even years ago. Members of our forum, ridleybradout, Johnny Busher, Michael Costa, and Alex, for your work to keep all of us in the best sounding and best versions of everything Pearl Jam has ever played. It was a giant part of making this book possible.

Nick Korte, Eli Triona, Chris Barr, Shannon Walsh, Angi Hale, and Joseph Clark, my comrades in arms and the people who gave me the reigns to become part of the "Pearl Jam Illuminati."

Those who provided inspiration and gracious support, the crew behind Two Feet Thick; John Reynolds, Kathy Davis, and Jessica Letkemann; Guerilla Candy's Travis Hay; Victor Nogales; and Donny Anderson.

And, of course, Pearl Jam, for supplying me and my friends with hours upon hours of the greatest music imaginable and an endless source of discussion, arguments, lists, and rankings.

Brian Stipelman and Brandon Rector
Frederick, Maryland, and Chapel Hill, North Carolina
May 2024

Contents

Introduction

One of the last surviving, and arguably greatest, of the grunge bands that emerged in the 1990s, Pearl Jam always lacked the cynicism and despondency of their contemporaries. Their music never wallowed in its pain, never leaned into escapism, and never gave up, no matter how pressing the darkness around it was. Largely absent was the desperation of Alice in Chains, the jagged edges of Nirvana, and the tectonic scope of Soundgarden. Instead, looking to their mentors, Pearl Jam offers the clarity of purpose of U2, the questing uncertainty of R.E.M., the humanism of Bruce Springsteen, the textured distortion of Neil Young, the reckless energy of punk, and the transformational sweep of the '60s and '70s classic rock era.

Pearl Jam understands that true solidarity cannot have an "us" and "them," and, thus, Pearl Jam is the rock and roll manifestation of "we." That is partly the source of their enduring power, but it is not the whole story. From the opening notes of "Once," to the closing notes of "Setting Sun" thirty years later, Pearl Jam's music is an ongoing journey of self-discovery that attempts to carve meaning from the absurdity of suffering and the beauty of love.

Their incredible success and remarkable legacy were hardly foregone conclusions. Pearl Jam was the last of the major Seattle grunge bands to find their audience. Alice in Chains' debut record *Facelift* was the first to hit gold on September 11, 1991. Nirvana's *Nevermind*, released on September 24, 1991, became a generation-defining phenomenon on the back of "Smells Like Teen Spirit," and dethroned Michael Jackson's *Dangerous* at the top of the *Billboard* charts in January 1992. At the same time, Soundgarden's *Badmotorfinger* (October 8, 1991) was nominated for the Grammy Award for Best Metal Performance, as was its predecessor, *Ultramega OK*.

Pearl Jam was born simultaneously as a new band and an elder statesman of a burgeoning musical movement. Founding members Stone Gossard (guitar) and Jeff Ament (bass) were in the pioneering Seattle band Green River, whose sound produced the "grunge" descriptor applied to seemingly every Seattle rock band and fellow traveler of the '90s. When Green River broke up in 1988, Stone and Jeff's follow-up group, Mother Love Bone, was one of the first bands in the Seattle scene to sign with a major label. Tragically, singer Andrew Wood's death by heroin overdose ended the band shortly before the debut of their first album, *Apple*.

Stone processed Wood's death by writing and eventually joined up with Seattle-area guitarist Mike McCready to record demos of darker, more aggressive material—songs that would eventually become "Alive," "Once," "Footsteps," "Black," "Breath," "Even Flow," "Animal," and "Alone." At Mike's insistence, Jeff was brought in to play bass, along with Soundgarden (and future Pearl Jam) drummer Matt Cameron. Hoping he would sign on as the permanent drummer of this nascent band, they sent a tape of five demos to former Red Hot Chili Pepper band member Jack Irons. Jack declined—eventually joining in late 1994—but passed along the demo to a young San Diego singer named Eddie Vedder.

What followed has achieved mythic status in Pearl Jam lore. After completing a late-night shift at a gas station spent listening to the demos, Eddie went surfing, and alone in the vastness of the ocean, wrote the lyrics to "Alive," "Once," and "Footsteps." He recorded vocals, returned the tape, and within a week had joined the band.

He arrived in Seattle in mid-October 1990 just as Stone, Jeff, Mike, and Matt were in the studio with Chris Cornell (Andrew Wood's roommate) recording *Temple of the Dog*, in tribute to Wood. When Eddie arrived, Chris was struggling to turn a single verse into a coherent song. In another moment of mythmaking, Eddie cautiously stepped up to the mic, sang Chris's words back to him, and created the duet "Hunger Strike"—the album's single and Eddie's first official release as a vocalist, eventually peaking at No. 4 on the *Billboard* Mainstream Rock Tracks chart (over a year after its initial release).

With Dave Krusen on drums, the band adopted the placeholder name Mookie Blaylock (named after the NJ Nets basketball player) and played their first show in October 1990, less than a week after forming. They would open for Alice in Chains later that year and, finally, took the name Pearl Jam after signing with Epic Records. Jeff suggested the name Pearl, with the Jam added after attending a Neil Young concert.

Pearl Jam's debut album, *Ten*—Blaylock's number—was recorded in March 1991, and Krusen left the band not long after, eventually being replaced by Dave Abbruzzese. Dave, the only person to involuntarily leave the band, would in turn be replaced by Jack Irons in 1994. Jack then left in 1998, and Matt Cameron stepped in following Soundgarden's breakup. Matt has been their drummer ever since, restoring the band to the original lineup that first recorded the demos sent to Eddie.

Ten was released a month before *Nevermind* (August 27, 1991), but it took time to find its audience. By 1992, their popularity exploded on the strength of intense live shows and radio hits like "Even Flow," "Alive," and "Jeremy." *Ten* entered the Top 10 of the *Billboard* Top 200 by May 30, 1992, peaking at No. 2. By February 1993, *Ten* was outselling *Nevermind,* and the two bands were canonized as twin icons of a revolution in rock music.

In 1993, Pearl Jam was the biggest rock band in the world, and their follow-up record, *Vs.*, became the fastest-selling album of all time, selling almost one million copies in its first week, more than the rest of the *Billboard* Top 10 combined—a record that would stand for five years until Garth Brook's 1998 album *Double Live.* For comparison's sake, Nirvana's follow-up, *In Utero,* sold 180,000 copies in its first week. This achievement is even more remarkable considering Pearl Jam's decision to stop making music videos—"Jeremy" would be their last until 1998's "Do the Evolution." They also refused to actively promote their music outside of live performances and rare interviews. Pearl Jam's third album, *Vitalogy,* was written on the road and released just over a year after *Vs.* It became the second fastest-selling album of all time after *Vs.*, moving almost 900,000 copies in its first week despite a far more abrasive sound. Its vinyl pre-release became the first vinyl album in ten years to chart on the *Billboard* 200 at No. 55. From 1992–1995, Pearl Jam was an inescapable cultural phenomenon.

Just as quickly—arguably by design—Pearl Jam morphed into something more akin to the world's largest cult band. 1996's *No Code* leaned even more heavily into the exploratory, anti-commercial instincts of *Vitalogy,* and from that point on, Pearl Jam's music never again enjoyed the effortless ubiquity of the early '90s, when songs like "Black" and "Better Man" could become massive hits despite never being released as singles, and with virtually no promotion.

Post *Vitalogy*, Pearl Jam was known for the idea of Pearl Jam as much as their music. They built and sustained a reputation as one of the world's great live bands, replacing the ferocity of earlier performances with a live experience that felt as much a revival as a rock concert—playing marathon shows, never repeating a set list, and drawing from the entirety of their catalog. They built an intimately reciprocal relationship with their fans, and the power and meaning of their songs were transformed by their shared experience. This reputation was cemented in 2000 when they began the practice of commercially releasing almost every live performance. Additionally, they twice set a record for the most albums on the *Billboard* 200 by a single band, with five European and, later, seven U.S. shows.

Besides the live experience, Pearl Jam was known for their non-hierarchical spirit and willingness to nurture new artists and bring exposure to veteran acts that never quite made it big. They became a byword for integrity within the industry and were renowned for their unapologetic progressive politics. Above all, they were defined by their unwavering belief in the transformative power of music. While their first ballot induction into the Rock and Roll Hall of Fame in 2017 was clearly on the back of their early records, Pearl Jam has avoided becoming a legacy act, and each new album is greeted by fans with the potential to be as consequential as what was released during their imperial phase.

Although Pearl Jam is greater than the sum of its parts, Eddie Vedder, through the power and intimacy of his voice and writing, provides the clearest entry point into understanding Pearl Jam's music. Ronen Givony, in *Not for You: Pearl Jam and the Present Tense,* offers a summary of Eddie's point of view:

> His lyrics tend to be about people confronting ordinary circumstances and falling short—out of fear; duty; or inertia. The problems that his characters face are inevitably the hardest of all: how to let go of the past, how to persist in the face of suffering; and how to grow with grace. His protagonists evolve, by the end of the lyric—but just barely. His lyrics work best when you can feel him reaching for the empathy, insight, and predicament of other people. To these qualities he adds an optimism, a sincerity, and an absence of irony that were unusual in the early '90s and uniquely all his own.[1]

Pearl Jam's music is defined by its empathy, its humanism, and its solidarity. It is emotionally complex but never oblique, and its sentiment is unapologetic. Eddie's lyrics are "startlingly intimate, the mark of a writer who feels everything he sees."[2] Each song exists as a statement, free of cynicism, resentment, and detachment. Animating Pearl Jam's music is a bone-deep conviction that any locked door can be opened, and even our darkest moments are illuminated by a faith that we can rise above them.

Pearl Jam's empathy helps them avoid some of the excesses of the grunge genre despite the epic scope and sweep of their anthemic moments. The listener is invited to be a fellow passenger in the emotional journey rather than observing or undertaking it in parallel. Eddie's power as a writer, performer, and icon is in his ability to convey a singer-songwriter's authenticity and intimacy at scale.

Pearl Jam's music builds and strengthens solidarity in a world that undercuts it. It welcomes anyone who arrives in good faith. For a politically engaged band, their music contains little judgment, and when it occasionally does, it is ill at ease within the larger catalog. Pearl Jam's music is best experienced as a journey, a decades-long search for meaning. Initially, there were no promises of discovery, just the commitment to search together, and a deeply rooted faith that answers are out there. Over time, there emerges a growing confidence in the wisdom derived from the experience of the journey, and a need to share what has been found along the way.

The character of the music is only part of its enduring resonance. Pearl Jam explores the same core set of themes over the life of the band, asking and answering the same questions in response to the ever-shifting context of their personal lives and our shared experiences. Each album exists in a conversation with itself while questioning and reassessing the conclusions of earlier records. Their music processes anger, grief, and disappointment over our personal and shared failure to live up to our expectations for each other and ourselves. Our biggest collective sin is stripping our fellow travelers of their humanity, and Pearl Jam's long history of social and political action, including their pro-choice, pro-democracy, pro-environmentalism, feminist, and anti-war commitments, is best understood in that context.

Pearl Jam's music recognizes we are all lost and in need of a guide. It is focused on creating unity, forgiving ourselves for not being better than we are, and never losing faith that someday we might be. This faith adds a level of catharsis to Pearl Jam's darkest moments—even at our lowest, there is a refusal to submit, a driving need to keep pushing knowing something better waits for us. Their music argues love is the grounds of solidarity, and the need to be worthy of it compels us to resist the absurdity of our world.

Beyond that core commitment, Pearl Jam's music is skeptical of answers and finds uncertainty empowering. It imbues the necessarily unknowable with a sense of possibility, a blank canvas upon which we can dream. And, once the music begins to draw conclusions, it flips the script, with later albums reexamining those same questions and themes with new concerns about legacy so that we can avoid reproducing the same mistakes. Pearl Jam's later work strives to pave the road the next generation must travel so that their journey might be a little easier.

I Am No Guide

I Am No Guide is a detailed exploration of Pearl Jam's central ideas and themes, and their evolution across the arc of the band's career. It tells the story of the music. This is not a history of Pearl Jam, though it is informed by that history. We assume the reader shares at least a passing familiarity with the band. If not, a few minutes on Pearl Jam's Wikipedia page can tell you everything you will need to get started, and Cameron Crowe's *Pearl Jam Twenty* documentary is also highly recommended. Instead, this book is a map of sorts, a way to revisit old songs in new ways and contextualize each moment within the larger catalog.

It is focused on the journey chronicled in the primary albums. We do not explore the songs that did not make it onto Pearl Jam's first twelve albums unless those B-sides or outtakes provide further insight into the larger discussion or are too important to ignore.

So much of Pearl Jam's identity is bound up in their approximately 1,000 live shows, each one a unique set list and experience. As Cameron Crow notes in *Pearl Jam Twenty*:

A Pearl Jam concert today is about much more than music. It's about the kind
of clear-eyed spirit that comes from believing in people and music and its power
to change a shitty day into a great one, or looking at an injustice and feeling less
alone about facing it.[3]

Pearl Jam's music is animated by its faith that, through solidarity and love,
people can change the world. It is reflected in their ongoing commitment to the
democratic process and embodied in the act of sharing music. To honor that
importance, each entry will identify some essential live performances and, when
appropriate, discuss how songs evolved through that shared experience.

We do not claim any insider insight. We have just been listening to, thinking
through, and talking about their music for over thirty years, growing and
evolving alongside Pearl Jam and the fan community. We cannot call these
definitive interpretations. Eddie has argued they do not exist, and we are inclined
to agree. If someone chooses "Better Man" for the first dance of their wedding
they probably missed the point, but, beyond that, the listener's experience of a
song is real and true to them. We also treat each song on its own terms, rather
than from the standpoint of our personal preferences. Every song is someone's
favorite, and we wish to respect the fandom's deep engagement with the catalog.
But please stop by the Red Mosquito forum to rank and debate them with us.[4]

Writing this book has changed how we understand the band and, if possible,
made us love them even more. If you are new to Pearl Jam, welcome to the
journey. If you are already a fan, we hope it can help you understand how and
why Pearl Jam has impacted your own life. You may draw connections you had
not seen, articulate what you have always felt but could not put to words, look
at the familiar in new ways, or simply throw on a record you have not heard in a
while and remember why Pearl Jam matters so much to so many of us.

1

Ten

Released: August 27, 1991, Epic
Musicians: Eddie Vedder, vocals
                     Stone Gossard, guitar
                     Mike McCready, guitar
                     Jeff Ament, bass
                     Dave Krusen, drums
                     Rick Parashar, piano, organ, and percussion
                     Walter Gray, cello
Producer: Pearl Jam and Rick Parashar
Engineering: Dave Hillis with Don Gilmore, and Adrian Moore
Remixed and re-released on March 24, 2009, with production by Brendan O'Brien
Studio: London Bridge Studios in Seattle, Washington, U.S.A.
Art Direction: Jeff Ament
Cover Art: Lance Mercer
Peak Chart Position: No. 2 on the U.S. *Billboard* 200, No. 18 U.K. Top Albums

Pearl Jam's iconic debut album remains their most culturally resonant and commercially successful. *Ten* indelibly attached Pearl Jam to a sound they almost immediately distanced themselves from. It also spawned countless imitators of both the anthemic punk and classic rock-influenced music and Eddie Vedder's distinctive baritone. Although slower to find an audience than some of the other breakthrough grunge albums of the era, *Ten* would go on to sell over 14 million copies and stay on the *Billboard* 200 for almost five years. It regularly appears on lists of the greatest albums of all time, occasionally tops lists of the greatest debut albums, and is unquestionably the record most associated with Pearl Jam.

    Ten is a remarkably self-assured debut. This is partly a reflection of Stone Gossard and Jeff Ament having collaborated across three bands. It owes something to Eddie's once-in-a-generation talent manifesting on the record as a fully formed force of nature. The DIY feel of *Green River* and the stadium-sized ambitions of *Mother Love Bone* made Stone and Jeff uniquely situated to merge those two approaches in a way that is perfectly aligned with Eddie's musical sensibilities, a combination no subsequent imitator has ever successfully reproduced.

Ten stood out from its peers due to the scope of its influences—the barn-burning statement-making of classic rock bands like The Who and Led Zeppelin, the lived-in authenticity of '80s punk, and some subtler funk and R&B influences from bands like the Jackson 5. Eddie's performance blended a singer-songwriter intimacy with the elemental power of his voice, and all this seamlessly infused into an album full of huge riffs and sweeping melodies. The abrasive middle finger of a song like "Not for You" was several years in the future. *Ten* is a joyful celebration of the healing power of music, and these songs, for all their intensely personal experiences, are intended to be shared. The darker moments of the record are collective challenges to overcome, rather than brooding spaces in which to linger.

Over thirty years after its release, *Ten* contains the strongest collection of memorable riffs in the catalog, along with some of the most full-throated and unapologetic performances of their career, whose soul-bearing immediacy was never muted by the frame story device that structures many of the lyrics. *Ten* was the only time Pearl Jam could be Pearl Jam without fear of repeating or parodying themselves. Everything is triumphant and new. Every moment swings for the fences and exults in the opportunity, bearing the weight of a lifetime of things to say and only one chance to say them. A highlight of so many of *Ten*'s best songs are their fearless commitment to remain in vulnerable spaces without forcing a resolution, exploring them with an unstructured primal intensity. Even after the lyrics are concluded, Eddie's voice weaves in and out of the music, tying those final moments to the emotional journey that carried them there. It paradoxically makes the music grandly cathartic, but also personal and intimate.

As Eddie noted in his *I Am Mine* audiobook, many of the songs on *Ten* have additional layers of narrative and characters in order "to make an interesting story of it." In hindsight, it reflects a lack of confidence in his abilities as a songwriter and performer or a fear of the naked vulnerability present in the themes and performance. This approach to storytelling is most evident in the "Momma-Son" trilogy of songs that Eddie describes as chapters in a larger narrative—an incest survivor ("Alive") driven to the breaking point by his inability to process the experience ("Once"), and ultimately left recounting his regrets ("Footsteps").

But, the strength of these songs is not found in their narrative, which is vague and occasionally misguided. Their power comes from their ideas, emotional authenticity, and commitment to rising above their pain and confusion. *Ten* is an intensely personal album, and a hallmark of Eddie's early writing—personal, quasi-autobiographical explorations of emotional experiences behind characters and stories that obscure their confessional nature.

Ten also successfully introduces key themes that will be explored throughout the catalog. *Ten* is about the feeling of betrayal—the crushing disappointment of a world that fails to live up to its promise and obligation. It seeks an honest exploration of the disenchantment that follows and is willing to have frank conversations about things like homelessness, bullying, parental neglect, rape, and suicide that few records of its size are capable of.

Ten is an empathically humanistic record. It does not condemn us when we fail or judge us for who we are. It holds fast to the hope that something better waits for us, and searches for solidarity in the face of betrayal. Song after song explores the harm that follows a catastrophic loss of trust—personal, familial, relational, and social—and how that experience undermines the creation of safe spaces where self-exploration and reflection are possible.

The search for agency defines the content and substance of Pearl Jam's music, explored on *Ten* with an intoxicating righteousness. "Breath," written during these sessions but not released until the *Singles* soundtrack a year later, encapsulates this commitment with its climactic lyric: "If I knew where it was, I would take you there. There's much more than this." No conclusions are drawn, or secret wisdom shared. Pearl Jam's early records—*Ten* through *Vitalogy*—make no promises at all. Instead, they recenter our expectations around a shared journey. A commitment to seeking answers together.

"ONCE"

Lyrics:	Eddie Vedder
Music:	Stone Gossard
Live Debut:	Off Ramp Cafe in Seattle, Washington, U.S.A., October 22, 1990
Alternate Versions/ Notable Performances:	"Mamasan Demo Tape" (part of the 2009 "Super Deluxe Boxed Set")
	2004 Remix, *Rearviewmirror (Greatest Hits 1991–2003)*
	Palladium in Los Angeles, California, U.S.A., October 6, 1991
	Borgata Events Center in Atlantic City, New Jersey, U.S.A., October 1, 2005
	Adelaide Entertainment Centre in Adelaide, South Australia, Australia, November 21, 2006

Ten begins and ends with excerpts from the "Master/Slave"' dreamscape instrumental, giving the album a cyclical quality that highlights the eternal nature of the unanswerable questions it raises. The music is searching and meditative, producing an underlying feeling of tension that we do not fully recognize until the buzzsaw riff of "Once" violently cuts through it. The juxtaposition is provocative in its shattering of a fragile spiritual peace, immediately drawing blood.

"Once" is an anthem of self-destruction. It is a song for the frantically lost convinced they cannot be found. "Once" happens when we cannot see ourselves as distinct from our pain. Placed at the start of the record, it feels like a warning. But its full thematic power becomes clearer at the end of *Ten's* journey when, in a world with no evident destinations, we are forced to start all over again.

The character in "Once" is desperate and bewildered.[1] We do not know what drove them to this point, the operatic "Momma-Son" narrative notwithstanding, but their history is a gaping wound they repeatedly try and fail to bandage. A nonchalant dismissiveness in the verses is exposed as a lie by the explosive chorus. "Once upon a time, I could control myself. Once upon a time, I could lose myself."

The heart of "Once" is about the loss of self. The nursery rhyme structure ("once upon a time") speaks to an innocence the subject clings to, like a child clutching a security blanket. The aggression in the music and the explosive solo in the bridge make the stakes clear—the destructive consequences of the inability to process loss, grief, or betrayal. Appropriately for a band whose lyrical content and performance focus so much on solidarity, "Once" does not draw a stark contrast between harm to self or harm to others. When the final chorus adds two more lines ("Once upon a time, I could love myself. Once upon a time, I could love you") the scope of the song expands. With the loss of autonomy and certainty comes the total collapse of human connection. And, as the song concludes with Eddie's frantic, repeating cry of "once…" we are left all too aware of the cost.

"Even Flow"

Lyrics:	Eddie Vedder
Music:	Stone Gossard
Single Release Date:	April 6, 1992
Peak U.S. Chart Position:	3
Live Debut:	Off Ramp Cafe in Seattle, Washington, U.S.A., October 22, 1990
Alternate Versions/Notable Performances:	"Even Flow" single and *Rearviewmirror (Greatest Hits 1991–2003)*, recorded in 1992 with Dave Abbruzzese on drums
	Moore Theater in Seattle, Washington, U.S.A., January 17, 1992 (filmed by Josh Taft for the video)
	Deutschlandhalle in Berlin, Germany, November 3, 1996
	Nassau Veterans Memorial Coliseum, East Garden City, New York, U.S.A., April 30, 2003
	Palaisozaki in Torino, Italy, September 19, 2006

Inspired by Eddie's interactions with a homeless veteran during the recording of *Ten*, "Even Flow" juxtaposes one of *Ten*'s thematically darker songs with one of its warmest, most inviting compositions.[2]

"Even Flow" begins with one of the more evocative images in the catalog: "Freezin', rests his head on a pillow made of concrete." The lyrics explore the physical and existential cold flowing from the nameless subject's isolation and invisibility within society. They are sustained by vague, ephemeral hopes. The charity they receive is devoid of human warmth and contact. It is defensive in scope—a way to ward off guilt rather than recognize the humanity of the recipient. That loss of humanity is further explored in the second verse—feelings of helplessness, shame, and isolation.

The chorus balances fantasies of hope and redemption ("someday yet he'll begin his life again"), imagery of beauty and transience ("thoughts arrive like butterflies"), and things that lurk in the dark ("whispering hands" and faceless interactions). The even flow is a state of passivity and loneliness.

It may be impossible to overstate the absolutism of Eddie Vedder's belief in the transformative power of music, and "Even Flow" is the first of many Pearl Jam songs to utilize that platform in service of social critique. Eddie's vocal performance empathizes with the homeless subject, the song rebuking any listener who would render the suffering of others invisible.

This moment of judgment, personal and political is further highlighted in the re-recorded version featured in the "Even Flow" video. The lyrics climax with a call to "never vote Republican"—not surprising, given the band's larger political commitments and the continued gravitational pull of Reaganite conservativism in 1991. Thirty years on, the lyric still makes an appearance in every live version of "Even Flow," which remains Pearl Jam's most played song (only "Alive" comes close). But even more significant are the rerecorded outro lyrics: "I died. I died and you stood there. I died and you walked by and said, 'No. I'm dead.'"

It is an idea Eddie grappled with before Pearl Jam in his prior bands, such as Bad Radio's "Homeless." But it appears in every song on *Ten* and is arguably its thesis statement: Failing to recognize the humanity in others is an act of violence.

"Alive"

Lyrics:	Eddie Vedder
Music:	Stone Gossard
Single Release Date:	July 7, 1991
Peak U.S. Chart Position:	16
Live Debut:	Off Ramp Cafe in Seattle, Washington, U.S.A., October 22, 1990
Alternate Versions/ Notable Performances:	2004 Remix, *Rearviewmirror (Greatest Hits 1991–2003)*

Cow Palace in Daly City, California, U.S.A., December 31, 1991

Drop in the Park, Warren G. Magnuson Park in Seattle, Washington, U.S.A., September 20, 1992

Constitution Hall in Washington, D.C., U.S.A., September 19, 1998

Immagine in Cornice, Mediolanum Forum in Milano, Italy, September 17, 2006

Rock & Roll Hall of Fame Induction Ceremony: Barclays Center in Brooklyn, New York, U.S.A., April 7, 2017 (Dave Krusen on drums)

"Alive" and "Release" are *Ten*'s two most thematically critical songs. They represent moments of prospective redemption, culminating in declarations of faith that the future offers possibilities closed off in the present. "Alive" deals with the immediate aftermath of an intimate, familial betrayal. "Release" approaches the same hurt from a place of reflective distance. Both speak to a generational trauma that Eddie will explore in length in later albums when he has children of his own.

The theme of family runs through *Ten* and remerges in a major way in the *Backspacer* -> *Dark Matter* albums. The idea of family is at the heart of Pearl Jam's music. Family create and sustain safe spaces. They are sources of unconditional love and acceptance, both for who you are and who you are becoming.

"Alive" explores the shattering and semi-autobiographical revelation that the person the subject thought was his real father, who consistently failed in the role, was a fake. His real father passed on before he could know him. The void will never be filled. Even worse is the casual way his mother shares that revelation. In "Alive," the singer discovers that everything he took for granted about his world is a lie, and the world expects him to move on, delegitimating his experience. Although the revelation is about his father, the question is almost exclusively about his mother's compulsive need for everything to be okay. "Is something wrong?" she says. And, of course, there is.

The opening guitar riff to "Alive" is crisp, clear, and musically defiant, a statement of purpose and clarity when everything is confused. The lyrics turn the statement "I'm still alive" into a question. Now what? Yet, the riff is redemptive, the solo cathartic, and Eddie's voice offers answers.

The song's beginning is modest, given how transformative the moment is. With casualness bordering on indifference ("have I got a little story for you"), the mother demolishes the foundations of her child's universe. The solidity of family is gone. Actually, it was already gone. She just finally got around to telling him. She is, frankly, relieved. One can readily imagine her sigh as she says, "I'm glad we talked." This conversation has been about and entirely for her benefit, and he must find the courage to rise above his trauma, alone.

Eddie ends the song with a series of wordless cries. They weave in and out of a triumphant musical outro, Mike's expressive solo and Eddie's cathartic performance releasing its anger, frustration, and fear, and finding the strength to continue. "Alive" is for anyone searching for the will to survive and love again.

"Alive" has undergone some remarkable transformations in its live presentation, the meaning of the song evolving in tandem with Pearl Jam's relationship with its fans. "I'm still alive" became "You're still alive," the song a gift from someone who once desperately needed it to any who might need it now. "Alive" transformed from a hyper-specific personal experience into a larger vehicle for processing grief and tragedy. Eventually, "you're still alive" became "we're all still alive" and stands today as a collective celebration of solidarity and having survived together.

"Why Go"

Lyrics:	Eddie Vedder
Music:	Jeff Ament
Live Debut:	Moore Theatre in Seattle, Washington, U.S.A., December 22, 1990
Alternate Versions/ Notable Performances:	Markthalle in Hamburg, Germany, March 10, 1992
	Sportspaleis Ahoy in Rotterdam, Netherlands, July 16, 1993
	Fox Theater in Atlanta, Georgia, U.S.A., April 3, 1994
	Late Show with David Letterman: Ed Sullivan Theatre in New York, New York, U.S.A., May 4, 2006

"Why Go" was inspired by the story of a girl Eddie knew who was institutionalized after her parents caught her smoking pot—incarcerated for her "benefit" by parents who refused to engage their child.

"Why Go" is dangerous and foreboding in a way most of the songs on *Ten* are not. Its hostile bass line explodes into a wash of dissonant guitars pounding in the subject's head as she carves her thoughts into the stone walls of her (metaphorical?) cell. It grows in righteous intensity as she ponders her circumstances—trapped and violated by the people who should unconditionally love and accept her.

The vocal performance is ferocious, but there are slightly muted moments, the anger softened by the subject's confusion about how she got here and how she can get herself out. Her anger is secondary to her clenched incomprehension, the rage building throughout the chorus until it reaches the fever pitch that creates an outlet for her anger. The lyrics to "Why Go" are claustrophobic, but the song is explosive enough to destroy her prison walls.

The song serves a crucial thematic purpose: Nobody on *Ten* can go home. Everyone's circumstances are broken, their lives shattered. And, if you cannot go home again, if they took that from you, why would you want to? It is the first clear instance of a theme that future records will explore with greater depth and nuance—victory by way of escape.

"Black"

Lyrics:	Eddie Vedder
Music:	Stone Gossard
Live Debut:	Off Ramp Cafe in Seattle, Washington, U.S.A., October 22, 1990
Alternate Versions/ Notable Performances:	2004 Remix, *Rearviewmirror (Greatest Hits 1991–2003)*
	MTV Unplugged: Kaufman Astoria Studios in New York, New York, U.S.A., March 16, 1992
	Fox Theatre in St. Louis, Missouri, U.S.A., April 3, 1994
	United Center in Chicago, Illinois, U.S.A., June 29, 1998
	Bridge School Benefit: Shoreline Amphitheatre in Mountain View, California, U.S.A., October 21, 2001
	Duomo Square in Pistoia, Italy, September 20, 2006

Pearl Jam's early records offer few songs about romantic relationships—primarily "Black" and "Oceans". But, where "Oceans" anticipates a reunion, "Black" embodies the experience of being left behind.

"Black" is about as melodramatic as Pearl Jam gets, masterfully inching right up to the line without crossing over. It is self-aware enough to know the world is not ending but empathetic enough to know that, for the person caught in this moment, it feels like it is. Eddie has described it as being about first relationships, and there is purity and innocence in its grief, alongside an idealization of a now unrequited love. It is not until *Vitalogy* that Eddie starts to write about lived-in relationships between imperfect people.

The introduction to "Black" is sepia-tinged, its muffled opening notes evoking distance and memory. The first verse is likewise wistful and bittersweet, probing the edges of a still bleeding wound. It speaks of promise and possibilities, of stories yet to be told and lives waiting to be lived. Only the subtle hint of the past tense gives any indication that none of this will come to pass.

Then the guitars distort, the music hints at steadily building pressure, and a small growl enters Eddie's voice. Still, the vocals ring strong and confident. Even in the chorus, where the lyrics speak of total collapse ("and now my bitter hands cradle broken glass of what was everything. All the pictures have all been washed in black ... tattooed everything"), he still sounds like he is in control. The hurt is present but mastered.

The tension becomes more prominent in the second verse. Each new confession reveals more than intended as "Black" gradually begins its descent into a total breakdown. Once confident vocals transform into a pleading midnight howl. It is not just the pictures and the memories that are lost to the growing darkness.

The final declaration is heartbreaking: "I know someday you'll have a beautiful life. I know you'll be a star in somebody else's sky, but why, why, why, can't it be, can't it be mine?" She shines for someone else while he remains here, trapped in the dark. "Black" ends with his exhausted, wailing howls, sobbing guitars, and bitterly sad melody, the sound of a life utterly collapsing. And we are left inside the experience, begging the universe to justify our perfect grief.

"JEREMY"

Lyrics:	Eddie Vedder
Music:	Jeff Ament
Single Release Date:	September 27, 1992
Peak U.S. Chart Position:	5
Live Debut:	Off Ramp Cafe in Seattle, Washington, U.S.A., February 1, 1991
Alternate Versions/ Notable Performances:	Cabaret Metro in Chicago, Illinois, U.S.A., July 21, 1991 (featured in the film, *Let's Play Two*) MTV's Video Music Awards: Pauley Pavilion, UCLA in Los Angeles, California, September 9, 1992 "No Jeremy," Red Rocks Amphitheatre in Morrison, Colorado, U.S.A., June 20, 1995 Great Western Forum in Inglewood, California, U.S.A., July 13, 1998 Fenway Park in Boston, Massachusetts, U.S.A., September 4, 2018

"Jeremy" is the only song on *Ten* inspired by non-biographical, real-world events, fictionalizing the classroom suicide of a high school student named Jeremy Wade Delle, who shot himself in front of thirty students on January 8, 1991. "Jeremy" was also influenced by a student Eddie knew in junior high who tried to shoot up a school, the details of the second verse semi-autobiographical.[3] "Jeremy" is a character study, exploring what might drive someone to commit violence against themselves or others, and the collective responsibility we bear for the choice they made.

"Jeremy" is another song of isolation. Jeremy is utterly alone, shunned by his peers, ignored by his family, and misunderstood by his teachers. The powerlessness he feels in the real world is juxtaposed against the fantasy he creates to experience a measure of control. He dreams of dominance, revenge, and a need to harm others before they can harm him again. Jeremy's world is full of coiled predators and unhinged jaws. Nobody is safe.

Consider the wonderful ambiguity in the unpunctuated lyric: "King Jeremy the wicked ruled his world." Is King Jeremy wicked? Does he torment his subjects? Or does Jeremy himself have no way out? Even in his fantasies, it is the wicked who shun and isolate him, who are in command. King Jeremy. The wicked ruled his world.

Like "Black," the unstructured climax of "Jeremy" serves as a musical accompaniment to the complete breakdown of a person. Urgent, pounding, and flailing, the outro empathically navigates its way into Jeremy's headspace, capturing his descent into violent surrender.

The chorus is brilliant for all its seeming simplicity: "Jeremy spoke in class today." When the quiet, brooding outsider finally speaks, what does he have to say? Jeremy's iconic, award-winning video makes it tragically clear, although there is enough ambiguity in the lyrics for there to be competing interpretations. He believed the only way to sear the trauma of his isolation into the minds of his tormentors was to take his own life and to do so in a place of safety and innocence. His final act was a sacrifice of sorts, and a prophetic warning—the cruelty of isolation never stays contained. The next time, the violence may not be turned inward. The song mocks our desire to ignore it. "Try to forget this," it snarls. "Try to erase this from the blackboard." The blackboard is the iconic image of school and education—but, while knowledge is supposed to be permanent, the information on a blackboard is temporary. It is written, discussed for a time, and then erased to move on to the next disposable moment.

Jeremy understood and sought to leave a message we could not forget. The song re-imagines his loss as a challenge to the rest of us: Do better for the abandoned and the lost, the homeless and the heartbroken.

"Oceans"

Lyrics: Eddie Vedder
Music: Stone Gossard, Jeff Ament, and Eddie Vedder
Additional Musicians: Tim Palmer, fire extinguisher and peppershaker
Live Debut: Town Pump in Vancouver, British Columbia, Canada,
                           January 11, 1991
Alternate Versions/
Notable Performances: Marcus Amphitheater in Milwaukee, Wisconsin, U.S.A.,
                           July 8, 1995
                           Orpheum Theatre in Boston, Massachusetts, U.S.A.,
                           April 12, 1994
                           Scotiabank Saddledome in Calgary, Alberta, Canada,
                           September 4, 2005
                           Viejas Arena in San Diego, California, U.S.A., July 7, 2006

"Oceans" inverts the betrayal theme running through *Ten* by focusing on the empowering risk that arises from having faith in others. It is an unabashed love song, even though the word "love" is never mentioned. "Oceans" deals with the fear and uncertainty that surrounds love, the need for trust and its attendant vulnerability, and the strength we draw from its promise. In "Oceans," it is under threat from distance, a metaphor for stress and uncertainty. It reminds us of love's fragility, and the need to protect it.

"Oceans" is also a plea for faithfulness. When Eddie sings "the sea will rise. Please stand by the shore. I will be, I will be there once more," there is a delicate resolve to his vocals, amplified during the wordless vocalizations that serve as a chorus. He knows how difficult it is to hold onto love, and how lost he is without it. His performance is simultaneously tenuous and assertive, and this tension propels the song.

The music is warm and gentle, but with a sense of motion and instability, moments of calm battered about by currents beyond the control of the people adrift. It sounds like rolling waves, and it creates an image of a vast, limitless space to be bridged by faith and longing. Eddie's vocals swim just below the waterline, making the moments where the performance breaches the surface more powerful. We are left with two people standing on distant shores who must carry their love across an endless, uncertain expanse, reminded that separation is a trial to be endured because what would be lost is too precious to let go.

"PORCH"

Lyrics: Eddie Vedder
Music: Eddie Vedder
Live Debut: Moore Theatre in Seattle, Washington, U.S.A., December 22, 1990
Alternate Versions/
Notable Performances: *MTV Unplugged*: Kaufman Astoria Studios in New York, New York, U.S.A., March 16, 1992
                                 Saturday Night Live: Studio 8H, NBC Studios in New York, New York, U.S.A., April 11, 1992
                                 Pinkpop Festival: Megaland Park in Landgraaf, Netherlands, June 8, 1992
                                 Live at Easy Street, East Street Records in Seattle, Washington, U.S.A., April 29, 2005
                                 Brendan O'Brien Remix, 2008

Eddie has said "Porch" was inspired by the panicked feeling of not being able to contact his then-girlfriend after an Iggy Pop concert. In a life before cell phones, she never called him, and he had convinced himself something terrible had happened.[4] That breathless, frantic feeling is captured in "Porch"—born in desperate motion, infused with second-chance intensity. In concert, it would blossom through improvisation, most famously becoming a pro-choice anthem when the band appeared on *MTV Unplugged* and *Saturday Night Live*.

A porch evokes the liminal space between the safety of home and uncertainty of the world outside. "Porch" is about the annihilation of that safety. Its galloping energy, a hallmark of Eddie's future compositions, struggles to stay ahead of the wave threatening to overwhelm him. "Porch" is simultaneously a declaration of independence and about the fear of being alone, fortifying the self for struggles that we may need to face on our own.

The fear of loss demands that you live fully within each moment, no matter what happens, and the climax of "Porch" is empowering like no other sequence on *Ten*. It is an emancipatory moment amidst a terrible crisis, an act of creation as the world falls apart. "Porch" concludes with the righteousness of the last stand against overwhelming odds, with nothing to offer but yourself and the conviction that you will be enough.

"Garden"

Lyrics:	Eddie Vedder
Music:	Stone Gossard and Jeff Ament
Live Debut:	Florentine Gardens in Los Angeles, California, U.S.A., February 7, 1991
Alternate Versions/ Notable Performances:	Albani Bar of Music in Zurich, Switzerland, February 19, 1992
	Fox Theater in Atlanta, Georgia, U.S.A., April 3, 1994
	Forum Milan in Assago, Italy, June 22, 2000
	Gorge Amphitheatre in George, Washington, U.S.A., July 23, 2006

"Garden" is a quiet moment for meditation on an otherwise relentless record, an attempt to make sense of a senseless world, echoing Plato's "Allegory of the Cave." The dissatisfaction driving "Garden" explores how the sensory overload of our lives interferes with our ability to create meaningful personal relationships and sustain attachments that provide real value rather than the simulacrum we are forced to accept. Nothing grows in a garden of stone.

In that respect, "Garden" is about resisting temptation, learning to look past the bright lights, the sales pitch, and the shiny objects of a superficial and disposable culture. Truth and love are found by peering into the shadowy depths that call our prior certainties into question, offering only the possibility of something more substantial in trade. This applies to our relationship with society and each other. We cannot separate the two—our personal connections are forever bound to their situated context. An impermanent world of smoke and mirrors will never allow us to grasp something tangible. Love and understanding require taking risks and letting go of familiar truths and comforts. Opening ourselves up to something more meaningful requires a surrender of sorts, a painful, threatening vulnerability. Love requires the death of old attachments so that we can be reborn into something new.

"Deep"

Lyrics:	Eddie Vedder
Music:	Stone Gossard and Jeff Ament
Live Debut:	God Save the Queen in Los Angeles, California, U.S.A., February 9, 1991
Alternate Versions/	
Notable Performances:	Moore Theatre in Seattle, Washington, U.S.A., January 17, 1992
	Drop in the Park, Warren G. Magnuson Park in Seattle, Washington, U.S.A., September 20, 1992
	Aladdin Theater in Las Vegas, Nevada, U.S.A., November 30, 1993
	Wachovia Spectrum Arena in Philadelphia, Pennsylvania, U.S.A., October 30, 2009

"Deep," a series of dark, sinister vignettes, is *Ten*'s most violent moment. It opens in an explosive, crashing freefall. Each verse chronicles a life in mid-disintegration. The first subject contemplates suicide, then settles for the slow death of addiction. The second is trapped by both the small town that offers him nothing and his fixation on resentment. The imagery ("he sinks the burning knife deep") evokes addiction and self-harm. Whatever is being done with that knife is being done just to feel something.

The final story is the most chilling of the three—the story of a young, innocent ("Christmas clean") girl in the process of being raped, though the act is implied rather than graphically presented. Another human being is treating her as nothing but a means to an end. The desecration is both physical and spiritual, the taking of her body and the rejection of her humanity.

In all three cases, the person is too far along to find a way out. The constant falling and the pervasive feeling of insignificance has left the subjects alone and failing with nowhere to turn. Like all of *Ten*, the catharsis comes from Eddie's voice, sharing his outrage that we allow people to feel this alone. There is, simply, no resolution here. Just a refusal to pretend these people and their experiences do not exist. A refusal to not see them.

"RELEASE"

Lyrics: Eddie Vedder
Music: Stone Gossard, Jeff Ament, Dave Krusen, Mike
                           McCready, and Eddie Vedder
Live Debut: Off Ramp Cafe in Seattle, Washington, U.S.A., October
                           22, 1990
Alternate Versions/
Notable Performances: Tivoli in Utrecht, Netherlands, March 4, 1992
                           Verizon Wireless Amphitheater in Bonner Springs,
                           Kansas, U.S.A., June 12, 2003
                           Bill Graham Civic Auditorium in San Francisco,
                           California, U.S.A., July 18, 2006
                           Stadio Olimpico in Roma, Italy, June 26, 2018

"Release" is the only song on *Ten* not to include lyrics in the liner notes. It is the most directly personal song on the record, and the only one not mediated through a character. Its intimacy is not bound by any time, place, or event. The whole record to this point has chronicled acts of betrayal and violence against the self, alongside attempts to rise above them. The experiences are exhausting, and "Release" begins from a place of stillness.

"Release" is best listened to at night, in a quiet, still space. Eddie is searching for the peace, love, and meaning that has alluded him, and he is finally asking for help. "Release" is a prayer called out in the silent darkness for deliverance. But he is not looking to God, as God must shoulder some responsibility for the mess we have made of things (a theme that will emerge in later records). He looks to the father he never knew—the person who should have taught him how to make sense of the world, offered him guidance, and prepared him for what was to come. His unknown father's love is unconditional, its promise never tainted by reality. He is the purest form of hope and deliverance Eddie can claim for himself.

"Release" culminates with his powerful, defiant plea to his father—or whatever we wish to substitute—for rescue. He refuses to surrender. He will hold the pain the world inflicts upon him, and he will deal with the isolation while searching for an answer. And, finally, he will make himself vulnerable. He will allow himself to trust again, to love again, and to keep doing so no matter how often he is hurt and violated, for as long as it takes until his faith is rewarded. "Release me" is a simple chorus, but it encapsulates the hope and need that runs through the entire record. No matter how violent and difficult the world becomes or how alone we are, we cannot surrender. We must hold on to the emergent possibility of a deeper love that can carry us through.

"MASTER/SLAVE"
Uncredited Hidden Track
Music:　　　Jeff Ament and Eddie Vedder
Live Debut:　None

"Master/Slave" serves as a soundscape bridge between "Release" and "Once," creating an experience that offers cathartic breaks and future possibilities but no resolution.

Selections from the Back Catalog: *Ten* Era

"Jeremy" Single
Released:　　　September 27, 1992
Musicians:　　　Eddie Vedder, vocals; Stone Gossard, guitar; Mike McCready, guitar; Jeff Ament, bass; Dave Krusen, drums.
Producer:　　　Pearl Jam and Rick Parashar
Engineering:　　Rick Parashar
Studio:　　　London Bridge Studios in Seattle, Washington, U.S.A.

"FOOTSTEPS"
Lyrics:　　　Eddie Vedder
Music:　　　Stone Gossard
Live Debut:　Ventura Theater in Ventura, California, U.S.A., May 12, 1992
Alternate Versions/
Notable Performances: "Times of Trouble" (1990 instrumental demo featuring Matt Cameron on drums, which later became "Footsteps" and the Temple of the Dog song with its original name, "Times of Trouble")
Alternate Take, used on the *Lost Dogs* compilation album
Volkshaus in Zurich, Switzerland, June 18, 1992 (part of "The Mamasan Trilogy" played live, in order)
Bridge School Benefit: Shoreline Amphitheatre in Mountain View, California, U.S.A., October 30, 1999
Cynthia Woods Mitchell Pavilion in The Woodlands, Texas, October 15, 2000

"Footsteps" concludes the "Momma-Son" trilogy. It is a raw, naked, acoustic song featuring a self-hating protagonist in the aftermath of a terrible act—murder in the context of the narrative. The singer is desperate to blame someone else: "I did what I had to do. If there was a reason, it was you." But they recognize the deflection by the end of the song. Responsibility for our actions lies with ourselves. "Footsteps" is one of the darkest compositions to come out of the *Ten* sessions, a self-hating song for those who have given up, and, unsurprisingly, it was omitted from an album that stubbornly refuses to surrender.

"YELLOW LEDBETTER"
Also appears on the *Lost Dogs* compilation album and *Rearviewmirror (Greatest Hits 1991–2003)*

Lyrics:	Eddie Vedder
Music:	Mike McCready and Jeff Ament
Peak Chart Position:	21 on Mainstream Rock Tracks
Live Debut:	Mesa Amphitheatre in Mesa, Arizona, U.S.A., November 6, 1993

Alternate Versions/
Notable Performances: Tibetan Freedom Concert: Downing Stadium in Randall's Island, New York, U.S.A., June 8, 1997
Sporthalle in Hamburg, Germany, June 26, 2000
Live at Benaroya Hall, Benaroya Hall in Seattle, Washington, U.S.A., October 22, 2003
Wuhlheide in Berlin, Germany, June 30, 2010

Arguably the most beautiful composition to come out of the *Ten* sessions, "Yellow Ledbetter" remains enigmatic thirty years after its release. As Mike McCready described:

> That was written around the time of the first record [*Ten*]. I think that was the second thing Ed and I wrote together. It came out of a jam in the studio and Ed didn't really have any lyrics. He came up with some ideas right there on the spot, and that's what we recorded.[5]

And, as Eddie noted, "The lyrics to 'Yellow Ledbetter' do constantly evolve. I admit that, at times, I have sung total nonsense." But Eddie clearly had an image in mind.

> The song was originally written about the first Gulf War, and I'd created this image of a young guy with long hair and grunge-wear clothes who had just got a yellow telegram telling him that his brother had been killed in action. He's walking by these conservative-looking, older folks on a porch, flying an American flag. He waves to them in a show of solidarity, and they brush him off and give him the finger. So, you know, what did his brother die for?[6]

Perhaps that story is present in the lyrics. But the beauty of "Yellow Ledbetter" is that it does not need it. That a song never formally released as a single, only appeared as a B-side, and featured indecipherable lyrics could peak at twenty-one on the charts speaks to the power of the performance. The yearning for transcendence—for the world to be better than it is—and the faith in that possibility are all on display. "Yellow Ledbetter" captures the emotional intent of *Ten* and the transformative aspirations of the band as well as any song in the catalog. Unsurprisingly, it is the most common song to close out the live shows, which attempt to reproduce over several hours the same journey the band has been on for over thirty years.

Singles: Original Motion Picture Soundtrack

Released:	June 30, 1992
Musicians:	Eddie Vedder, vocals; Stone Gossard, guitar; Mike McCready, guitar; Jeff Ament, bass; Dave Abbruzzese, drums
Producer:	Pearl Jam and Rick Parashar
Engineering:	Rick Parashar
Studio:	London Bridge Studios in Seattle, Washington, U.S.A.

"BREATH"

Also appears on *Rearviewmirror (Greatest Hits 1991–2003)*

Lyrics:	Eddie Vedder
Music:	Stone Gossard
Live Debut:	Off Ramp Cafe in Seattle, Washington, U.S.A., October 22, 1990
Alternate Versions/ Notable Performances:	"Breath and a Scream," original version recorded during the *Ten* sessions with Dave Krusen on drums, appears on the 2009 *Ten* reissue Andrew's Amphitheater in Honolulu, Hawaii, U.S.A., September 26, 1992 E-Centre in Camden, New Jersey, U.S.A., September 1, 2000 Madison Square Garden in New York, New York, U.S.A., July 8, 2003

Although written for *Ten*, "Breath" made its first official appearance on the *Singles* soundtrack. An explosive, joyous anthem, "Breath" is the most unabashedly hopeful song to come out of the *Ten* sessions—like "Alive" if the music was a little more rugged and stripped of everything but its transformational aspirations. "Breath" celebrates that life never stops offering new possibilities if you are willing to reach for them. It features one of the most moving bridge sequences in the entire catalog, culminating with the mission statement lyric: "If I knew where it was, I would take you there. There's much more than this." A better world is possible, and while we do not know how to get there yet, we do not have to search for it alone. Love, solidarity, transformation, redemption, and possibility are articulated by, if not found through, the power of music.

"STATE OF LOVE AND TRUST"

Lyrics: Eddie Vedder
Music: Mike McCready and Jeff Ament
Live Debut: RKCNDY in Seattle, Washington, U.S.A., May 25, 1991
Alternate Versions/
Notable Performances: *Rearviewmirror (Greatest Hits 1991–2003)*, recorded in 1990 with Dave Krusen on drums
"Rough Mix," recorded on April 21, 1991 with Dave Krusen, appears on the 2009 *Ten* reissue
Drop in the Park, Warren G. Magnuson Park in Seattle, Washington, U.S.A., September 20, 1992
MTV Unplugged: Kaufman Astoria Studios in New York, New York, U.S.A., March 16, 1992
Fox Theater in Atlanta, Georgia, U.S.A., April 3, 1994
Immagine in Cornice, Mediolanum Forum in Milan, Italy, September 17, 2006

"State of Love and Trust," typical of the early records, is a dark song that refuses to wallow in its darkness. The lyrics are angry and suspicious, chronicling the rapid decline of trust in people and institutions, and it features some of the first religious imagery to appear in a Pearl Jam song. There are intimations of suicide ("the barrel shakes aimed directly at my head") and mental panic as the song careens across the edge of a psychological breakdown, with pleas to "help me from myself." As with "Black," normally upbeat and innocent vocalizations ("hey nah nah nah nah") are repurposed with desperate intent. But, as the singer mourns the loss of innocence and "a state of love and trust," there is a stubborn refusal to give up. Although he swears to "do this one myself," there is still the cry for help, a recognition that you can start your journey alone, but you cannot complete it that way. Resolution and meaning are mutually generated and collectively experienced. We cannot move forward alone.

Vs.

Released:	October 12, 1993, Epic (vinyl-only release), October 19, 1993, Epic (CD/cassette release)
Musicians:	Eddie Vedder, vocals Stone Gossard, guitar Mike McCready, guitar Jeff Ament, bass Dave Abbruzzese, drums
Producer:	Pearl Jam and Brendan O'Brien
Engineering:	Brendan O'Brien with Nick DiDia, Adam Kaspar, and Kevin Scott
Studio:	The Site in Nicasio, California, U.S.A., and Potatohead in Seattle, Washington, U.S.A.
Art Direction:	Joel Zimmerman
Cover Art:	Jeff Ament
Peak Chart Position:	No. 1 on the U.S. *Billboard* 200, No. 2 U.K. Top Albums
Recommended Reading:	*Vs.* by Clint Brownlee (2021)

Given the runaway success of *Ten*, there was an impossible amount of pressure surrounding the release of *Vs.*, Pearl Jam's sophomore album. The world was waiting to see how Pearl Jam, arguably the biggest band in the world, would define itself. The music would need to do the talking, as the band was engaged in a partial media blackout and refused to make videos. Within its first week, it set the record for fastest selling album of all time, and at the end of that week, *Time* magazine anointed Eddie Vedder the "voice of his generation."

The original album title, *Five Against One*, and, later, the more efficient *Vs.* speaks to the embattled challenge of being asked to serve as the definitive voice of a musical movement whose artists could not define themselves. The album cover features a sheep hurling itself against a wire fence, a caged animal violently railing against confinement and craving freedom despite not knowing what to do with it.

Vs. has a frightened, hunted quality only hinted at on *Ten*. It is an album that lashes out, sometimes indiscriminately, as it desperately tries to clear a path to escape. It is a wounded, cornered beast of a record, mirroring the state of the band—or, at least, Eddie.

If *Ten* was defined by a huge, atmospheric, reverb-drenched sound that tried to wrap itself around the world, *Vs.* is tight and lean. The songs are focused but claustrophobic, and sometimes border on incomplete. Rather than embrace its ideas with confidence, *Vs.* barrels forward on intensity and assertive nerve.

That driving energy is appropriate for an album that is itself an inarticulate howl of protest against the human tendency to retreat from conflict or embrace ignorance in the face of a crisis—a major theme of later records. It is an angrier record than *Ten*, frustrated by its inability to fully comprehend its enemies. Despite being progressive for the era and standing in stark and flattering contrast against its more apolitical peers, *Vs.* does not chronicle an individual's alienation from society. Instead, it explores our war with ourselves. The songs feature stories about being torn apart and trying to put yourself back together; about contradictory fears of engagement and isolation; about not understanding the message or messenger and finding the collective courage and strength in others to light the way forward for ourselves: "We will find a way. We will find our place." *Ten* had similar concerns, but *Vs.* begins to ask questions about obligation: How will the biggest band in the world use its platform? Will it have something to say and take responsibility for the message?

Vs. also serves as an instructional manual for future Pearl Jam records; new themes will continue to emerge, but, as here, their exploration will be evolutionary and discursive. Albums will both build on and respond to their immediate predecessor. By rejecting the temptation to remake *Ten* (which the band has, to its credit, never done), *Vs.* established that Pearl Jam would persevere by remaining in a perpetual state of transition. It prepared the listener for a future that would be more stylistically diverse but would never sacrifice immediacy and empathy on the altar of experimentation.

And, as always, the evolution of the songs in concert speaks to the evolution of the band. The music refuses to stay static, growing and changing alongside the lived experience of both the band and fan base. Songs like "Animal" and "Daughter" have transformed over time into collective, celebratory experiences that offer exactly the release they blindly reach for here.

"Go"

Lyrics:	Eddie Vedder
Music:	Dave Abbruzzese
Single Release Date:	October 25, 1993
Peak U.S. Chart Position: 3	
Live Debut:	Slim's café in San Francisco, California, U.S.A., May 13, 1993
Alternate Versions/ Notable Performances:	Fox Theater in Atlanta, Georgia, U.S.A., April 3, 1994
	Live on Two Legs, Continental Arena in East Rutherford, New Jersey, U.S.A., September 8, 1998
	Let's Play Two: Original Motion Picture Soundtrack, Wrigley Field in Chicago, Illinois, U.S.A., August 20, 2016
	Maracana Stadium in Rio de Janeiro, Brazil, March 21, 2018

Arguably the heaviest song in the catalog, "Go" captures the panic and righteous indignation of "Once" and "Why Go" without the crutch of a framing story. The ominous, rumbling bass and skittering guitars erupt into an inexorable pile driver of a riff, punctuated in the chorus by blistering six-string sirens. It is a riot in full swing, a sonic combination of a mob surging forward and the authorities pushing back. It somehow argues both for and against acts of mutual self-destruction and establishes the primal and wounded ferocity of *Vs.*

Eddie delivers a perfect mix of growling threat, pleading intensity, and questing fury, the sound of someone railing against a formerly just desire. Adding to the stampeding energy and sense of urgent communal need is a chorus of backup voices intoning a single haunted word: "please." The panic is made personal with the addition of "don't go on me."

Eddie has said that the inspiration for "Go" comes from him begging his truck to start, which may be true in the same way that "Porch" is inspired by a phone call that never came. Each is a moment of prosaic panic and mundane—and therefore human—desperation that serves as a vehicle to explore a more elemental experience. The lyrical content is vague, referencing prior mistakes, unintended abuse, and an unnamed nemesis. Instead, the band distills "Go" down to a desperate, regretful desire to rectify a wrong that can no longer be put right. The performance captures the sense of being at war with oneself, of being torn in two. It collapses the distinction between abuser and abused.

Given the way Eddie was grappling with imposter syndrome during the writing of *Vs.*, his discomfort with the privilege afforded by fame and success, his guilt over other artists he held in high esteem toiling away in comparative obscurity, and the emergent toxicity of the crushing weight of fame, "Go" may be about Eddie's relationship to himself. The two subjects of "Go" represent the authentic person he aspires to protect and the public role he is forced to play, ready or not.

"Go" defies easy classification. It commits the listener to *Vs.* with its power and immediacy, and through the absolute conviction with which Eddie sings about something even he may not fully understand.

"ANIMAL"

Lyrics:	Eddie Vedder
Music:	Stone Gossard
Single Release Date:	April 4, 1994
Peak U.S. Chart Position:	21
Live Debut:	Slim's Cafe in San Francisco, California, U.S.A., May 13, 1993
Alternate Versions/ Notable Performances:	MTV Video Music Awards, Gibson Amphitheater in Los Angeles, California, U.S.A., September 2, 1993 Aladdin Theater in Las Vegas, Nevada, U.S.A., November 30, 1993 Nassau Coliseum in Uniondale, New York, U.S.A., April 30, 2003 *Live on Ten Legs*, Bern Arena in Moutier, Switzerland, September 13, 2006

Befitting its bestial title, the music of "Animal" is a growling assault, its hanging notes offering a momentary breath between attacks. It is relentless despite its shifting moods, alternating between predator and prey. The questions it asks are practically howled: "Why would you want to hurt me? So frightened of your pain?" but the song immediately retreats into a doubled-over, clenched ache. A sardonic, almost dismissive tone flits in and out of the main vocal that seems to welcome the hurt and resent the need.

"Animal" and "Go" are companion songs, two sides of the same coin. Where "Go" invokes the language of an abuser, "Animal" is a song about being abused, complete with intimations of physical and emotional violation. Like "Rats," "Animal" condemns the things we do to each other to escape from ourselves. Each act makes us less than human and worse than animals—something more akin to a monster. Like "Go," Eddie's nuanced performance does some of the heavy lifting. Anger and desperation mix with undertones of judgment—and the main solo snarls back at him like an accusation. He even pities the attackers for the loss of their humanity. A wounded animal not yet ready to forgive but trying to understand.

Both "Go" and "Animal" are stripped of the thin layer of narrative artifice used to explore these themes on *Ten*, focusing instead on the intensity of the experience and obscuring the difference between victim and victimizer. In both cases, life becomes defined by a sense of violation and betrayal, cutting everyone off from their shared humanity and leaving them lost, diminished, and bereft of possibility. We are trapped in a world frightened of its own pain, one that lashes out in violence rather than confront the cause. We risk less by killing off the part of us that wants more.

"Daughter"

Lyrics:	Eddie Vedder
Music:	Stone Gossard
Live Debut:	Bridge School Benefit, Shoreline Amphitheatre in Mountain View, California, U.S.A., November 1, 1992
Alternate Versions/ Notable Performances:	Seattle Center Arena in Seattle, Washington, U.S.A., December 8, 1993
	Saturday Night Live: Studio 8H, NBC Studios in New York, New York, U.S.A., April 16, 1994
	Live on Two Legs, Constitution Hall in Washington, D.C., U.S.A., September 19, 1998
	Forum Milan in Assago, Italy, June 22, 2000
	Live at Benaroya Hall, Benaroya Hall in Seattle, Washington, U.S.A., October 22, 2003

Eddie has said "Daughter" is about a child with a learning disability, or about being different in a time that lacks the vocabulary to understand that difference.[1] At the core of either description is the absence of acceptance. Something that was not chosen and cannot be controlled is perceived as rebellious and willful. It is used to justify rejection during our most innocent and formative experiences, ensuring we carry that hurt with us.

"Daughter" is disarming in its presentation. The music is warm and inviting, a blank slate filled in with simple but evocative images that set the scene for the familial psychodrama of the lyrics. There is an immediate contrast between the peaceful tranquility of the music and the desolation of the scene: "Alone, listless, breakfast table in an otherwise empty room. A young girl, violins(ence), center of her own attention." The imagery throughout the song is of family and home, places of peace and security, but it hints at a deeper undercurrent of hidden fractured dysfunction ("the shades go down, it's in her head"). The subject is dependent on their abuser to define the terms of her world.

There is a physical, emotional, and even spiritual emptiness present in "Daughter." Whatever connectivity she feels to the world and the people around her is illusory, made more devastating by the subject's desire for love and her eagerness to please. Yet, even if the belonging is not real, the need to find it, to rise above that broken world, is there. The understanding that we can reject the people who degrade or destroy us is tentative, even illicit, but the seed is planted. The climactic declaration "She holds the hand that holds her down ... she will rise above" is punctuated by a brief but cathartic solo that promises to cast aside her chains. That catharsis evaporates, and then *Daughter* does too. It spools out as a tentative whisper in the encroaching dark. "The shades go down" it repeatedly mutters to itself. We are reminded that shades are designed to block the light and keep things hidden from view. The listener is put in the mind of someone walking away from hope and into a dim, uncertain future.

Live versions of "Daughter" contain significant changes that recast the impact of the song. The audience joins in on the key lyric "rise above," sharing ownership of that emancipatory sentiment, empowering it beyond the distant promise of the studio performance. And "Daughter" regularly features an extended outro jam that is itself an unformed, open space in which singer and audience can call back and forth, sharing an often wordless but loving musical exchange. Like a caring father might do with a daughter who has a learning disability.

"Glorified G"

Lyrics:	Eddie Vedder
Music:	Stone Gossard and Mike McCready
Live Debut:	University Theatre in Missoula, Montana, U.S.A., June 16, 1993
Alternate Versions/ Notable Performances:	Orpheum Theater in Boston, Massachusetts, U.S.A., April 12, 1994
	Soldier Field in Chicago, Illinois, U.S.A., July 11, 1995
	Bon Secours Wellness Arena in Greenville, South Carolina, U.S.A., April 16, 2016

"Glorified G" is a drunken BBQ rant about firearms inspired by then drummer Dave Abruzzese's love of guns. It views them as tools for murder—that is all. Guns are not toys, and their owners are not sportsmen. Yet, we live in a society that celebrates their existence, and the etymological roots of "glorify" are found in the praise and worship of God, which is intentional. The lyrics rail against the inability of Americans to see a world outside their immediate horizons. If I can personally trust myself to use a gun responsibly, or so the logic goes, then there is no problem. But how many of us distrust our intentions and ourselves?

A loss of perspective is a theme that runs through much of the record, both as personal tragedy and social critique. One of the things that *Vs.* attacks is this personal and public blindness, and regaining perspective is the key to the redemptive moments on the record.

But too many of us applaud our own lack of vision, turning our stubborn blindness into a badge of honor and a mark of our freedom. "Glorified G" captures this in the novel *1984*'s allusion "doublethink/dumb is strength" and the casual sanctimony of "that's okay man, cuz I love god." The subject of "Glorified G" lacks a single shred of self-awareness, blithely confident in the justness and rightness of the mastery over life and death conferred by the possession of a gun.

The sentiment is more nuanced than the execution, which is reductive and even innocently simplistic, with a chorus ("glorified version of a pellet gun, feel so manly when armed") that reduces complicated questions raised by the song to "guns = compensation." It diminishes the gravity of the subject matter and does not fully engage with America's spoiled tolerance of violence. Then again, neither do we and perhaps that is the point.

"DISSIDENT"

Lyrics:	Eddie Vedder
Music:	Stone Gossard, Mike McCready, and Jeff Ament
Single Release Date:	May 16, 1994
Peak U.S. Chart Position:	3
Live Debut:	Slim's Cafe in San Francisco, California, U.S.A., May 13, 1993
Alternate Versions/ Notable Performances:	Delta Center in Salt Lake City, Utah, U.S.A., November 1, 1995
	Constitution Hall in Washington, D.C., U.S.A., September 19, 1998
	New England Dodge Music Arena in Hartford, Connecticut, U.S.A., May 13, 2006

The soaring and liberating guitars of "Dissident" stand in opposition to its weighty subject matter. "Dissident" offers a vague narrative of a woman sheltering a political dissident, deciding to turn him in rather than taking on the burden and responsibility of political change. She is haunted by her guilt, and "Dissident" is a tragedy stemming from human weakness, not human wickedness. It is a restatement of one of the album's principal arguments: human suffering has a human cause and solution.

"Dissident" runs into some of the storytelling challenges found in "Alive"— the narrative is too thin to withstand deep scrutiny. But, like "Alive," the song's power stems from the questions it asks rather than the story it tells. Do we have the courage of our convictions? Will we rise when we are called upon?

Most of us will not. As Eddie reminds us in one of his most consequential lyrics, "escape is never the safest path" even though it is the one we regularly choose.

Safety over risk. Concession over confrontation. Stability over change. These choices come at a cost and with a warning. The spirits of missed opportunities and lingering regrets haunt the bridge of "Dissident."

Its music stands in opposition to its narrative because it is meant to inspire. It wants to help us find strength the next time we are forced to choose between our principles and our security. The security of that safest path is an illusion because it costs us the very thing we are afraid to lose—our integrity and sense of self. When Eddie alternately swaps "place" for "path" ("escape is never the safest *place*"), he highlights how navigating this conflict is both a journey and a destination. The struggle itself has value even when it cannot be won.

So much of *Vs.* chronicles the process of preparing yourself to shoulder burdens you have no choice but to embrace. Being unprepared or feeling unworthy does not absolve you of the need to carry them. The willingness to take the weight determines our worth.

"W.M.A."

Lyrics:	Eddie Vedder
Music:	Dave Abbruzzese and Jeff Ament
Additional Musicians:	Brendan O'Brien, Mellotron
Live Debut:	Slim's Cafe in San Francisco, California, U.S.A., May 13, 1993
Alternate Versions/ Notable Performances:	Fox Theater in Atlanta, Georgia, U.S.A., April 3, 1994
	Scottrade Center in St. Louis, Missouri, U.S.A., October 3, 2014
	Oakland Arena in Oakland, California, U.S.A., May 13, 2022 (Richard Stuverud and Josh Klinghoffer on drums)

"W.M.A." (White Male American) is one of Pearl Jam's first attempts at serious engagement with concrete social issues—racialized police violence and white privilege. It captures a swirling mixture of anger and tragedy, and the composition has a tribal, ritualistic pulse. "W.M.A." feels ceremonial in a way no other Pearl Jam song does, a communal attempt to purify something unclean. Its extended outro and fade-out give it an ageless quality. Racism is America's original sin, and we have been trying to purge ourselves of it for a long, long time.

"W.M.A." explores the existential and physical violations of racial violence—of white power exercised with impunity against marginalized communities. The liner notes contain a concrete reference to the 1992 case of Malice Green, an unemployed black steel worker who was pulled from his car and beaten to death by three Detroit police officers. The Pavlovian nature of institutional racism is captured in lyrics like "trained like dogs, color and smell, walks by me to get to him," which were directly inspired by Eddie witnessing Seattle police harassing a black man he was talking to.[2]

"W.M.A." reprises themes raised in "Glorified G": the obliviousness and entitlement that forms the core of mainstream (read: white) American life in the early 1990s. Starting from the opening lyric "he won the lottery by being born," there is an indictment of white privilege—a conferral of unearned institutional advantage that reflects what philosopher John Stuart Mill called "the accident of birth." The privilege of knowing your exalted place in the world ("Jesus greets me. Looks just like me") is hardwired into our fundamental perceptions, and they are so deeply embedded in society as to be invisible.

While Eddie's writing sometimes struggles in explicitly political songs, "W.M.A." offers a delicate and subtle presentation. It is infused with the sense of opposition and defiance that gives *Vs.* its character. But, here, unlike "Glorified G," it observes and tries to understand. It hopes for something better—even if it is not ready to forgive.

"BLOOD"

Lyrics:	Eddie Vedder
Music:	Stone Gossard and Mike McCready
Live Debut:	Slim's Cafe in San Francisco, California, U.S.A., May 13, 1993
Alternate Versions/ Notable Performances:	*Pearl Jam Twenty: Original Motion Picture Soundtrack*, Mount Smart Stadium in Auckland, New Zealand, March 25, 1995
	Dodge Music Center in Manchester, Connecticut, U.S.A., October 2, 1996
	Immagine in Cornice, Arena di Verona in Verona, Italy, September 16, 2006

"Blood" is a twitching musical electrocution that is a little too slick and shiny to take seriously. The '70s-style funk guitar brightens the mood, standing in stark contrast to the dark, venomous lyrics. That is not to say it is a lightweight song. It is too angry for that. But, if "Blood" is not meant to be tongue in cheek, at least it can smile while it screams.

"Blood" is a song about feeling violated—the cry of sacrificial victims strapped to the altar of entertainment media and the co-option of Seattle's music, artists, and culture. The reporter wielding the pen replaces the priest wielding the knife or the junkie wielding the needle. Eddie's life fills their pages, and he needs to bleed to keep the content machine fed. His blood is just another lucrative substance marked for extraction. That he has become involuntarily complicit in sustaining a machine he hates makes this entire process even more perverse, and there is a quiet moment in the bridge where Eddie acknowledges the irony.

"Blood" is as self-destructive as it is self-protective. Eddie shreds his own vocal cords to prove his voice needs protection. Music had always been a salvation for Eddie Vedder, but in the scope of 1993's fame, it was also an act of self-harm.

Eddie will deal with the same themes in a more sophisticated way on *Vitalogy*, but "Blood" is a primal scream. Songs like "Last Exit," "Not for You," "Corduroy," "Satan's Bed," and "Immortality" will be more nuanced. None will be this elemental.

"REARVIEWMIRROR"

Lyrics: Eddie Vedder
Music: Eddie Vedder
Additional Musicians: Eddie Vedder, rhythm guitar
Live Debut: Slim's Cafe in San Francisco, California, U.S.A., May 13, 1993

Alternate Versions/
Notable Performances: Red Rocks Amphitheatre in Morrison, Colorado, U.S.A., June 20, 1995
                         Deer Creek Music Center in Noblesville, Indiana, U.S.A., August 17, 1998
                         Jones Beach Music Theatre in Wantagh, New York, U.S.A., August 25, 2000
                         Pacaembu in São Paulo, Brazil, December 2, 2005

"Rearviewmirror" provides *Vs.* with its true thematic anchor. After seven flailing tracks, it is the album's first real moment of revelation. The subject finally sees who they were and where they have been, if not where they can go and who they might become. That part of the journey will commence with *No Code*.

"Rearviewmirror" documents the moment of discovery, not the aftermath. It is an experience of emancipation, its power found in the breathless savoring of that moment. The music tells much of the story. A stubborn grittiness to the main riff conveys a sense of fluid movement and a promise of freedom. The rest of the band follows unobtrusively, adding weight without distraction. Experience piles on experience. Life piles on life. Still, the subject pushes through, unbowed and defiant.

Their determination is finally rewarded when the bridge releases the oppressive weight that defined the first half of the album, taking on an ethereal, dreamlike quality. Burdens recede. There is suddenly space to breathe and reflect. The past is disconnected from the present, and the song reels back and offers a long, exultant scream of triumph. It is not clean. There is a lingering hatred of the vanquished foe scarring this celebration of hard-won freedom. It makes for a complicated finale that never leaves the trenches.

Eddie chooses a car as his central image. It is a symbol of aggressive, protected freedom—fast, safe, and powerful. The subject is running from abuse, both mental and physical. There are references to beatings, but there is psychological abuse too. It is not clear if the physical beatings were always there, or if they finally served as a catalyst, a way to crystallize the mental torture they had been "forced to endure." It is easy to imagine "Rearviewmirror" as revisiting characters depicted in "Go," "Animal," or "Daughter." There is even a formal callback to "Daughter" as the shades that went down are finally raised, the fulfillment of a child's promise to rise above, their escape a memorial to the cost of survival.

"Rearviewmirror" is about revelation, bought with bitter currency. The descriptions of abuse convey a sense of slow suffocation, the claustrophobia that comes from being the victim of someone else's crimes: "I couldn't breathe, holding me down, hand on my face, pushed to the ground." The final lyrics in the chorus ("united by fear, tried to endure what I could not forgive") ground their foundational relationship in fear rather than love. This is unsustainable and toxic despite the misguided efforts of the subject to make it work—a theme Eddie will return to in "Better Man."

When the subject finally flees, they are no longer the cornered, wounded animal from earlier in the record. They recognize they have been victimized, that they deserve better, and that they have an opportunity to free themselves and start again. We do not know how they will recreate themselves. "Rearviewmirror" does not try to define them, choosing instead to celebrate the moment of release that makes future exploration possible.

"Rats"

Lyrics:	Eddie Vedder
Music:	Jeff Ament
Live Debut:	Slim's Cafe in San Francisco, California, U.S.A., May 13, 1993
Alternate Versions/ Notable Performances:	Orpheum Theater in Boston, Massachusetts, U.S.A., April 12, 1994
	The Vic Theatre in Chicago, Illinois, U.S.A., August 2, 2007

"Rats"' tongue is planted firmly in its cheek. The stalking music is stridently playful, the performance almost self-parody. Metaphorical cannibalism pervades the song and makes everything seem that much more sordid. Despite some clever wordplay, "Rats" feels slightly disposable. But its giddy energy and its curious solidarity with creatures that society has classified as vermin make it an oddly appropriate postscript to the journey undertaken in "Rearviewmirror"— someone in a common cause with their fellow survivors—and it helps explains the inclusion of the "Ben, the two of us need look no more" lyric.

Ben was an early '70s horror movie (a sequel to *Willard*, which was about killer rats). The main character befriends the titular Ben, the leader of a pack of telepathic rats. Ben keeps the boy company and acts as his friend while he confronts childhood bullies. Eventually, most of the pack is destroyed and the movie ends with the main character nursing Ben back to health. It is remembered mostly for Michael Jackson's incongruously sweet song about the movie— Jackson being an important musical influence on Eddie. It echoes the "I'd rather be with an animal" sentiment from earlier in the record, that the singer needs to look for comfort in odd places since humanity can be so disgusting.

"Elderly Woman Behind the Counter in a Small Town"

Lyrics: Eddie Vedder
Music: Eddie Vedder
Additional Musicians: Eddie Vedder, rhythm guitar
Live Debut: University Theatre in Missoula, Montana, U.S.A., June 16, 1993

Alternate Versions/
Notable Performances: "Acoustic Version" from the "Go" Single (1993)
                               Fox Theater in Atlanta, Georgia, U.S.A., April 3, 1994
                               Scotiabank Place in Ottawa, Ontario, Canada, September 16, 2005
                               Let's Play Two: Original Motion Picture Soundtrack, Wrigley Field in Chicago, Illinois, U.S.A., August 20, 2016

For a gentle song, "Elderly Woman…" possesses a strange and subtle urgency. This is a song about lifetimes, and the richness of the acoustic canvas reflects a lost opportunity, or a dream revived only to fade away again.

The evocative title sets the scene. We envision an older woman ground down by life and the dreams she deferred. This is a song about standing still while the rest of the world passed you by, until an unexpected second chance. Although he sings in the first person, the song is not about Eddie, who stands apart while offering empathy and forgiveness. He refuses to condemn someone for not being able to overcome what so many of us cannot—echoes of "Dissident." Part of maturation is learning not to resent people when they cannot transcend who they are.

It begins trapped in gauzy recollections. The hesitantly phrased "I seem to recognize your face. Haunting, familiar, yet I can't seem to place it. Cannot find a candle of thought to light your name" intimates light, heat, awareness, and passion just beyond reach. It is the experience of having a name on the tip of your tongue last forever. The song slides into wistful regret that "lifetimes are catching up with me, all these changes taking place, I wish I'd see the place, but no one's ever taken me." These hurts are too old to kindle immediate pain, but they are sadder for it, as the passive loss encompasses a lifetime. That passivity is important. She waited for someone to show her the world rather than seek it out, and no one ever came.

The gentle decay of the chorus ("hearts and thoughts they fade … fade away") punctuates the tragedy of a life ill lived. The delivery is effectively understated, more melancholy than bitter or sad—emotions too immediate for the moment. "Elderly Woman…" is not a crime in progress or even its aftermath. Eddie is visiting long-abandoned ruins, disturbing their forgotten slumber with his unwanted intrusion. Perhaps it is better to let them lie.

There is a moment when we imagine she might escape the gravity of her past: "I just want to scream 'Hello!' My god it's been so long, never dreamed you'd return. But now here you are, and here I am." It is the emotional climax of the song and a powerful, communal moment in a live setting. But she holds herself back as she always has. Memories are not enough. There needs to be someone accompanying you on the journey. We rarely overcome our inertia. Engaging the world around us is easier with someone to share in our triumphs and offer their strength when we stumble. Instead, "Elderly Woman…" returns to the fading repetition of the chorus, as thoughts once again fade away. What awoke could not be sustained, because it was alone.

"LEASH"

Lyrics:	Eddie Vedder
Music:	Stone Gossard and Mike McCready
Live Debut:	Bender Arena in Washington, D.C., U.S.A., November 9, 1991
Alternate Versions/ Notable Performances:	Pinkpop Festival: Megaland Park in Landgraaf, Netherlands, June 8, 1992
	Aladdin Theater in Las Vegas, Nevada, U.S.A., November 30, 1993
	TD Garden in Boston, Massachusetts, U.S.A., May 25, 2006

"Leash," originally written during the *Ten* sessions, ecstatically celebrates the solidarity at the heart of Pearl Jam's music with the promise that "I am lost, I am no guide, but I'm by your side. I am right by your side." If we keep searching together, we will find our destination.

"Leash" articulates its insights with catharsis, joy, and relief. Eddie sings as if his heart is going to burst, a complex release of long-held tension. When Eddie declares "Will myself to find a home, a home within myself, we will find the way, we will find our place," he reveals that the journey is the destination, and its meaning is given definition through shared experience.

He is screaming simply to celebrate the fact that he can scream, and that there is an audience listening that wants to scream too. It is not a coincidence that the "Leash" chorus/outro has some of the most prominent backing vocals in any Pearl Jam song.

For all its energy, "Leash" is not an angry song and instead leans into the righteous purity of youth and the freedom that comes from the experience of solidarity. "Leash" wants us to hold onto and draw strength from the feeling of being part of something larger than ourselves. A long road remains before us, but for the first time, there is the confidence that someday, together, we will arrive.

"INDIFFERENCE"

Lyrics:	Eddie Vedder
Music:	Jeff Ament and Stone Gossard
Live Debut:	University Theatre in Missoula, Montana, U.S.A., June 16, 1993
Alternate Versions/ Notable Performances:	*Self Pollution Radio* FM Broadcast from Seattle, Washington, U.S.A., January 8, 1995
	Live at the Garden, Madison Square Garden in New York, New York, U.S.A., July 8, 2003 (with Ben Harper)
	Pearl Jam Twenty: Original Motion Picture Soundtrack, PalaMalaguti in Bologna, Italy, September 14, 2006

"Indifference" is the sleepless night of *Vs.*, when the rage is spent and the promise of redemption that seemed so real by day fades in the late, lonely, quiet hours. The gentle rain of cymbals against the keys transports the listener to a space where the veil is lifted, and we cannot hide from the question haunting the record: "How much difference does it make?" The song spends its time making a slow and careful study, reluctant to draw any conclusions. Jeff's bass slowly carries us across a world without illusions, with the guitar accents acting as flashes of light that reveal without judgment.

Eddie's vocals match the pace and mood. Where a song like "Release" rails against the darkness, "Indifference," gently probes its hidden corners. There are moments of rising urgency and careful retreat, but what really characterizes his performance is its caution. Eddie is unwilling to touch anything for fear of breaking the spell. Even as he gathers confidence, he quickly pulls back, afraid to commit. "Indifference" explores a graying world in a state of transition, one that can be simultaneously cold and warm, distant and close, barren and lush.

To the song's credit, it allows the listener to answer its core question for themselves. The profound simplicity of the ask, alongside a series of striking images, makes this one of Eddie's most evocative lyrics.

The opening notes capture the sound of the match striking, the quick burst of light, and the shadowy illumination of a lonely flame pushing back against the darkness. There is someone next to him, a tenuous and uncertain source of comfort. But he turns his thoughts away from her, and when the light goes out, he is on his own. Maybe she was never there at all. Maybe what he so desperately needed to glimpse was his own determination to keep fighting.

> I will hold the candle, till it burns up my arm.
> I'll keep takin' punches, until their will grows tired.
> I will stare the sun down, until my eyes go blind.
> I won't change direction, and I won't change my mind.

The rest of the song is a litany of stubborn defiance and refusal. To hold onto the light no matter the pain and exhaust the world through force of will: "I'll swallow poison until I grow immune. I will scream my lungs out 'til it fills this room."

Defiance feeds defiance, and there is a sad beauty in the declaration of martyrdom. But he cannot help going back to those core-underlying questions: Is the sacrifice worth it? Does the struggle have meaning? "How much difference does it make?" *Vs.* teaches us that the instinct to lash out against uncertainty is natural and seductive but ultimately unsatisfying. It is a stimulus response, not a solution.

Vs. argues that there is more to life than injustice, and that struggle has meaning. But we cannot struggle alone. We cannot find or maintain the light by ourselves. The truth is revealed in the live experience of "Indifference." To declare, alongside thousands of others, that "I will scream my lungs out until it fills this room" is to understand that there is magic in that sound, the power to make illusions real.

Selections from the Back Catalog: *Vs.* Era

Chicago Cab: Original Motion Picture Soundtrack

Released:	August 25, 1998
Musicians:	Eddie Vedder, vocals; Stone Gossard, guitar; Mike McCready, guitar; Jeff Ament, bass; Dave Abbruzzese, drums
Engineering:	Nick DiDia
Studio:	Bad Animals Studio in Seattle, Washington, U.S.A.

"HARD TO IMAGINE"

Lyrics:	Eddie Vedder
Music:	Stone Gossard
Live Debut:	Great Woods Center in Norton, Massachusetts, U.S.A., August 07, 1992

Alternate Versions/
Notable Performances: Alternate Vocal Recording, used on the *Lost Dogs* compilation album

Orpheum Theatre in Boston, Massachusetts, U.S.A., April 12, 1994

Molson Centre in Montréal, Quebec, Canada, August 20, 1998

"AOL Sessions," recorded in Studio X in Seattle, Washington, U.S.A., February 27, 2006

Although "Hard to Imagine" was not formally released until the *Chicago Cab* soundtrack (1998), it is one of Pearl Jam's oldest songs, played live before the release of *Vs*. A meditative, veiled elegy to lost innocence, it is an early attempt at articulating ideas that will become the core of *No Code*. Eddie challenges the listener to "paint a picture using only gray" and try to process the emotional and existential fallout of living in a world without easy answers. The original recording directs that angst toward the injustice embedded in human experience ("fuck tradition, no one's safe from harm"), though the re-recorded vocals appearing on *Lost Dogs* are more interested in interrogating the self ("tear into yourself, count tales upon your arm"), as if wondering what to do with his power rather than lamenting his powerlessness.

In both cases, the singer is grappling with how to engage with the vastness of the world, a passage from the innocent expectations of youth into the obligations and necessities of adulthood. As he sings "things were different then, all is different now, I've tried to explain, somehow," there is a survivor's weariness, a reflective distance that recognizes the difference between past and present measured by our awareness of complexity. And, as the song approaches its muted crescendo, there is a plaintive conviction that if we open our eyes, together, we can imagine something better.

Vitalogy

Released: November 22, 1994, Epic (vinyl-only release),
                      December 6, 1994, Epic (CD/cassette release)
Musicians: Eddie Vedder, vocals, guitar
                      Stone Gossard, guitar, mellotron
                      Mike McCready, guitar
                      Jeff Ament, bass
                      Dave Abbruzzese, drums
Producer: Pearl Jam and Brendan O'Brien
Engineering: Nick DiDia with Caram Costanzo, Adam Kasper, Trina
                      Shoemaker, John Burton, and Kevin Scott
Art Direction: Noel Zimmerman
Cover Art: Eddie Vedder
Studio: Bad Animals Studio in Seattle, Washington, U.S.A.; Southern
                      Tracks Recording in Atlanta, Georgia, U.S.A.; and Kingsway
                      Studio in New Orleans, Louisiana, U.S.A.
Peak Chart Position: No. 1 on the U.S. *Billboard* 200, No. 4 U.K. Top Albums

Vitalogy was largely written on the road while touring in support of *Vs.*, and those origins are encoded into its DNA. It is Pearl Jam's most unfiltered, immediate record. *Vitalogy* is an exposed nerve—a raw, bloody, experience that plays like a band standing unveiled and vulnerable before its audience, asking for help but afraid to receive it: Protective of its voice but determined to be heard, uncertain of its future but committed to going down fighting for its principles. Each song feels like it is about to fall apart but somehow manages to hold together and stumble toward an end. While not yet abandoning the anthemic aesthetic of *Ten* and *Vs.*, *Vitalogy* marks the pivot into the more introspective style of writing and performance that, except perhaps *Yield*, will characterize the run of albums from *Merkin Ball* through *Riot Act*.

No Pearl Jam album is as thematically dense as *Vitalogy*, which deals with philosophically complex ideas manifested as abstract questions, lived experience, and personal therapy. It addresses the opportunities, obligations, and costs that follow from being one of the biggest bands in the world. Yet, it never feels self-indulgent. Following the runaway success of *Ten* and *Vs.* and the subsequent loss of control over the reach and meaning of their music—the idea of Pearl Jam as something existing independent of the band's control—*Vitalogy* explores, without cynicism or ironic detachment how the culture industry's inevitable commodification of their music undermines its emancipatory possibilities, ravaging the creator in the process.

Vitalogy grapples with the consequences of turning a subject into an object—the objectification of art and artist. It is also about the loss of agency, of the ability to exert control over external forces in your life and imbue your actions with self-directed meaning. The artist is at the mercy of the industry that produces them, the celebrity culture that mythologizes them, and the audience that depends on them. At one show Pearl Jam played shortly after the death of Kurt Cobain, a female fan screams, "I love you Eddie," to which he responds, "You don't love me. You love who you think I am and the image you have created in your mind."[1] Can Eddie Vedder the person co-exist alongside Eddie Vedder the symbol?

Blessings and obligations follow from the gift of a platform. But the sheer size and scope of that platform destroys the intimacy and connection between the artist, his work, and the people it affects. It becomes mediated through industry and shorn of authenticity. "Stripped and sold," transformed into something consumable, reproducible, and designed for maximum profit and disposable engagement.

As a central figure in an influential musical movement and cultural moment, Eddie would have been particularly sensitive to this dynamic. That he is a true believer in the transformational power of music makes that sensitivity especially acute. He spent his life wishing and hoping for the chance to reach an audience with his art and establish a connection through which we can experience meaningful forms of community, solidarity, and love. For a few brief moments, he was a part of a vital music scene that did just that, and just as quickly, that moment was gone—turned into "grunge," mass-produced as fashion, image, and form as fast as imitators could be found, devoid of the sentiment, mission, and community originally animating it.

What does it mean to dissent when dissent is good for business? How do you respond to the co-option of intensely personal and authentic self-expression? How do you deal with the existential guilt of being chosen and not feeling worthy? How do you reassert personal agency in a world that continuously strips it from you? What happens if you cannot? *Vitalogy* is an album about life and death—and was originally going to be called *Life*. There is a palpable sense of suicide hanging over the entire record, granted new urgency by the death of Kurt Cobain prior to its release, the only other artist of the period grappling with the same questions on the same scale. Sometimes, death is the last authentic act available to us. *Vitalogy* reads like a suicide note but in the uncertain hand of someone who has not yet given up. It is a last desperate chance to navigate the paths before him. There is the spiritual surrender that comes from accepting things the way they are. There is the literal death of the body, in defeat or as a defiant act of forfeit. Or there is the choice to pick yourself up and fight back, to construct new forms of meaning, and reclaim what was taken.

Vitalogy does not answer which path the singer chooses, which is part of its power. The record is in conversation with itself. The listener can read their own battles into the music and draw conclusions appropriate to their own experience. But a response lingers just beneath the surface. A snarling, spitting defiance runs through the record, as well as the crystallization of one of Pearl Jam's central ideological commitments—that meaning is derived from the struggle, not the outcome, and we achieve our greatest success in the struggles we undertake together. The band's subsequent actions make their response explicit. Establishing a charity named after the record (the Vitalogy Foundation), the fight against Ticketmaster to keep live music accessible, the scaling down of the fan base, the no video, minimal media exposure policy—all are attempts to recenter the meaning of Pearl Jam on its music, its power to impact the world, and the shared and reciprocated humanity of the artists who create it and the listeners who derive hope and meaning from that creation.

A quick word on the album's artwork, a critical part of the *Vitalogy* experience. The band paid 50 cents per printing of *Vitalogy* (costing them $2.5 million in the first year alone), as the irregularly sized album booklet was thirty-four pages long and featured liner notes carefully interwoven with excerpts from its 1899 namesake.[2] That *Vitalogy* was a book of wellness quackery offering rules for "life prolonged indefinitely," and its images captured in the album booklet explore the corruption and "self-pollution" that threaten our health and virtue.[3] But it is also clear that the promise of a timeless purity is a lie, achieved through the annihilation of the self and the passions that make us human. *Vitalogy* the album rejects the book and asks us to accept that the life we have may be short and difficult, but it can be honest, and it can be ours.

"LAST EXIT"

Lyrics:	Eddie Vedder
Music:	Dave Abbruzzese and Stone Gossard
Live Debut:	UNO Lakefront Arena in New Orleans, Louisiana, U.S.A., November 16, 1993
Alternate Versions/ Notable Performances:	Constitution Hall in Washington, D.C., U.S.A., January 14, 1995

Pearl Jam Twenty: Original Motion Picture Soundtrack,
Taipei International Convention Center in Taipei,
Taiwan, February 24, 1995
Verizon Wireless Amphitheatre in Irvine, California,
U.S.A., June 2, 2003
Gorge Amphitheatre in George, Washington, U.S.A.,
September 1, 2005

"Last Exit" begins with a discordant tune-up, as if the band walked into a room, picked up their instruments, and the record spilled out of them. Given that much of *Vitalogy* was written in spare moments on tour, that may not be too far from the truth. "Last Exit" is the first half of a suicide note ("Immortality" being its second part), a piece of bewildered anger and fraying commitment. *Vitalogy* will try to work through whether the commitment is to life or death.

Musically, "Last Exit" is an act of violent desperation. The crashing drums and the jagged guitars look to cut and scar so that the pain might bring focus. Its various peaks and climaxes lack the clarity (even in the face of uncertainty) present throughout the first two records, mirroring the frantic confusion in the lyrics.

The first verse captures a life spiraling out of control ("Lives opened and trashed, look ma watch me crash, no time to question, why'd nothing last?"), experiences made dangerous by their runaway energy. The parallels to the rise of the band and the destruction of Eddie the human and the birth of Eddie the symbol are intentional and cut across the entirety of *Vitalogy*. Intimations of death and suicide are made more explicit in alternative lyrics found in the liner notes, where he writes: "Once resigned, dictating your demise seems only fair. Built-in effect of the system … control. If one cannot control his life, will he be driven to control his death…" In a world that systematically takes away authentic choice, our only act of agency may be choosing the circumstances surrounding our death.

The question becomes what kind of death? Death as suicide is present as a subtext throughout the song, especially with the "three days" lyrics—the image of a body lying for days waiting for discovery and the soul lingering to learn how the act will be received. Parallels of Kurt Cobain's suicide immediately come to mind, though "Last Exit" was written before it. But death can also be interpreted as a moment of rebirth—a phoenix dying to rise again. Imagery of elemental purification present throughout—the sun, the ocean, masks burned away, the past drowned, skin shed—remind us that renewal awaits on the other side of pain and loss. The resignation present in the alternate lyrics is absent, but the threat remains real. "Last Exit" and *Vitalogy* stand at a crossroads. We may walk away stronger. We may be broken by the journey. But a path must be chosen. Eddie's plea to "let my spirit pass" acknowledges this is the last exit off a road heading inexorably toward annihilation.

"Spin the Black Circle"

Lyrics:	Eddie Vedder
Music:	Stone Gossard
Single Release Date:	November 8, 1994
Peak U.S. Chart Position:	18
Live Debut:	Paramount Theater in Denver, Colorado, U.S.A., March 6, 1994
Alternate Versions/ Notable Performances:	*Self Pollution Radio* FM Broadcast from Seattle, Washington, U.S.A., January 8, 1995
	Saratoga Performing Arts Center in Saratoga Springs, New York, U.S.A., August 27, 2000
	Live on Ten Legs, Copps Coliseum in Hamilton, Ontario, Canada, September 13, 2005

"Spin the Black Circle" is an ecstatic celebration of the generative power of music. It fixates on vinyl (the titular black circle), in part because of its status, in 1994, as a relic, an artifact of an earlier time when listening to music was made sacred by the ritualized experience of playing a record.

Music offers love and communion without requiring transactional reciprocity. It allows you to take what is needed without demanding anything in return. It offers something unconditionally yours. This remembrance is essential in the context of *Vitalogy*, which grapples with the complex relationship between artist and audience, the way the latter always complicates and sometimes compromises the act of creation and expression undertaken by the former, especially when mediated through the industry.

"Spin the Black Circle" features a swinging chainsaw of a riff and Eddie's most vocally shredded performance to date, loving so much it hurts. Given the public conception of grunge as fundamentally dour, a performance this aggressive should be about an inescapable pain. The lyrical imagery speaks to addiction—but one that heals and affirms. It is a wonderful misdirection, a song about life sung in the key of destruction.

"Spin the Black Circle," which won Pearl Jam their first Grammy (Best Hard Rock Performance with Vocals), is also essential for making sense of "Not for You," whose hostility is out of place without first sharing in this moment of exultation.

"Not for You"

Lyrics:	Eddie Vedder
Music:	Eddie Vedder
Single Release Date:	March 21, 1995

Peak U.S. Chart Position: 12
Live Debut: Paramount Theater in Denver, Colorado, U.S.A.,
                                                  March 7, 1994
Alternate Versions/
Notable Performances: Orpheum Theatre in Boston, Massachusetts, U.S.A.,
                                                  April 12, 1994
                                                  Saturday Night Live: Studio 8H, NBC Studios in New
                                                  York, New York, U.S.A., April 16, 1994
                                                  Pearl Jam Twenty: Original Motion Picture
                                                  Soundtrack, Folk Arts Theater in Manila, Philippines,
                                                  February 26, 1995
                                                  Touring Band 2000, Greek Theatre in Los Angeles,
                                                  California, U.S.A., October 24, 2000

In 1994, Eddie told the *LA Times*: "There is something sacred about youth, and the song ['Not for You'] is about how youth is being sold and exploited. I think I felt like I had become part of that too." "Not for You" argues for a purity of meaning and experience open to anyone willing to surrender to rather than exploit it.

The slow powder-keg burn of "Not for You" feels like the crackling, deceptively calm moments before an explosion. There is an undercurrent of barely contained rage, released during the chorus ("This is not for you ... never was for you ... fuck you"), quickly bottled back up during the verses before burning itself out in the outro. There is temporary relief found in catharsis, but no resolution. Then again, a resolution is not the point.

The liner notes reference twentieth-century French existentialist Albert Camus's essay *The Myth of Sisyphus*, who was punished by the gods for trying to cheat death. Sisyphus is cursed to forever push a boulder up a steep hill only for it to roll back down. Camus argues the only proper orientation to the absurdity of life is to revolt against it. Even if the revolt can never be successful, the act of rejecting absurdity conveys significance. "Not for You" is directed at the people who forgot the power of that rejection and abandon their youthful ideals once they become difficult, uncomfortable, or unwinnable.

"Not for You" builds upon the assertion in "Spin the Black Circle" that music is sacred and speaks the language of solidarity. Others have experienced what we have experienced, and we find comfort and strength in the music we share. Music embodies the voice of optimism, the promise of accountability, and the demand for justice. And, it never has more power than in those critical moments when we form our adult identities.

This is why Pearl Jam's live shows feel so much like revivals, and what makes the "corruption" of music and the commodification of art and artist so damning. Rather than a source of authenticity, community, and transcendence, music is hijacked into the service of empty exploitation, moving away from an affirmation of life toward, if not death, then a type of marketed half-life. It rejects transformation in the name of an empty acceptance of everything it once opposed.

Eddie is an ancient thirty at the time of the song's recording, and from that vantage, he launches an accusing salvo directly at the people who have acquired power, but in the process forgotten what that power is for.

> All that's sacred comes from youth
> Dedications, naïve and true
> With no power, nothing to do
> I still remember why don't you?

"Leash" urges us to "delight in our youth." Just one year later, Eddie feels youth belongs to others, but he can still defend its purity. Eddie pleads for us, and himself, to never forget where we came from and what we have left behind, to hold onto the shared vocabulary of revolution and solidarity, the intimate obligation to treat one another as human beings and not as things.

"TREMOR CHRIST"

Lyrics:	Eddie Vedder
Music:	Jeff Ament and Mike McCready
Live Debut:	Aladdin Theater in Las Vegas, Nevada, U.S.A., November 30, 1993
Alternate Versions/ Notable Performances:	Seattle Center Arena in Seattle, Washington, U.S.A., December 8, 1993
	Palaisozaki in Torino, Italy, September 19, 2006

"Tremor Christ" begins in the aftermath of a metaphorical shipwreck, and the music evokes the storm. The subject had succumbed to the superficial ease of temptation, the promise of reward without cost. Slight innocuous surrenders of principle lead to consequences that quickly spiral out of control: "Little secrets, tremors turn to quake. The smallest oceans still get big big waves." The price is always steep, paid in love and integrity. Both the art and the artist suffer for the easy choices, for the refusal to see the hidden price of playing the game instead of moving Sisyphus's rock. We are left with an exhausted artist, their passion bled dry, the emancipatory promise of the music gone: "Gorgeous was the savior, sees her drowning in his wake."

The second verse chronicles his journey to this desolate shore. The devil's bargain is seductive, and it is rare our better angels see clearly enough to resist before it is too late. And, if you cannot avoid the devil, you need to refuse him (a recurring theme in "Whipping," "Corduroy," and "Satan's Bed").

The subject is wounded, but they are not dead yet. Like "Last Exit," a choice remains, and the second half of the song is a fighting creed, a declaration to resist, forgo temptation, endure hardship, and do what is necessary to regain control over their soul. "Tremor Christ" ends with the eerily calm determination to face down the ocean's trackless expanse armed only with love and a willingness to resist.

That Camusian theme runs throughout *Vitalogy*'s defiant moments. Never a guarantee, or even expectation, of victory, but the willingness to fight is what preserves our humanity. The willingness to accept responsibility for the mistakes we have made, and to keep searching for the possibility of a wavering, uncertain salvation—the "Tremor Christ."

"Nothingman"

Lyrics:	Eddie Vedder
Music:	Jeff Ament
Live Debut:	Crisler Arena in Ann Arbor, Michigan, U.S.A., March 20, 1994
Alternate Versions/ Notable Performances:	Demo, included in the 2011 *Vs./Vitalogy* reissue, recorded October 14, 1993, featuring Richard Stuverud on drums
	Live on Two Legs, Sandstone Amphitheater in Bonner Springs, Kansas, U.S.A., July 3, 1998
	Touring Band 2000, Key Arena in Seattle, Washington, U.S.A., November 6, 2000

"Nothingman" sounds like a memory, from the opening guitar gliding into focus to the final goodbye. It is fragile and regretful, and it works well as a love song—the story of a man who took for granted a powerful, dynamic woman, stifling her until she had no choice but to free herself from him. He did not understand what he had until their love was beyond recovery: "Some words when spoken can't be taken back." He is left with nothing but regret and memories. "Nothingman" gives the female partner an equal voice within the song, highlighting her rising independence and ability to break free from their dying life together: "Empty stares from each corner of a shared prison cell. One just escapes, one's left inside the well."

But, given the larger issues Eddie was grappling with at the time of its composition, "Nothingman" can also be read another way—the woman standing in for any gift we take for granted and abuse. "Nothingman" picks up right after "Tremor Christ," serving as a warning. What happens when the ship is turned around too late for redemption, when passion is permanently tainted by commodification and objectification, a mockery of its transcendent potential? He no longer deserves the gifts ("Caught a bolt of lightning. Cursed the day he let it go"), and the muse has moved on. "Nothingman" is animated not just by loss but also by an overpowering sense of guilt. So, where does this leave the subject? The closing lyrics recall "Last Exit" and foreshadow "Immortality." There is the reference to the sun, fame, celebrity, inauthenticity, and a false light under which nothing grows. He is trapped there, blind, and slowly burning away into nothingness. Left only with the memory of what could have been, his life a living warning not to make the same mistakes.

"WHIPPING"

Lyrics:	Eddie Vedder
Music:	Eddie Vedder
Live Debut:	Slim's Cafe in San Francisco, California, U.S.A., May 13, 1993
Alternate Versions/ Notable Performances:	Fox Theater in Atlanta, Georgia, U.S.A., April 3, 1994
	Constitution Hall in Washington, D.C., U.S.A., September 19, 1998
	Riverport Amphitheatre, Maryland Heights, Missouri, U.S.A., October 11, 2000

"Whipping" is Pearl Jam's first straight protest song, a defiant call to arms. The album art clearly draws attention to the pro-choice abortion movement and the rise of anti-abortion terrorism and violence, but it is not a song about abortion per se. It is a template to be used when and as necessary.

"Whipping" conjures the racialized image of master and slave, the punishment for disobedience, and the literal transformation of a person into a thing.[4] It is full of images of protracted suffering. It openly wears its institutional distrust on its sleeve, too suspicious to ask for help after having been burned so many times. There is anger at the people who author and enforce the systems that control us. There is a sense that conflict is inevitable. Too late to turn back. No choice but to push forward. Yet, as the song presses on, it moves from solitary acts of defiance to a greater sense of solidarity. "I's" become "we's"—"why must we trust," "I'm just like you, think we've had enough," "we all got scars, they should have 'em too." Even if our only choice is to push the rock, we do not need to push it alone, and the enemy is not the rock, but the system that placed it before us.

"PRY, TO"

Lyrics:	Vedder
Music:	Dave Abbruzzese, Jeff Ament, Mike McCready, and Stone Gossard
Live Debut:	None

"Pry, To," an interstitial pause, features a muted declaration that "p-r-i-v-a-c-y is priceless to me," which gradually morphs into a claustrophobic cry for help. Appropriately, the corresponding *Vitalogy* liner notes explore nightmares. The call for privacy, peace, and space, is responding to a powerful sense of dread that culminates with "Immortality."

According to Pearl Jam fan folklore, if you play "Pry, To" backward, Eddie is allegedly chanting something like "Peter Townsend how you saved my life." It is not clear if that is intentional, but if true, the fact that the message is hidden is significant. Music, once an immediate form of escape and release, is perverted, taken away, its healing properties now buried and difficult to extract.

"Corduroy"

Lyrics:	Eddie Vedder
Music:	Eddie Vedder
Live Debut:	Fox Theatre in St. Louis, Missouri, U.S.A., March 15, 1994
Alternate Versions/ Notable Performances:	Alternate Take, included in the 2011 *Vs./Vitalogy* reissue
	Constitution Hall in Washington, D.C., U.S.A., January 15, 1995
	Bridge School Benefit: Shoreline Amphitheatre in Mountain View, California, U.S.A., October 19, 1996
	Virginia Beach Amphitheatre in Virginia Beach, Virginia, U.S.A., August 3, 2000
	The Fans Are Alright, Duomo Square in Pistoia, Italy, September 20, 2006

No other song fully encapsulates Pearl Jam's energy and philosophy like "Corduroy," arguably the most important song in their catalog. The *Vitalogy* liner notes offer important context for unlocking "Corduroy," though the actual entry contains no lyrics. Instead, it features a picture of Eddie's teeth, in bad shape and, as he said in an interview with the *LA Times*, "analogous to my head at the time." In the same interview, he calls it a relationship song, but the relationship between an individual and the mass public—an individual who opens himself up for others and finds himself under assault for that act of intimacy. Is that the inevitable price of making yourself vulnerable, especially when meaningful relationships require vulnerability?

The liner notes surrounding "Corduroy" are instructive. There is a discussion of "self-pollution," and "Corduroy" is worried about the pollution of the soul. The next page discusses the sanctity of childbirth, the crime that comes from bringing unwelcome children into the world, the importance of being grounded and at peace before beginning an act of creation, and the value of self-knowledge: knowing who you are, where you are going, and why you want to be there. Equally important is the origin of the track's unassuming title—Eddie's cheap corduroy jacket becoming an overpriced fashion statement, the jacket symbolic of seeking meaning and identity in celebrity.[5]

"Corduroy" opens with its slow, ominous build, tentative at first, but rising in power—steeling itself for the fight ahead before crashing into the first verse and its iconic opening lines, delivered with weary defiance: "The waiting drove me mad. You're finally here and I'm a mess." What happens when dreams arrive tainted? "Corduroy" is about purging yourself of corruption and starting over, the details kept vague so the listener can read their own struggles and demons into the lyrics.

"Corduroy" is a process of rejection and emancipation. The "rewards" that come from surrendering your integrity and authenticity are not worth the cost: "I don't want to take what you can give. I would rather starve than eat your bread." The Sisyphean language of a struggle for its own sake is embedded throughout. The singer is engaged in a battle with himself to restore his own humanity by resisting what degrades it. Strength is drawn from the realization that even if you must choose alone, you are not alone in having to make a choice.

There is a call to trust your own experiences and intuition rather than accept what you are told, and to define your own worth rather than allow others to define it for you. "Corduroy" adopts the language of both slave and martyr, and there is a willingness, almost an insistence, to suffer physically if that suffering affords a chance to restore your humanity and, through your example, inspire others. On the surface, it sounds like a defeat but is best understood as a restoration, a chance to start over.

The stakes are clear in the song's emancipatory bridge, recognizing that freedom offered by others is illusory: "Everything has chains, absolutely nothing's changed." Life is a constant struggle to preserve your authenticity and self from forces seeking to seduce or bludgeon you into submission. But that struggle is offset by that moment of solidarity so important in Pearl Jam's music. The world is full of people facing the same devils and pushing the same rocks. By embracing that shared experience, we can embrace each other's power. And music can bridge the distances between people, reminding us that we are part of a shared community, speaking a common language, and collaborating around the creation of shared meaning.

Over time live versions of "Corduroy," like "Alive," have become shared celebrations, rather than a declaration of war against long odds, because we know how the story ends—or at least that the worst is over, and we have come through it together. The studio version lacks that celebratory tone because the journey is just beginning, the happy ending a distant possibility, but worth fighting for.

"BUGS"

Lyrics:	Eddie Vedder
Music:	Eddie Vedder
Additional Musicians:	Eddie Vedder, accordion
Live Debut:	Wachovia Spectrum Arena in Philadelphia, Pennsylvania, U.S.A., October 31, 2009

Alternate Versions/
Notable Performances: Ziggo Dome in Amsterdam, The Netherlands, June 27, 2012

Wrigley Field in Chicago, Illinois, U.S.A., July 19, 2013

"Bugs" is a difficult, jarring listen. It is a sarcastic spoken word piece accompanied by an out-of-tune accordion and percussive crunching, as if someone is stomping through a field of roaches. While playful, it is a depressing piece to follow the tentative but somehow triumphant "Corduroy." "Bugs" is a song of descent that gradually surrenders the hard-earned victory of "Corduroy."

The bugs symbolize any force destructive of agency, authenticity, and life. They are faceless, identical, amoral, and inevitable ("waiting ... waiting ..."), in the service of endless consumption and reproduction. There are too many to kill, too many to reason with, and ultimately no choice but to give in. The subject never fully does, but the listener leaves "Bugs" wondering how long they can fight—especially if they remain alone, staring down the swarm. "Bugs" ends with the subject resigned to the inevitability of the forces arrayed against them. As the accordion cuts out, the mind's eye lingers on the image of the subject enveloped by a skittering darkness.

And yet, the inclusion of songs like "Bugs" (and "Stupid Mop") push back against its message, the decision to include something this discordant as a follow-up to the fastest-selling album of all time is itself an act of resistance, an assertion of self. The choice of the accordion embeds an undercurrent of defiance in an otherwise defeatist song. It declares that something intangible is at work, a core to the music that cannot be commodified, and a refusal to be a party to any attempt at doing so.

"SATAN'S BED"

Lyrics:	Eddie Vedder
Music:	Stone Gossard
Additional Musicians:	Eddie Vedder, bass; Jimmy Shoaf, Drums
Live Debut:	Fox Theater in Atlanta, Georgia, U.S.A., April 3, 1994

Alternate Versions/
Notable Performances: *Self Pollution Radio* FM Broadcast from Seattle, Washington, U.S.A., January 8, 1995

Bryce-Jordan Center in State College, Pennsylvania, U.S.A., May 3, 2003
Arlene Schnitzer Concert Hall in Portland, Oregon, U.S.A., July 20, 2006

"Satan's Bed" offers a dirty, raunchy, argumentative celebration of imperfect authenticity. The music repudiates the surrender of "Bugs" as the lyrics embrace a refusal to be anything other than who we are. The song's relaxed playfulness offers a welcome break from the tension on the rest of the record. The urgency is present, but its swagger pushes through *Vitalogy*'s heavy pressure, lifting a huge weight so the singer can finally breathe easy.

The first verse explores the easy allure of surrender. The temptation is always there—constant ("Sundays Fridays Tuesdays Thursdays the same"), uninvited ("sometimes the special guest he don't like to leave"), and powerful ("funny how I always want to give in"). What stops him from surrendering? The answer, as usual, is love—a purer, healthier, more authentic kind of love, whatever its form, unmediated by the temptations and expectations of our corruptors.

The second verse further develops the theme of authenticity, rejecting superficial materialism and social standards of a celebrity consumer culture, and reminding us that authentic and unmediated love is beyond these illusionary standards and may only be achievable by actively rejecting them. We do not need to look to heroes. It requires no messiah. Love is something we find and create for ourselves.

The bridge briefly recalls "Bugs," a reminder that existence is an endless, punishing cycle of torture and rewards. Whether you surrender or commit to moving the rock, life remains a series of victories and defeats, rewards and punishments, joy and sadness. But we can endure and occasionally find moments of triumph if we are not alone.

The third verse returns to the Satan metaphor and reaffirms the need to live imperfectly but true to ourselves. If we are going to fall, we will choose to jump. If we are going to rise, we will do so under our own power. It will be difficult, but we are going to have to learn to live for ourselves, to save ourselves, in the service of a better kind of love.

"Better Man"

Lyrics:	Eddie Vedder
Music:	Eddie Vedder
Additional Musicians:	Brendan O'Brien, pipe organ and Hammond organ
Live Debut:	Slim's Cafe in San Francisco, California, U.S.A., May 13, 1993

Alternate Versions/
Notable Performances: *Bad Radio* demo (recorded by the band Bad Radio,
                        1988)
                        "Guitar/Organ Only," included in the 2011 *Vs./Vitalogy*
                        reissue
                        Fox Theater in Atlanta, Georgia, U.S.A., April 3, 1994
                        Bridge School Benefit: Shoreline Amphitheatre in
                        Mountain View, California, U.S.A., October 31, 1999
                        Idaho Center in Boise, Idaho, U.S.A., November 3, 2000
                        Rock & Roll Hall of Fame Induction Ceremony: Barclays
                        Center in Brooklyn, New York, U.S.A., April 7, 2017

"Better Man," written before Eddie was twenty-one, is a near-perfect piece of pop songwriting—insightful, devastating, flawlessly performed, and featuring one of the most remarkable tonal shifts in the catalog. It moves seamlessly from an achingly resigned sadness to revelatory breathless energy. Yet, producer Brendan O'Brien had to fight to include it since the band (or, at least, Eddie) was anxious to avoid hits.

"Better Man" is about being trapped in a destructive relationship, its dedication "to the bastard that married my momma" immortalized in the April 3, 1994 Fox Theater radio broadcast. It explores the lies we tell ourselves to justify our circumstances, recalling the pre-emancipatory moments of "Rearviewmirror," and it is easy to imagine both songs being about the same person. Yet, it is simultaneously wistful and tender, recognizing that underneath its complicated wreckage is a desperate desire to love and to be loved, and an all too human fear of being alone that compels us to make poor choices—in addition to gendered dynamics centered around fear, power, expectation, and opportunity.

The first verse, accompanied by a gentle guitar and wistful organ, contains some of Eddie's finest narrative table setting, introducing our main character, her circumstances, her dreams and nightmares.

> Waiting, watching the clock, it's four o'clock, it's got to stop.
> Tell him, take no more. She practices her speech
> As he opens the door she rolls over.
> Pretends to sleep as he looks her over.

One verse, one scene, a lifetime of regret amplified by an evocative, heart-wrenching chorus.

> She lies and says she's in love with him.
> Can't find a better man.
> She dreams in color. She dreams in red.
> Can't find a better man.

She lies to convince herself that this is the life she chose, the life she wants. But the truth is revealed in her dreams, as red is the color of anger and violence—the feelings she dares not voice in real life—as well as the color of health, courage, and love, representing the person she wishes she could be. As "Better Man" progresses the song shifts to her lost potential and unrealized life, culminating with the revelation that she stays with this person because she feels needed, the desire to matter and belong overriding her abusive, co-dependent treatment.

The track's prevailing emotion is not judgment but empathy. It explores why people surrender to forces that threaten to destroy them, out of a combination of fear, powerlessness, naiveté and need. It recognizes that once the initial surrender is made, it is difficult to hold onto the best part of who we are and could be (shades of "Elderly Woman..."). But rather than mourning or condemning, the version of "Better Man" found on *Vitalogy* (as opposed to the melancholy original recording) chooses to turn its ending into an empathetic, almost joyful celebration of the frailty that makes us human.

Unsurprisingly, it was the live experience that cemented this transformation, as the second half of the studio version is built from live performances of "Better Man" captured during the 1994 Atlanta concerts, the reciprocal energy between band and audience transforming guilt and tragedy into forgiveness and possibility.[6]

"Aye Davanita"

Lyrics:	Eddie Vedder
Music:	Dave Abbruzzese, Jeff Ament, Mike McCready, Stone Gossard, and Eddie Vedder
Live Debut:	Great Woods in Mansfield, Massachusetts, U.S.A., September 16, 1998 (a recording was used as the opening music for the 1998 tour)

"Aye Davanita" is a loose and easy transition between the triumphal ending of "Better Man" and *Vitalogy*'s intense conclusion, a product of the band going "interlude crazy," according to producer Brendan O'Brien.

"Immortality"

Lyrics:	Eddie Vedder
Music:	Eddie Vedder
Live Debut:	Boston Garden in Boston, Massachusetts, U.S.A., April 11, 1994
Alternate Versions/ Notable Performances:	Soldier Field in Chicago, Illinois, U.S.A., July 11, 1995
	Sports Palace in Barcelona, Spain, November 21, 1996

Air Canada Centre in Toronto, Ontario, Canada,
October 5, 2000
Nagoya-shi Koukaidou in Nagoya, Japan, March 6,
2003
Time Warner Cable Arena in Charlotte, North Carolina,
U.S.A., October 30, 2013

Vitalogy's liner notes contain a glossary, which defines immortality as the "ability to live by dying." "Immortality" embraces and explores the contradiction in the definition—that we can end up being so overwhelmed by life that we can only live through negation, the dark promise in the alternative lyrics of "Last Exit." But it can also embrace the more life-affirming theme that runs throughout Pearl Jam's catalog—the need for release from the expectations and demands of others to find space for reflection, healing, and new beginnings. Immortality as an act of rebirth. "Immortality" (and *Vitalogy*) explores the tension between these two competing definitions, and one way or another, the journey that began in "Last Exit" ends here.

The music is laden with foreboding expectations while still being open enough to allow for movement and possibility. The lyrics begin with "vacate is the word," and to vacate is to make empty, which has different connotations than "to leave." The first verse explores an emotionally hollow and performative life ("cannot find the comfort in this world. Artificial tear, vessel stabbed, next up, volunteer?"), one in which it is impossible to find purpose and definition ("vulnerable, wisdom can't adhere"). A lonely verse for a lonely existence.

The chorus centers on the subject as a truant, and the home he finds in the context of *Vitalogy* is the community created by music. He wants to linger there. The sun imagery takes us back to the chorus of "Last Exit." The sun's light illuminates and punishes, warms and burns—we cannot live without it. But too much exposure is self-destructive, a metaphor for the culture industry that made Pearl Jam possible. There is a way out—a trapdoor in the sun—but we cannot know what is on the other side. That is the question *Vitalogy* struggles to answer. Like "Last Exit," it is difficult not to think of "Immortality" in the context of Kurt Cobain, and while Eddie insists the song was not written about him (and that to do so would have been exploitative) "there might be some things in the lyrics that you could read into and maybe will … help you understand the pressures on someone who is on a parallel train."[7]

The second verse situates "Immortality" squarely in the context of the record—acknowledging the costs of the public objectification of self. The industry is merciless, and when you are no longer useful, you find yourself "swept out through the cracks beneath the door," denied a graceful, dignified exit. Earlier on *Vitalogy*, the subject contemplated surrender—abandoning Sisyphus' rock—but it is clear in the end that this is no real option. The part of you that surrenders is "executed anyhow," and what is authentically yours fades away, the "scrawl dissolved."

A quiet, meditative solo gradually builds in urgency, and the whispered thought of immortality leads to the final, quietly panicked verse. The subject is unable to stop the thought of suicide and the need for escape. He is utterly lost, "running in the dark" (despite the proximity of the sun) and recognizing that the time for choosing is at hand. Life or immortality. As is typical for Eddie's early writing, we do not know what he decides or what we should do. The music leaves us paused at the crossroads.

Still, *Vitalogy* does help us draw some conclusions. Throughout the record, there are moments of resistance, if not hope. It chooses life because the grinding struggle for authenticity and love is where we derive meaning. The possibility of love makes the struggle, no matter how difficult, something we can endure until something finally changes.

"HEY FOXYMOPHANDLEMAMA, THAT'S ME" (AKA "STUPID MOP")

Lyrics: Eddie Vedder
Music: Jeff Ament, Stone Gossard, Jack Irons, Mike McCready, and
               Eddie Vedder
Live Debut: None

Vitalogy's arc completes with "Immortality." You can choose to stop listening before the sound collage that is "Stupid Mop." But "Stupid Mop" serves a purpose as another road not taken. The subject of "Stupid Mop" lacks the love, meaning, and purpose that *Vitalogy* fights so hard to preserve. What makes the song so disturbing is the desperate, sad desire of the main character for love and clarity. The closest they can approximate to love is violence (shades of "Better Man") and trauma as a substitute for intimacy, a desire expressed through incoherent ramblings. It is a cold, clinical song, intentional in the way it discomfits the listener.

"Stupid Mop" is a character study and an empathetic warning. It adds some interesting flavor at the end, where Eddie could have ended up without love and music, and without *Vitalogy*, his last exit.

4

Merkin Ball

Released:	December 4, 1995
Musicians:	Eddie Vedder, vocals, guitar
	Jeff Ament, bass
	Jack Irons, drums
	Neil Young, guitar, pump organ, vocals
Producer:	Brett Eliason
Engineering:	Brett Eliason
Studio:	Bad Animals in Seattle, Washington, U.S.A.
Art Direction:	Gary Burden
Cover Art:	Jeff Ament, Eddie Vedder, Barry Ament, Joel Zimmerman, and Emek
Peak Chart Position:	No. 7 on the U.S. *Billboard* Top 100, No. 25 U.K. Top Singles

After *Vitalogy,* Pearl Jam, in particular Eddie, continued to struggle with their identity as a band besieged by obligations and expectations imposed by the industry, fans, and themselves. It was at this particularly low moment that Neil Young, musical influence, and the inspiration for half of their name, staged a much-needed intervention. Both were playing at Voters for Choice in support of reproductive rights when Neil asked if they would like to record together. The band jumped at the opportunity, and Neil headed up to Seattle. Over the course of four days in January and February 1995, they wrote and recorded the album *Mirror Ball*, though legal conflicts between labels prevented Pearl Jam's name from appearing on the album. Neil Young served as the principal songwriter and vocalist, though Eddie made a brief appearance on the song "Peace and Love."

Eddie's exclusion was not by design. He was struggling with a particularly intense situation with a stalker (partially chronicled on *No Code's* "Lukin") and "leaving the house wasn't the easiest thing to do."[1] He did attend some of the later sessions, writing and recording the tracks that would become the *Merkin Ball* companion EP, featuring some of Eddie's most visceral performances to date. Although released as a Pearl Jam album, only Eddie and new drummer Jack Irons appear on both tracks. Jeff plays bass on "Long Road," and neither Stone nor Mike feature at all. Producer Brendan O'Brien plays bass on "I Got Id," and Neil Young plays lead guitar on "I Got Id" and pump organ on "Long Road."

Despite the intentionally rushed, snapshot nature of the *Mirror Ball/Merkin Ball* sessions, the band credits the experience as essential for their survival. According to Stone, playing with a hero like Neil Young "came at a time when we needed it.... He made it all right for us to be who we were."[2] Following *Mirror Ball/Merkin Ball*, Pearl Jam felt capable of exhaling for the first time in years. *No Code's* softer distance is the result, and likely not possible without their four transformative days in the studio with "Uncle Neil."

"I Got Id" (aka "I Got Shit")

Also appears on *Rearviewmirror (Greatest Hits 1991–2003)*

Lyrics:	Eddie Vedder
Music:	Eddie Vedder
Additional Musicians:	Neil Young, guitar and pipe organ; Brendan O'Brien, bass
Engineered:	Brett Eliason
Live Debut:	Kosei Nenkin Kaikan in Osaka, Japan, February 21, 1995
Alternate Versions/ Notable Performances:	Soldier Field in Chicago, Illinois, U.S.A., July 11, 1995 *Give Way* (reissued 2023), Melbourne Park in Parkville, Victoria, Australia, March 5, 1998 *Touring Band 2000*, Molson Centre in Montréal, Quebec, Canada, October 4, 2000

Neil asked Eddie to write a song for inclusion in *Mirror Ball*, and although it did not make the album, "I Got Id' (generally known as "I Got Shit") was the result. There is a frayed energy to the music and a harsh, desolate beauty to the vocal performance. The song documents an emotional collapse. But, unlike "Black," which struggles to contain the devastating aftermath of a singular experience, "I Got Id" explores an ongoing decomposition that leaves the singer with nothing.

There is no ambiguity about the singer's mental state: "My lips are shakin' my nails are bit off. It's been a month since I've heard myself talk." The lyrics flirt with self-loathing in a way unique to *Merkin Ball*: "I fight back in my mind. Never lets me be right. I got memories, I got shit." Compare this with "Black," where the memories are a carefully guarded treasure. Or, later, "I'll just lie alone and wait for the dream where I'm not ugly and you're looking at me." The song builds to a moment of salvation through human connection: "I walked the line when you held my hand that night" before revealing "I paid the price, never held you in real life." Not only is that moment a fantasy, but the obsession came at the cost of other experiences, other lives lived, leaving him trapped in the prison of an unrequited dream, with Neil Young's wailing outro laying bare a deeply rooted and twisted pain.

"I Got Id" presents itself as a love song, but it is not a stretch to read in reflections on Eddie's relationship to his art and music—"I Got Id" was written shortly after *Vitalogy* and is very much still in that headspace—or imagine it written from the perspective of his stalker. Regardless, it is one of Eddie's most wounded and isolated performances. He has felt this hurt, but never sounded this alone.

"LONG ROAD"

Lyrics:	Eddie Vedder
Music:	Eddie Vedder
Additional Musicians:	Neil Young, guitar and pipe organ
Engineered:	Brett Eliason
Live Debut:	Red Rocks Amphitheater in Morrison, Colorado, U.S.A., June 20, 1995
Alternate Versions/ Notable Performances:	Dead Man Walking: Not In Our Name, Shrine Auditorium in Los Angeles, U.S.A., March 29, 1998 (with Nusrat Fateh Ali Khan)
	"America: A Tribute to Heroes," Television City Studios in Los Angeles, U.S.A., September 21, 2001
	The Molo Sessions (Eddie Vedder with the Walmer High School Choir), Recorded at Studio Litho, Seattle Washington, U.S.A., September 8–9, 2004

While recording *Mirror Ball*, Eddie learned his former high school drama teacher and personal mentor, Clayton Liggett, passed away. Eddie wandered off by himself and picked up a guitar. He began chiming a single chord, marking Liggett's passage. He sat there, alone with his droning eulogy, until Jeff, Neil, and Jack found him, and wordlessly joined in. "Long Road" emerged from the sharing of grief. A simple, moving performance that tries to process the finality of death while celebrating the immensity of a life and its impact on the people forced to live in its absence. The call and response outro "Will I walk the long road? We all walk the long road" simultaneously captures our inability to comprehend the totality of loss while rooting it in an inevitable, communal, and, above all, human experience.

Later that year, "Long Road" was re-recorded for the *Dead Man Walking* soundtrack as a duet with Pakistani Qawwali singer Nusrat Fateh Ali Khan. It is a beautiful recording. After September 11, Eddie and Neil Young performed "Long Road" for the "America: A Tribute to Heroes" televised concert. Playing a song that Eddie had previously recorded with an Islamic singer felt like a statement in that moment. Khan had died several years earlier.

Like so many of Pearl Jam's songs that stare into a void, demanding answers that aren't coming, "Long Road" is transformed when played live. A surprising number of these compositions serve as concert openers ("Oceans," "Release," "Wash," "Hard to Imagine," "Long Road," "Pendulum"), signifying that the questions and the need driving the ask are universal, and that we should look to each other, and the community created through music, for answers. They are experienced as a collective unburdening, a shared release that builds bridges across spaces that we can only navigate together.

5

No Code

Released:	August 27, 1996
Musicians:	Eddie Vedder, vocals, guitar
	Stone Gossard, guitar
	Mike McCready, guitar
	Jeff 2Ament, bass
	Jack Irons, drums
Producer:	Brendan O'Brien and Pearl Jam
Engineering:	Nick DiDia and Brendan O'Brien with Matt Bayles, Jeff Lane, and Caram Costanzo
Studio:	Chicago Recording in Chicago, Illinois, U.S.A.; Litho Studio in Seattle, Washington, U.S.A.; and Southern Tracks Recording in Atlanta, Georgia, U.S.A.
Art Direction:	Barry Ament and Chris McGann
Cover Art:	Eddie Vedder as Jerome Turner
Peak Chart Position:	No. 1 on the U.S. *Billboard* 200, No. 3 U.K. Top Albums

No Code marks an intentional pivot from Pearl Jam's earlier records, stepping back from the expansive, effortlessly anthemic feel of even the murkier moments on those albums. *No Code* looks inward, stumbling in a way that is simultaneously cautious and experimental, redefining who and what Pearl Jam is.[1] It represents both a logical follow-up to and thematic departure from *Vitalogy*, their first musical answers to the increasingly desperate questions asked across the first three records. It is arguably their first "adult" album, one that champions youth but no longer identifies with it, fixating instead on a return to an Edenic state of innocence to cope with the trauma of surviving in a corrupt and disenchanted world.

No Code marks the first time Pearl Jam writes from a place of potential wisdom, the perspective of seekers far enough along on their journey to begin tentatively mapping the path they follow, even if they cannot be sure of the destination. *No Code*'s title is misleading in that respect. Amid all the confusion and uncertainty, there is a code—or, at least, the outline of one. We have guideposts. We may even have a guide. The album cover is a seemingly random collection of pictures, but when you unfold it and step away, approaching it from a distance, a design emerges from the chaos.[2]

After *No Code*, Pearl Jam will continue to build upon the idea that music should offer answers, not just questions and companionship. While solidarity and love remain at the core of their music, there will be an increased commitment to action, growing comfort with uncertainty as something to be embraced rather than overcome, and an eventual grappling with new questions of intergenerational legacy and responsibility. But that growth begins with *No Code*, where every song either offers an answer or clears the space to find one. *No Code* is the first Pearl Jam record that is as much about the destination as it is the journey. It stands in marked contrast to the transitory, rootless urgency of *Vitalogy* by grounding its songs in particular moments, places, or relationships.

Still, these songs are hesitant and preliminary. They lack the iron core running through even the most lost and confused moments on the earlier albums. There is a palpable sense of longing and questing—an underwater quality to the record that mutes its climactic moments. *No Code* stalks something elusive just beyond its peripheral vision. Eddie's performance is more measured, the music distanced and difficult to track, but while *No Code* is detached, it does not retreat. Instead, it creates safe spaces where we can, for the first time, share in the insights of someone who has experience rather than someone who is experiencing, even if their journey is far from over.

No Code is one of Pearl Jam's most conceptually ambitious albums, equal parts question and answer, a record about the moment where journey and destination become one in arrival. It offers the wisdom of an adult by honoring the innocence left behind. Making peace is harder than making war, and *No Code* takes the first tentative steps down a new road. We stumble. We double back. But we travel, finally, in service of an end.

"SOMETIMES"

Lyrics:	Eddie Vedder
Music:	Eddie Vedder
Additional Musicians:	Mike McCready, piano
Live Debut:	The Showbox in Seattle, Washington, U.S.A., September 14, 1996
Alternate Versions/ Notable Performances:	Reunion Arena in Dallas, Texas, U.S.A., July 5, 1998 Air Canada Centre in Toronto, Ontario, Canada, October 5, 2000

Tweeter Center in Mansfield, Massachusetts, U.S.A.,
July 11, 2003

"Sometimes" is a dramatic departure from the bombastic opening tracks of previous records and quietly puts the listener's prior expectations on notice. "Sometimes" is best understood as an anti-prayer. It reproduces prayer's vulnerable surrender to something greater than yourself, the acceptance of your own insignificance, and the child-like hope that a force you can neither comprehend nor master will make it all okay. Yet, it looks inward to the self rather than outward to God to find its answers.

"Sometimes" feels wet and purifying, like a soft rain or gliding waves. The effect is not religious but feels spiritual—sacred, even playful in a distanced way. Eddie's vocals best capture this feeling during the recitation of "sometimes..." where his prior rage is swallowed and disarmed, sliding alongside him instead of propelling him forward. "Sometimes" comes from a place of meditative stillness that allows you to look safely inside yourself.

"Sometimes" recognizes the world is a vast and impersonal place, emphasizing our smallness and imperfections. After two verses—there is no chorus, as "Sometimes" discovers its conclusion in real time—the song moves immediately into the whispered intensity of its anti-climax, where the singer asserts their agency by accepting their imperfection and, as a result, their humanity. We get a litany of opposites, good and bad, rise and fall, knowledge and ignorance, culminating with the declaration, "Sometimes I reach to myself, dear God." If we can learn to love ourselves in our messy totality, we do not need God. We do not even need answers. We just need ourselves.

"Hail, Hail"

Lyrics:	Eddie Vedder
Music:	Stone Gossard, Jeff Ament, and Mike McCready
Live Debut:	Civic Center Augusta in Augusta, Maine, U.S.A., September 26, 1996
Alternate Versions/ Notable Performances:	Ed Sullivan Theater in New York, New York, U.S.A., September 20, 1996
	Live on Two Legs, Arco Arena in Sacramento, California, U.S.A., July 16, 1998
	E-Centre in Camden, New Jersey, U.S.A., September 2, 2000
	John Labatt Centre in London, Ontario, Canada, September 12, 2005

"Hail, Hail" is more cerebral than passionate, more reflective than instinctive. Consistent with the album's larger designs, "Hail, Hail" is initially more interested in rationalizing and justifying love than in experiencing it. And, despite some penetrating insights, it accepts that love is an experience that defies the imposition of reason. It embraces the vulnerability that flows from being under the power of another as essential to the fulfillment of the self.

The main riff, dirty and tenacious, offsets the muted vocals, grounding the abstractions and reminding the head of the heart. And, by the time "Hail, Hail" concludes, *No Code*'s musical grammar is clear. The vocals are again an exercise in restraint, allowing for greater contrast with the music, appropriate for the head/heart dynamic of the song and the album. This tension frequently manifests as dueling traditional "masculine" (rational, self-regarding, assertive) and "feminine" (emotional, other-regarding, appeasing) perspectives that require synthesis for fully realized relationships—with others, and with the self, though the record privileges the feminine perspective.

"Hail, Hail" is the story of a relationship in crisis, a couple bound together out of habit, hamstrung by baggage they cannot put down, and the realization that love requires acceptance of imperfection and risk. It understands that love is about negotiating dominance and submission—willingly giving someone power over you and accepting responsibility for the power you have over them. Independence is found in interdependence, manifesting in the culminating question, "Are you woman enough to be my man, bandaged hand in hand?"

The song's dominant images are shackles and restraints, all of which the singer initially chafes against ("Are we bound out of obligation? Is that all we got?"). But the ties that bind are eventually recognized as a source of strength rather than weakness. Nor do they require any justification. We are empowered through that acceptance, a theme immediately reprised in *No Code*'s iconoclastic first single "Who You Are."

"WHO YOU ARE"
Also appears on the *Chicago Cab: Original Motion Picture Soundtrack* and *Rearviewmirror (Greatest Hits 1991–2003)* with a minor lyrical change

Lyrics:	Eddie Vedder
Music:	Stone Gossard and Jack Irons
Additional Musicians:	Eddie Vedder, electric sitar
Single Release Date:	July 30, 1996
Peak U.S. Chart Position:	31
Live Debut:	The Showbox in Seattle, Washington, U.S.A., September 14, 1996
Alternate Versions/ Notable Performances:	Deutschlandhalle in Berlin, Germany, November 3, 1996 Bonnaroo in Manchester, Tennessee, U.S.A., June 14, 2008

"Who You Are" was a bold and divisive choice for the lead single of a band of Pearl Jam's stature, and it acted as a litmus test for the fandom. It is impish and sloppy, making it a thematically, if not commercially appropriate choice for the first single. It playfully embraces its flaws and imperfections, privileging the messy context in which we look for answers rather than what we find.

Its musical components arrive discreetly from a distance, searching for where and how they fit with each other. The backdrop that brings them together is disrupted by a discordant main riff, like someone starting to grasp enlightenment but too full of nervous energy to give it structure. The multi-tracked vocals sound like a proliferation of voices coalescing into one. And, during the climax and outro, the song disintegrates into its components without ever losing the memory of what it briefly was, confident that despite the complexity of the journey, "you've got a part."

"Who You Are," like "Sometimes" and "Hail, Hail," is about liberating the self by embracing our limitations, asking us to love ourselves as messy beings in a state of transition, with a self-aware lightness and sincerity. The lyrics are about travel along well-worn paths, which is the point. When you follow where others have been, you do not journey alone, and if you are willing to embrace the detours along the way, you will enjoy the ride a whole lot more.

"In My Tree"

Lyrics:	Eddie Vedder
Music:	Stone Gossard, Jack Irons, and Eddie Vedder
Live Debut:	The Showbox in Seattle, Washington, U.S.A., September 14, 1996
Alternate Versions/ Notable Performances:	*Give Way* (reissued 2023), Melbourne Park in Parkville, Victoria, Australia, March 5, 1998
	Live at the Garden, Madison Square Garden in New York, New York, U.S.A., July 8, 2003
	Goffertpark in Nijmegen, Netherlands, June 27, 2010

"In My Tree" explores the tension between the terrifying promise of growth and the comforting safety of innocence, embodying that dynamic within the music's propulsive stillness. "In My Tree" arrives from a great height, precarious and expansive, but at peace. The overall composition offers a clarity of vision that can only come when immediate details fade away. The world recedes and we are left with no companions but the leaves, who listen without judgment. The perfect space to talk through the ever-changing puzzle of yourself.

Nineteenth-century English philosopher John Stuart Mill used the tree as a metaphor for human growth and development in his seminal work *On Liberty*:

Human nature is not a machine to be built after a model, and set to do exactly the work prescribed for it, but a tree, which requires to grow and develop itself on all sides, according to the tendency of the inward forces which make it a living thing.

If *No Code* has a central metaphor, it may be the tree, which never stops changing within the broad contours of its final form, bending and swaying in the face of opposition without surrendering its solidity. The chorus uses the sensation of dizzying heights ("up here so high the sky I scrape") to demonstrate how self-discovery is simultaneously exhilarating and terrifying, but the tree's deep roots ensure we are kept safe and protected in our explorations.

Prior to *No Code*, youth was sacred ("Leash," "Not for You"), but youth occupies the liminal space between childhood and adulthood. It is righteous but transitory, more concerned with anticipating what is coming than savoring what it has. *No Code* explores the totemic sacredness of innocence—a space devoid of judgment that exists in, rather than waits for, a state of unending possibility. We have left that innocence behind, or had it stripped and stolen from us, and *No Code* is fixated on recapturing what we can. At times, the desire is needful, but in the album's quieter moments, innocence is something to be celebrated even if it cannot be possessed. "In My Tree" offers the most explicit formulation of this idea. Not just in the direct naming of innocence, but the childlike wonder of the song, the intimations of nursery rhymes, solipsistic play, and imagination. There is not a sense of what to do with that innocence, just a conviction that we cannot grow without it.

"Smile"

Lyrics:	Eddie Vedder
Music:	Jeff Ament
Additional Musicians:	Jeff Ament, guitar; Eddie Vedder, harmonica; Brendan O'Brien, piano
Live Debut:	Wembley Arena in Wembley, United Kingdom, October 28, 1996
Alternate Versions/ Notable Performances:	Sports Palace in Barcelona, Spain, November 21, 1996 Greensboro Coliseum in Greensboro, North Carolina, U.S.A., August 6, 2000 Verizon Wireless Amphitheatre in Noblesville, Indiana, U.S.A., June 22, 2003

"Smile" (along with "Hail, Hail" and "Around the Bend") understands our individual worth is measured in part by the health of our relationships.

Like "Hail, Hail," "Smile" draws a balance between traditional understandings of masculinity and femininity, fusing them into something healthier and more complete. The music is traditionally masculine—tough, muddy, crunchy, dusty. It moves with rough and ready swagger. The vocals and the sentiment, on the other hand, are traditionally feminine. Eddie's singing is gentle and even demure. The lyrics have an intimate simplicity, full of requited longing and gratitude.

A fully realized human being does not live solely within themselves. We are social animals. And "Smile" understands that while we are diminished by the absence of the people we love, that absence is something to celebrate insofar as it documents the presence of something deep and enduring. The declaration "I miss you already" is more joyful promise than bittersweet longing.[3]

"OFF HE GOES"

Lyrics:	Eddie Vedder
Music:	Eddie Vedder
Additional Musicians:	Brendan O'Brien, piano
Single Release Date:	January 11, 1997
Peak U.S. Chart Position:	34
Live Debut:	The Showbox in Seattle, Washington, U.S.A., September 14, 1996
Alternate Versions/ Notable Performances:	*Live on Two Legs*, Great Western Forum in Inglewood, California, U.S.A., July 14, 1998 *Live at the Showbox*, The Showbox in Seattle, Washington, U.S.A., December 6, 2002 John Labatt Centre in London, Ontario, Canada, September 12, 2005

"Off He Goes" starts a four-song run marking the low point of *No Code*'s spiritual journey. It explores the failures that "Present Tense" will ask us to forgive. "Off He Goes" is one of Pearl Jam's more beautiful compositions—rich, vibrant, full of weary dignity, whose lyrics create a space for the listener to observe rather than participate. While Eddie has joked that it is a song about a shitty friend, digging deeper reveals that "Off He Goes" is about elements of his personality needing to be more fully reconciled into a stable self—including wanderlust, passion, judgment, and embattlement.

There is a rustic wood panel and picture frame feel to the music. The subject is lost in memories and bittersweet regrets. Someone he cares for deeply is too afraid of stopping to slow down for very long, too busy denying the world to live in it, imagery dominated once again by the language of travel and destination, this time colored with fatigue and exhaustion. The wear and tear of living in opposition to the world rather than embracing it. Still, the traveler holds onto a crumpled desire. He longs for peace and stillness. The "perfectly unkempt hope."

For a moment, the traveler returns home, and they are whole. No matter how complex and difficult our context becomes ("the surrounding bullshit") the core of that relationship is soft enough to surrender and strong enough to endure. It is a short-lived victory, however. An aspirational peace glimpsed only for a fleeting moment. The desire to run, the pull of the road, the fear of stopping, and the longing for escape are all too strong. So, "Off He Goes" ends where it begins. The battle is not over, so there can be no peace. At least, not yet.

"HABIT"

Lyrics:	Eddie Vedder
Music:	Eddie Vedder
Live Debut:	Tramps in New York, New York, U.S.A., April 27, 1995 (performed by Eddie Vedder, Mike Watt, and Dave Grohl)
Alternate Versions/ Notable Performances:	Red Rocks Amphitheatre in Morrison, Colorado, U.S.A., June 19, 1995 (first performance by Pearl Jam) Fiddler's Green Amphitheatre in Denver, Colorado, U.S.A., June 23, 1998 Selland Arena in Fresno, California, U.S.A., October 27, 2000

"Habit" stands in stark contrast, sonically and thematically, to most of *No Code*. That is not necessarily surprising since, alongside "Red Mosquito" and "Lukin," it was written early enough to be considered a postscript to *Vitalogy*.

"Habit" is dogmatic and judgmental in its exploration of addiction—understandable given the alarming number of Seattle musicians who died from overdoses. The riff is brash and almost petulant—an excellent platform for self-righteous lyrics and a vocal performance that shrieks itself hoarse. It is not interested in dialogue, and almost entirely abandons the empathy that is quintessential to Pearl Jam. There is little screaming on *No Code*, and the places where it appears are the songs standing in intentional opposition to the album's ultimate message. This is not a song about being happy with your righteous self. It is about judging those who have the audacity not to follow your example, those who choose self-abuse over love.

The ferocious ending, the song's highlight, reinforces its lack of empathy and moral complexity. It is loud, violent, cacophonous, but oddly self-serving. It draws no conclusions. It offers no new directions. It is a musical affirmation of angry and judgmental superiority.

"RED MOSQUITO"

Lyrics:	Eddie Vedder
Music:	Jeff Ament, Stone Gossard, Jack Irons, Mike McCready, and Eddie Vedder
Live Debut:	Delta Center in Salt Lake City, Utah, U.S.A., November 1, 1995
Alternate Versions/ Notable Performances:	*Live on Two Legs*, Blockbuster Music Entertainment Center in Camden, New Jersey, U.S.A., August 29, 1998 Gibson Amphitheater in Universal City, California, U.S.A., October 7, 2009 (performed with Ben Harper)

"Red Mosquito" features one of the more subtly evocative images in the catalog. A mosquito is a parasite, and a red mosquito will have fed, red the color of blood and sin. The bite itches, and scratching makes it worse, but not scratching will drive you mad. Under certain circumstances, it can kill. Swat one and another takes its place. And, for all its power, it is a small thing, practically invisible, revealing itself through an endlessly patient droning whisper, "reminding me of his presence, letting me know he's waiting."

Musically, "Red Mosquito" is a melodically cacophonous wall of fuzzy guitars. Mike's lead buzzing disrupts a gentle, even peaceful melody, harassing us out of our reverie. While the music gives license for Eddie to let loose, his performance remains restrained. He sings like someone resigned to the bitter permanence of fresh wounds. It presents as a cautionary tale, urging the listener to learn from his mistakes before it is too late. Before they are bitten. "Somewhere in the time between."

"Red Mosquito" structured like a fable, features some of the strongest lyrics on the record. It is about the forced cessation of movement and growth. Its subject is trapped, pining for something just out of reach, and only vaguely aware of the passage of time. The red mosquito follows him, symbolizing the price of temptation, the flaw embedded in the wish itself. The devil reference calls up images of a Faustian bargain. The stalker imagery of the second verse (offering a nice segue into "Lukin") is amplified by the inability to escape, barely ahead of the inevitable reckoning and slowly being bled. Locked down and unable to affect a change: "Two steps ahead of him, punctures in your neck, hovering just above your bed…"

Despite the presence of the third-party tormentor, the singer bleeds himself through his own tortured regrets. If he knew now what he knew then, things could have been different, a sentiment reprised from "Elderly Woman…" and "Hard to Imagine" and revisited in "I'm Open." Payment is due, and yet it is owed to himself, a debt he need not carry. He could not have known then what he knows now, and the only person he has harmed is himself. If he figures out a way to let go, to forgive himself, he can move forward. He can leave. *No Code* is written in response to this longing.

"Lukin"

Lyrics: Eddie Vedder
Music: Eddie Vedder
Live Debut: Moore Theatre in Seattle, Washington, U.S.A., February
                   5, 1995

Alternate Versions/
Notable Performances: Soldier Field in Chicago, Illinois, U.S.A., July 11, 1995
                   Deutschlandhalle in Berlin, Germany,
                   November 3, 1996
                   Live at Benaroya Hall, Benaroya Hall in Seattle,
                   Washington, U.S.A., October 22, 2003
                   "Slow Version," Pepsi Center in Denver, Colorado,
                   U.S.A., October 22, 2014

"Lukin" is firmly rooted in the tradition of Pearl Jam's escape songs but in its most instinctive and reactionary form—escape as an immediate need, stripped of any reflection. "Lukin" is a musical tantrum, and while it strives to be a primal scream, it recognizes its own inadequacy and points to the need for something deeper, more substantive, and permanent.[4]

Responding to the stalker situation that kept Eddie sidelined during the *Mirror Ball/Merkin Ball* recordings, "Lukin" features a claustrophobic punk performance, its walls closing in with a deceptive speed. The siren guitar accents are distant and gentle and create the curious sensation that "Lukin" is somehow slowing down. Eddie's shrieking vocals share the lack of empathy of "Habit," while the verses describe an intense feeling of invasive intimacy, like a virus from which there is no escape. Despite the narrative specificity of the lyrics, "Lukin" feels more like an unsustainable ground state rather than a difficult day, and it captures the state of mind that "Present Tense" and the remainder of *No Code* will try to put at ease.

"Present Tense"

Lyrics: Eddie Vedder
Music: Mike McCready
Live Debut: The Showbox in Seattle, Washington, U.S.A., September
                   14, 1996

Alternate Versions/
Notable Performances: Great Western Forum in Inglewood, California, U.S.A.,
                   July 13, 1998
                   Savvis Center in St. Louis, Missouri, U.S.A., April 22, 2003
                   Rod Laver Arena in Melbourne, Victoria, Australia,
                   November 16, 2006

The music of "Present Tense" is warm, probing, and safe, suggestive of new memories and old wounds ready to heal. The transition from "Lukin" is a bit abrupt, but the impact of "Present Tense" is diminished if it is not following a run of songs about broken people. There are callbacks to "Sometimes," both in the precision of the introduction and the spiritual journey of the outro. The chorus takes stock of individual moments and weighs them with the intent of naming our crimes so we can be forgiven rather than punished: "You can spend your time alone redigesting past regrets, or you can come to terms and realize you're the only one who can(not) forgive yourself." The catharsis of the second chorus feels organic—earned within the journey of the song, the record, and the catalog. The outro is exploratory and confident, transitioning from the past to the future by embracing the lived experience of every moment along the way. Eddie's vocals are restrained throughout, as is typical for *No Code*'s anthemic moments. There is an unwillingness to disturb its tranquility.

"Present Tense" reminds us that our lives are informed by the past and anticipate the future but are bound to neither. To hold on to regrets is to hold on to the fiction that the past is predictive. Fixating on regret absolves us of the responsibility to be better and abandons the possibility that we can. It prevents us from growing from our mistakes and fails to understand that freedom is found by embracing each moment as its own experience. "Present Tense" asks us to abandon the conceit that life can be controlled. It can only be lived.

"Mankind"

Lyrics:	Stone Gossard
Music:	Stone Gossard
Additional Musicians:	Stone Gossard, vocals and piano
Live Debut:	The Showbox in Seattle, Washington, U.S.A., September 14, 1996
Alternate Versions/ Notable Performances:	Air Canada Centre in Toronto, Ontario, Canada, October 5, 2000
	iWireless Center in Moline, Illinois, U.S.A., October 17, 2014

"Present Tense" wraps up *No Code*'s arc, its final three songs serving as an extended postscript. "Mankind" tells us that one way to live in the present is to disenchant it. If nothing is at stake in the world, you do not have to care too much about it. You can live a self-referential life. "Mankind" is a sardonic song, smiling at a joke lost on the uninitiated. Eddie does not deliver sarcasm particularly well, and so this is a perfect song for Stone to sing, as he effortlessly conveys the sense of being slightly removed from everyone else's wavelength and in possession of some secret insight as a result.

But something is unsettling about this approach. Although the song chronicles the artifice and "inadvertent imitation" of our lives, "Mankind" keeps wondering why people do not see it, or, if they do, why they keep pretending otherwise. It cannot simply be that we are all sheep following the herd ("a pattern in all mankind"). The song's posturing hides that we crave something real and sincere and offers a retroactive reminder of why *No Code*'s journey is necessary.

"I'M OPEN"

Lyrics: Eddie Vedder
Music: Jack Irons
Live Debut: New England Dodge Music Arena in Hartford, Connecticut, U.S.A., May 13, 2006

Alternate Versions/
Notable Performances: The Vic Theatre in Chicago, Illinois, U.S.A., August 2, 2007
                         Water on the Road: Eddie Vedder Live, Warner Theatre in Washington, D.C., U.S.A., August 17, 2008

"I'm Open" is a reprisal of the deep, raw longing that lies beneath most of *No Code*. There are no answers—just a willingness to strip ourselves of the past we carry so we might be ready to receive them.

Musically, "I'm Open" creates the same hazy dream space as "Present Tense" and "Sometimes," although slightly heavier, holding onto a stifling pressure it wants to let go. It lightens during the chorus, and we are invited to "come in" as the music gently ascends and we begin to set our weight aside.

The lyrics address a deep disenchantment with the world: the replacement of "magic for fact," where everything is what it is, and we are bound to what lies before us. You cannot dream in a world like that, let alone move beyond it. The singer feels trapped, having long ago surrendered their innocence, calling back to "In My Tree." However, if we are willing to reenchant the world, to look for ways to let the magic back in, we can recapture that innocence. "Around the Bend" concludes *No Code* with the clearest picture of what that might look like.

"AROUND THE BEND"

Lyrics: Eddie Vedder
Music: Eddie Vedder
Additional Musicians: Brendan O'Brien, piano
Live Debut: The Showbox in Seattle, Washington, U.S.A., September 14, 1996

Alternate Versions/
Notable Performances: *Live at Benaroya Hall*, Benaroya Hall in Seattle, Washington, U.S.A., October 22, 2003
Wachovia Center in Philadelphia, Pennsylvania, U.S.A., October 3, 2005

For a band that does not write too many explicit love songs, almost every Pearl Jam song is, at its core, a celebration of love or longing for it. "Around the Bend" tells us we can most easily rediscover the magic we search for within the people we love—the people who mean more to us than we mean to ourselves. Forgiving yourself for your transgressions lets you find magic in other people, and through the reciprocity of love, see it reflected back in yourself.

Written for Jack Iron's son, "Around the Bend" is Pearl Jam's first attempt at a lullaby. It captures the gentle longing and peaceful, fragile stillness of bedtime. A particular moment frozen in time as the rest of the world moves on. How each day lasts forever and passes so quickly. Most of the time, you are only aware of the grind, but the moments where you can live in stillness are magical. It is the incarnation of the present tense, and "Around the Bend" captures the aspirational warmth and need to make the world a better place because someone in your life deserves it.

Eddie's vocals are grateful for the chance to linger in this moment. It is an understated performance, but more realistic for it. These are quiet feelings, honest enough to not require much adornment. "Around the Bend," with its focus on parent and child, is intimate and feminine because the parent/child relationship more purely obliterates (for the parent) the distinction between self and other. And, because they are unified, the music lacks the tension present in *No Code*'s other love songs.

"Around the Bend" is overwhelmed by quiet gratitude for the moments we have with the people we love, prays the world becomes worthy of them, and vows to be worthy of them too. That is what *No Code* tries to teach us. If we learn to forgive ourselves, we can start to become the person our loved ones deserve. If we make our peace with the world, we can make the most of the time we have with them. There may not be a grand unifying theory of everything, no silver bullet solution to the ills that afflict us. But, if we can find a way to live, and live well, with the people we love, we have found enough.

6

Yield

Released:	February 3, 1998
Musicians:	Eddie Vedder, vocals, guitar
	Stone Gossard, guitar
	Mike McCready, guitar
	Jeff Ament, bass
	Jack Irons, drums
Producer:	Brendan O'Brien and Pearl Jam
Engineering:	Nick DiDia with Matt Bayles, Sam Hofstedt, and Ryan Williams
Studio:	Litho Studio in Seattle, Washington, U.S.A.; Studio X in Seattle, Washington, U.S.A.; and Southern Tracks Recording in Atlanta, Georgia, U.S.A.
Art Direction:	Stone Gossard, credited as Carpenter Newton
Cover Art:	Jeff Ament
Peak Chart Position:	No. 2 on the U.S. Billboard 200, No. 7 U.K. Top Albums

Yield, Pearl Jam's fifth album, was hailed as a return to form—a collection of soaring anthems and grand statements after *No Code*'s naval gazing. Warm, energized, even fun, *Yield* continued to redefine Pearl Jam's sound while making space for more lyrical voices. Jeff and Stone each contributed two full sets of lyrics after Eddie wrote 98 percent of the first four albums. Following a turbulent period in the band's history, they started talking to the press, released a making-of documentary, *Single Video Theory*, and produced an award-winning video for *Do the Evolution*. After the failure of the Ticketmaster anti-trust investigation, for which Jeff and Stone provided Congressional testimony, and a subsequent boycott that generated public support but no action on the part of their peers, there was a palpable sense that Pearl Jam was making peace with the world and carving out their space in it.

To yield is to give way to external forces, but a yield is also the result of creation and labor, and both definitions apply. *Yield* rejects the need to fight every battle in the interest of health and healing. An album focused on self-care, it turns small actions into sweeping gestures and makes walking away an act of resistance. This is an evolutionary development after the unshakable commitment of *Ten*, *Vs.*, and *Vitalogy* to find solidarity and meaning in a world that undercuts both.

No Code is Pearl Jam's most personal and least political record to date, and many of *Yield*'s songs continue that inner journey, doubling down on the need to create safe and supportive spaces for exploration, growth, and love. Unlike *No Code,* there is a social critique running through *Yield*. Being skeptical of our institutions, it touches on how their design intrudes upon the relationships at the core of meaningful human experiences. This is not new. What is unusual is the deep and persistent doubt we find underneath *Yield*'s placid surface. What if our institutional flaws are so firmly embedded in our collective identity that there is no way to resist them? Embracing them is not an option. Pearl Jam draws a bright line between personal acts of forgiveness and larger social obligations. What is left, then, but to disassociate and focus instead existing apart from the enervating and corrupting influences that conspire against us? Love is an important part of this story but as a private alternative to the challenges of our time rather than a public response to a broken world.

Author Daniel Quinn's seminal work *Ishmael* was so foundational to the band's thinking at the time that Eddie was quoted in their fan club newsletter saying, "you could almost go as far as saying the liner notes to the record are in [*Ishmael*]," and that same issue featured a contest asking fans to create artwork showcasing what *Ishmael* meant to them.

In *Ishmael* and subsequent novels, Quinn argues that humanity is imprisoned by a myth that the world was created specifically for humanity to rule and exploit as it sees fit. This has led civilization to disregard nature's demand for equilibrium and construct a social order predicated on limitless expansion—a cycle both unsustainable and irredeemable. No scientific solution and no magical discovery will enable us to reconcile balance with endless growth.

For Quinn, our current trajectory is doomed. He is not a reformist or incremental thinker. Humanity's only way forward is to move "beyond civilization" into something new, something sustainable that enables us to surrender our core commitments to growth, entitlement, and mastery. He counsels a restless abdication to build new, smaller, sustainable communities that gradually leave our current world behind.

It is hard to appreciate the impact a theory like this might have on a person like Eddie Vedder—generous, empathetic, and optimistic. Eddie is, at heart, more reformist than revolutionary. He would rather fix what is broken than give up on it. He has too much faith in the capacity of people to endure, change, and grow. He is a humanist, and his faith in humanity's potential to transform itself is at odds with Quinn, whose work is predicated on the belief that this very confidence is what threatens our species. How would someone like Eddie, who believes so profoundly that if you keep fighting you will eventually win, react to the possibility that failure is the inevitable outcome of systemic flaws that cannot be overcome?

This tension results in a record that is quietly at war with itself, its more optimistic, transformational moments appearing on its first half and receding as the rest of the album inverts the core premise of "Dissident." What happens if, safety aside, escape is the only path?

"BRAIN OF J"

Lyrics:	Eddie Vedder
Music:	Mike McCready
Live Debut:	Delta Center in Salt Lake City, Utah, U.S.A., November 2, 1995
Alternate Versions/ Notable Performances:	*Monkey Wrench Radio* FM Broadcast from Seattle, Washington, U.S.A., January 31, 1998
	Alexander M. Baldwin Amphitheatre in Maui, Hawaii, U.S.A., February 21, 1998
	Smirnoff Music Centre in Dallas, Texas, U.S.A., October 17, 2000

The performance of "Brain of J" is loose, swinging, and playful, signaling that *Yield* will not be taking itself too seriously. Everything we believe can and will be called into question in the service of creating something better. It is a dirty performance with a street preacher's crackpot manic energy.

The opening lyrics ask "who's got the Brain of JFK? What's it mean to us now?", referencing the disappearance of President John F. Kennedy's brain from the National Archives and the conspiracy theories that followed. The central message of "Brain of J" calls for the challenging of prior assumptions, dead dogmas, political conditioning, and other tools of social control: "You, you've been taught, whipped into shape, now they got you in line."

It is not a political message, though—not in the traditional sense of advocating for a particular platform or targeting a specific system of control. *Ishmael* offers a window into the song's intent, as its core argument is about challenging foundational myths that create the illusion of boundless mastery, the right to act without reflection or consequence. *Ishmael* argues that for humanity to survive, it must first learn to accept the same limitations as the rest of creation.

It is a powerful idea whose spirit is found in the song's joyful discovery that if everything is a lie, we are absolved of trying to rationalize the absurdity of our social order. A more satisfying and sustainable truth awaits our discovery ("the whole world will be different soon"). It is a declaration of faith in the possibility of something more, delivered by the newly converted, and unpacked further in "Faithfull."

"Faithfull"

Lyrics:	Eddie Vedder
Music:	Mike McCready
Live Debut:	Alexander M. Baldwin Amphitheatre in Maui, Hawaii, U.S.A., February 20, 1998
Alternate Versions/ Notable Performances:	*Pearl Jam Twenty: Original Motion Picture Soundtrack*, Duomo Square in Pistoia, Italy, September 20, 2006 (soundcheck)
	Give Way (reissued 2023), Melbourne Park in Parkville, Victoria, Australia, March 5, 1998
	Adams Field House in Missoula, Montana, U.S.A., August 29, 2005

"Faithfull" is an anti-spiritual meditation on the nature of faith, an agnostic's affirmation of love. Its sunny disposition asks its big questions in clean, unadorned spaces, without the atmospheric drama, tortured conflict, or hushed contemplation normally associated with the subject matter. An unapologetic composition, it questions the legitimacy of organized faith and those who lay claim to mastery in its self-aggrandizing stories. There are no hidden mysteries, no secret truths: "Plaque on the wall says that no one's slept here. It's rare to come upon a bridge that has not been around or been stepped on." Everything we need to understand our place in the world lies visible before us.

There is a metaphorical reference to God as "the man upstairs" who is "used to all of this noise," and Eddie takes his critique further in the chorus, describing prayer and someone's relationship with an externalized spirituality as an "echo nobody hears"—a self-referential conversation that seeks validation and, through that validation, absolution from our sins. Eddie never comments on whether God exists. But, if it does, it is not listening or intervening. We are on our own.

Ishmael is again helpful for unpacking "Faithfull," as Quinn's early works were about deconstructing stories that privilege man as the center of the universe. The better story we are searching for ("Brain of J") can only be found by first removing ourselves from the ones that cause harm. And this is one of the big ones. "We're faithful. We all believe it."

Eddie will flesh this out further in "Do the Evolution." But Eddie's humanism, rather than Quinn's critique, anchors the song's conclusion. If traditional religion is "belief in the game controls that keep us in a box of fear," then real faith is found in the human connections that define our identity. Traditional faith takes what is best about us, our capacity for love, forgiveness, and redemption, and externalizes it into something we bow down before. Instead, we must embrace that power within and between ourselves: "Just be darling and I will be too, faithful to you."

"No Way"

Lyrics:	Stone Gossard
Music:	Stone Gossard
Live Debut:	Star Lake Amphitheater in Pittsburgh, Pennsylvania, U.S.A., August 25, 1998
Alternate Versions/ Notable Performances:	Key Arena in Seattle, Washington, U.S.A., September 22, 2009
	HSBC Arena in Buffalo, New York, U.S.A., May 10, 2010

"No Way" reintroduces some of the funkier playing that emerges occasionally throughout the catalog. There is a wry sarcasm in the music, though it is never mean-spirited, and the moments where the song briefly ratchets up its tension are quickly deconstructed before segueing into its anti-anthem chorus. A mock confessional quality to Stone's tongue-in-cheek lyrics pokes fun at the band's self-seriousness reputation: "There's a token of my openness, of my need to not disappear" and "to the ocean, all my platitudes." During the bridge and outro, there is a sarcastic request to "call in an angel," the larger-than-life rock star presented as a supernatural being who both feeds and endures the oversized transformative expectations of their audience.

Like "Faithfull," "No Way" is clear that our apathy and anxiety is a question of scale. We cannot save the world, but maybe we can save each other. We do not need heroes. We just want and need "someone to be there for me." Or, as Stone said, "maybe we all need to just live life and quit trying to prove something."[1] It represents a significant contraction of the sweep and scope of Pearl Jam's traditional message, especially after the millennial expectations of "Brain of J." And it makes for a curious transition into the unapologetically messianic "Given to Fly."

"Given to Fly"

Lyrics:	Eddie Vedder
Music:	Mike McCready
Single Release Date:	December 22, 1997
Peak U.S. Chart Position:	21
Live Debut:	The Catalyst in Santa Cruz, California, U.S.A., November 12, 1997 (Pearl Jam performing as the Honking Seals)
Alternate Versions/ Notable Performances:	*Monkey Wrench Radio* FM Broadcast from Seattle, Washington, U.S.A., January 31, 1998
	Live on Two Legs, Great Western Forum in Inglewood, California, U.S.A., July 14, 1998

Sound Advice Amphitheatre in West Palm Beach, Florida, U.S.A., April 11, 2003
Pearl Jam Twenty: Original Motion Picture Soundtrack, McCready Instrumental (2010)
Rock & Roll Hall of Fame Induction Ceremony: Barclays Center in Brooklyn, New York, U.S.A., April 7, 2017

"Given to Fly" is a soft culmination of Pearl Jam's journey thus far, a beautiful composition that speaks of renewal and obligation, and whose dynamics capture the peaks and valleys that mark the complexity of human life—and reflect Mike McCready's struggles with addiction. It features Eddie's most powerful vocal on the record and offers a clarity of purpose *Yield*'s second half will quietly start to unravel.

The song's narrative offers a microcosm of the transformative potential embedded in the human experience. The subject begins disaffected ("alone in a corridor, waiting, locked out") but a restless, rolling energy resides within him. He rejects the platitudes and expectations that contain him: "He got up outta there, ran for hundreds of miles." A long, solitary journey, but a necessary one, with the familiar emphasis on escape as a precondition of liberation. It culminates at the ocean—a vast, indifferent power that erodes and destroys, a cradle of life that nurtures and cleanses—with a "smoke in a tree," calling back to the restoration of innocence and forgiveness found in "In My Tree" and "Present Tense."

The music ratchets up in speed and intensity as the ocean overpowers and transforms him. He is reborn, granted wings (recall the angel reference in "No Way"), and liberated from his past and our collective enervating mythology. From this high, clean place, he is afforded a new vision and made whole.

"Given to Fly" argues that with liberation and transcendence comes the obligation to pass it on: "He floated back down 'cause he wanted to share his key to the locks on the chains he saw everywhere." Like *Ishmael*, we may not be ready to receive this revelation. Love requires obligation and reciprocity— the surrendering of mastery and privilege, both jealously guarded. Eddie casts the subject as a prophet who suffers as "first he was stripped and then he was stabbed by faceless men," though he endures. "Given to Fly" reaches its climax around the message: to share love is the essence of what it means to be human.

And he still gives his love, he just gives it away.
The love he receives is the love that is saved.
And sometimes is seen a strange spot in the sky.
A human being that was given to fly.

It is a powerful message. Anti-mastery. Anti-capitalist. Humanist in its embrace of empathy, solidarity, and refusal to judge who is worthy of receiving them. We all are.

"Given to Fly" has become a live staple (only "Do the Evolution" is played more from *Yield*), and over time has transformed into a different song. On *Yield*, "Given to Fly" is a personal journey of affirmation and commitment. But live it leans into a galloping energy that turns it into a breathless collective experience of redemption through the mutual giving and receiving of love: "The love he receives is the love that is saved."

"WISHLIST"

Lyrics:	Eddie Vedder
Music:	Eddie Vedder
Single Release Date:	May 5, 1998
Peak U.S. Chart Position:	47
Live Debut:	The Catalyst in Santa Cruz, California, U.S.A., November 12, 1997 (Pearl Jam performing as the Honking Seals)
Alternate Versions/ Notable Performances:	Melbourne Park in Melbourne, Victoria, Australia, March 3, 1998
	Merriweather Post Pavilion in Columbia, Maryland, U.S.A., September 4, 2000
	The Vic Theatre in Chicago, Illinois, U.S.A., August 2, 2007
	Maracanã Stadium in Rio de Janeiro, Brazil, March 21, 2018

Although love is thematically present, or intentionally absent, in almost every Pearl Jam song, "Wishlist" is one of the first times the band leans into open sentimentality, however delicate and tenuous the exercise. It is unapologetic and aspirational in its description of the person Eddie wishes he could be, a logical coda to "Faithfull" and "Given to Fly"—the quiet, internal, monologue of someone who very much wants to be worthy of the love they have been given.

A simple composition, it is no less beautiful for its simplicity and the restraint necessary to avoid disturbing the quiet moment. It also features one of the first appearances of Mike's transcendent "prayer" solos, where his playing carries the message somewhere safe and sacred.

Wishlist was born of an eight-minute stream-of-consciousness exercise from which Eddie chose his favorite wishes.[2] Each evocative lyric highlights an absence, imperfection, or insecurity he hopes to overcome or a gift he wants to share. Some deal with Eddie the public figure who strives to be worthy of what people have invested in him: "I wish I was the evidence; I wish I was the grounds for fifty million hands upraised and open toward the sky."

Others speak to more personal and intimate sentiments—to be important in the life of just one person: "I wish I was a sentimental ornament you hung on the Christmas Tree. I wish I was the star that went on top," or "I wish I was the full moon shining off your Camaro's hood."

"Wishlist" is at its best when it speaks to a simple but profound longing to be useful and needed, to justify your space in someone else's life by putting in the work, even when it is hard. "Wishlist" gives. It never takes. And, while the culminating lyrics are a mouthful, they are delivered with such sincerity that they serve as the perfect aphoristic summation: "I wish I was the verb 'to trust' and never let you down."

The word "love" is never uttered, but it is the beating heart of every wish.

"PILATE"

Lyrics:	Jeff Ament
Music:	Jeff Ament
Live Debut:	Perth Entertainment Centre in Perth, Western Australia, March 20, 1998
Alternate Versions/ Notable Performances:	San Diego Sports Arena in San Diego, California, U.S.A., October 25, 2000
	Members Equity Stadium in Perth, Western Australia, November 14, 2009

"Pilate" marks a reset of sorts, a recognition that *Yield*'s prior conclusions are prematurely drawn. The gently swaying verses suffer small intrusions and moments of doubt that build toward a spikey, disruptive chorus. The lyrics track the music's progression and are full of vaguely disconcerting images: "Talk of circles and punching out," "talking out of turn," and "making angels in the dirt." "Pilate" peaks during its bridge, where the subject is "stunned by my own reflection. It's looking back, sees me too clearly and I swore I'd never go there again." It speaks of unfinished business and wistfully premature conclusions. Jeff said "Pilate" was inspired by *The Master and Margarita* by Mikhail Bulgakov, and the novel's conclusion of Pontius Pilate stuck on a mountain alone with his dog, haunted by "the loose ends in his life."[3]

Yield does not become a cynical album after "Pilate," as the familiar empathy and acceptance of imperfection remain, but it does lose its crusading spirit. It may take longer for the world to be different, and we may not be ready for it yet. Five years prior, Eddie argued "escape is never the safest path." *Yield*'s second half argues that safe or not, sometimes escape is the only path.

"Do the Evolution"

Lyrics:	Eddie Vedder
Music:	Stone Gossard
Additional Musicians:	Stone Gossard, bass and lead guitar
Single Release Date:	February 3, 1998
Peak U.S. Chart Position:	40
Recommended Reading:	*Pearl Jam: Art of Do the Evolution* by Joe Pearson (2020)
Live Debut:	The Catalyst in Santa Cruz, California, U.S.A., November 12, 1997 (Pearl Jam performing as the Honking Seals)
Alternate Versions/ Notable Performances:	*Monkey Wrench Radio* FM Broadcast from Seattle, Washington, U.S.A., January 31, 1998
	Live on Two Legs, Great Western Forum in Inglewood, California, U.S.A., July 13, 1998
	Live at the Garden, Madison Square Garden in New York, New York, U.S.A., July 8, 2003
	Colonial Center in Columbia, South Carolina, U.S.A., June 16, 2008
	Doheny State Beach in Dana Point, California, U.S.A., September 26, 2021

"Do the Evolution" marks a singular moment in Pearl Jam's catalog. A danceable, tetanus-infused garage riff backs a vocal that screams itself hoarse trying to believe its own bullshit. "Do the Evolution" is one of the more brutally cynical sets of lyrics Eddie has written, and the most *Ishmael*-influenced moment on *Yield*. It offers a near-nihilistic assessment of the self-aggrandizing story of mastery at the heart of capitalism, America, and an entire social order built on an unsustainable refusal to live in alignment with the world around it. It names and condemns a civilization that reifies both life and love in the interest of extraction and exploitation. While the song is too angry to have given up completely, absent is the usual call to arms accompanying its critique. This makes sense. As Daniel Quinn wrote for the 2001 issue of Pearl Jam's newsletter, the *Manual for Free Living*, "Liberation has to begin with understanding the nature of the wall that surrounds us." The first step to freedom is learning to see the bars of your cage.

Pulling from *Ishmael*, "Do the Evolution" frames evolution as an entitlement. By virtue of being "more advanced," the rules that govern others need not apply to us. "I'm at peace with my lust. I can kill 'cause in God I trust" because "It's evolution, baby." The world exists as a canvas for our own aggrandizement. Even the phrase "do the evolution" transforms a process of communal growth and adaptation into a system that can be exploited and controlled by power and privilege.

"Do the Evolution" marked Pearl Jam's return to videos, with a truly excellent very late '90s-style concept video by Todd McFarlane. It makes the political and economic critiques inherent in the song visible and uses organized religion as a stand-in for institutional hypocrisy. It also connects its imagery to "Faithfull" and "Push Me/Pull Me." "I'm a thief, I'm a liar there's my church I sing in the choir" followed by an anemic and sickly hallelujah chorus. There is a deeper Quinn tie-in here as well, as arguably the most compelling moment in *Ishmael* is the tracing of our self-destructive species narratives back to the Book of Genesis. Religion, exploitation, and mastery have been intertwined since the beginning of our civilization, and the church becomes an institution that feeds rather than opposes that dynamic.

There is a cynicism bordering on despair in "Do the Evolution" that its infectious groove blithely dances past. Our blind faith in our own superiority, our refusal to pause or reflect, and our celebration of our own tautological ignorance—man is the most evolved species, therefore anything man does is right because man does it—have marked us for extinction. And, until we can break this story and replace it with something sustainable (which would require us to move, in Quinn's words, "beyond civilization"), there is nothing we can do to stop it.

Eddie never fully embraces Quinn's entire message. His faith in our capacity for change is too strong. But, for the first time, we are offered a reprieve from pushing Sisyphus' rock. Escape has always served as a means to an end in Pearl Jam's music, a chance to recharge and reset so the struggle can begin anew. "Do the Evolution" asks a dangerous question: What if the struggle is futile? *Yield*'s retreat into the self speaks to Pearl Jam's unwillingness to interrogate this question just yet. For now, though, they are "through with screaming."

"The Color Red" (aka "Red Dot")

Lyrics: Jack Irons
Music: Jack Irons
Additional Musicians: Jack Irons, vocals
Live Debut: None

An interstitial track featuring Pearl Jam's first use of a steel drum, "The Color Red" offers a cooldown between the frantic conclusion of "Do the Evolution" and the engine revving up for "MFC."

"MFC"

Lyrics: Eddie Vedder
Music: Eddie Vedder
Live Debut: Alexander M. Baldwin Amphitheatre in Maui, Hawaii, U.S.A., February 20, 1998 (in live performances, "MFC" is

frequently paired with a song, originally an improvisation, given the name "Untitled" on the *Live on Two Legs* compilation album.)

Alternate Versions/
Notable Performances:*Touring Band 2000*, MGM Grand in Las Vegas, Nevada, U.S.A., October 22, 2000

Bill Graham Civic Auditorium in San Francisco, California, U.S.A., July 18, 2006 (with "Untitled")

Stadio Olimpico in Roma, Italy, June 26, 2018 (with "Untitled")

"MFC" (Mini Fast Cars) is Pearl Jam's finest example of musical onomatopoeia, with an opening riff that sounds like an engine gunning to life. It is rich with the promise of adventure and escape, and the music captures that sense of open road possibility, but post "Do the Evolution," that energy takes on a different flavor.

"MFC" feels liberating at the start, making up for lost time and broken promises through the long overdue embrace of life's inherent possibilities. And, since the chorus threatens "there's no leaving here," leaving becomes a form of resistance. The act of disappearance ("he/she/we've disappeared") speaks to pulling up roots—the abandonment of any binding ties drawing you back to a person or place.

In a hopelessly flawed system, there is value in lowering stakes: "They said that the timing was everything, made him want to be everywhere, there's a lot to be said for nowhere." No obligations and no connections other than to the people you let in. It is a Pearl Jam song, so almost all solitary acts eventually make space for other people.

As is typical, live performances transform a song about escape into a celebration of engaging with the immediate moment, as the "there's a lot to be said" lyric morphs from "nowhere" into "right here." The message is enhanced by the recurring "Untitled" semi-improvisational introduction that makes it clear the value of leaving comes from having someone to leave with, and recognizing that when you are with them, you are home.

"Low Light"

Lyrics: Jeff Ament
Music: Jeff Ament
Additional Musicians: Brendan O'Brien, keys
Live Debut: Bridge School Benefit: Shoreline Amphitheatre in Mountain View, California, U.S.A., October 21, 2001

Alternate Versions/
Notable Performances: *Live at Benaroya Hall*, Benaroya Hall in Seattle, Washington, U.S.A., October 22, 2003

Air Canada Centre in Toronto, Ontario, Canada, May 10, 2006

"Low Light" is a love song written shortly after Jeff met his future wife, and features the unstable abstractions that are a hallmark of his writing. It is a disarming composition that captures the slightly woozy feeling of an early relationship, where every moment feels like a discovery that could stretch out forever. Jeff has described the phrase low light as a sense of calm, peace, and gratitude. It conjures images of dusk and liminal spaces, marking the moment of transition where two lives become one, captured in Eddie's double-tracked harmonies.[4]

But like much of *Yield*'s second half, "Low Light" contains haunted undercurrents, with the sound of a discordant toy piano cutting through the gentle placidity, evoking a creeping fear of loss. There is an inability to imagine a life apart now that these once fractured pieces have converged into a new whole. The lyrics alternate between love and loneliness, peace and violence, in an ongoing, seemingly inescapable cycle circling around a central fear of being lost and alone. "Low Light" collapses any distinction between the two.

Rather than confront that fear, there is a retreat into the seductive fantasy of staying forever within that perfect moment when love exists independently of the complexity of life. "I need the light" or "Two birds is what they'll see. Getting lost upon their way." And, in the closing lyrics, "I'll find my way from wrong, what's real? Your dream I see." It is another form of escape, but refusing to come to terms with the possibility of loss or the necessity of growth keeps them trapped forever in that moment of transition. Eddie will return to similar conflicts years later in songs like "Come Back" and "Sirens."

"In Hiding"

Lyrics:	Eddie Vedder
Music:	Stone Gossard
Live Debut:	Alexander M. Baldwin Amphitheatre in Maui, Hawaii, U.S.A., February 20, 1998
Alternate Versions/ Notable Performances:	Great Western Forum in Inglewood, California, U.S.A., July 13, 1998
	Live on Ten Legs, Bill Graham Civic Auditorium in San Francisco, California, U.S.A., July 18, 2006

"In Hiding" is inspired by the beautifully misanthropic poet Charles Bukowski. Eddie's own words are illustrative.

"In Hiding" is actually written about Bukowski. Sean Penn gave me a quote that Bukowski had said to him once, and it was written directly from that. He told Sean that sometimes he just has to check out for a few days—no people, no nothing. So he goes in hiding, then he gets back and has the will to live once again. Maybe because society takes you down. For all the good things we offer each other, sometimes we beat each other down.[5]

It is a message consistent with *Yield*'s second half and the whole catalog. But, while most Pearl Jam songs present escape as a means to a larger end, "In Hiding" celebrates that moment of retreat as an end in itself.

It is a bold move to center that message in a composition with such an anthemic musical sweep. The lyrics are *Yield*'s most narratively straightforward. The singer seals himself off and enters a drug-fueled state of decompression, pushing away the overwhelming weight, pressure, and complexity of the outside world. It is clearly necessary, as the pre-chorus reveals someone tearing themselves apart over the masks the world forces them to wear, the temptation to lash out, and the sense of pervasive suffocation that infuses their life.

> I swallow my words to keep from lying
> I swallow my face to keep from biting
> I swallowed my breath and went deep, I was diving

Being able to step away and take a breath is transformative. There is rejuvenation in the stillness of isolation, catharsis to be found "in hiding."

After the first chorus, we meet a changed person, "no longer overwhelmed and it seems so simple now." The question that "In Hiding" does not answer is whether the person will linger in that safe space or re-engage. Eddie's explanation points to the latter. Yet Eddie's writing regularly features small lyrical changes that signify changes in perspectives, and here the pre-chorus and chorus remain the same. The music ends on a gradual deflation rather than a triumphant conclusion, focused on creating sustainable rather than transformational spaces and celebrating the unencumbered peace and joy of being alone. The live experience of "In Hiding" is much clearer as it transforms into a rafter-shaking singalong affirmation about solidarity and, ironically, no longer needing to hide.

"Push Me, Pull Me"

Lyrics:	Eddie Vedder
Music:	Jeff Ament
Live Debut:	Sydney Entertainment Centre in Haymarket, New South Wales, Australia, March 11, 1998
Alternate Versions/ Notable Performances:	Constitution Hall in Washington, D.C., U.S.A., September 19, 1998
	Wuhlheide in Berlin, Germany, June 30, 2010

"Push Me/Pull Me" captures the sense of bewildered dislocation experienced by anyone who has seen through the hollow narratives at the heart of our civilization. The song gets lost in the swirling contradictions that inevitably follow from attempts to impose order and meaning on an absurd world: the realization that mastery is illusory ("I had a false belief, I thought I came here to stay. We're all just visiting, all just breaking like waves"); nothing waits for us beyond this life ("If I behave can you arrange a spacious hole in the ground"); and all our striving leads to nothing ("Like a cloud dropping rain I'm discarding all thought. I'll dry up, leaving puddles on the ground").

The flat, unhurried spoken word delivery adds to that sense of futility. The best response to the absurdity of our situation is a sardonic self-awareness, and if presented with the chance to escape, the best option is to "pull me out," without a reference to those left behind.

Given the sequencing of the record, it is a curious choice to follow a song like "In Hiding," if the goal of that song is to recharge and reengage, especially as Eddie's final lyrics inform us "I've had enough, said enough, felt enough, I'm fine." *Yield* doubles down on this sentiment in its final track, concluding with its thesis statement.

"ALL THOSE YESTERDAYS"

Lyrics:	Stone Gossard
Music:	Stone Gossard
Live Debut:	Wolf Mountain in Park City, Utah, U.S.A., June 21, 1998
Alternate Versions/ Notable Performances:	Constitution Hall in Washington, D.C., U.S.A., September 19, 1998
	Madison Square Garden in New York, New York, U.S.A., July 11, 2003

"All Those Yesterdays" is Pearl Jam's first attempt at writing a Beatles-inspired ballad. The music begins in a lullaby adjacent space with Eddie's soothing question, "Don't you think you oughta rest? Don't you think you oughta lay your head down?" The second verse doubles down on this sentiment, reminding us we have done enough, have enough, and there is time to lay our burdens down. "Let it wash away, all those yesterdays." The call to put the past behind us is nothing new, but, once again, a link to the future is missing—rest becomes the end, rather than a waypoint on the road.

The music is in playful dialogue with the next verse, chiding us for our slavish acceptance of the dominant narratives and expectations of our society, its brutal pacing, and the human and emotional costs of participation. But "All Those

Yesterdays" transitions into a far more urgent conclusion as its frisky energy transforms into a pleading warning:

> You've got time to escape
> There's still time
> It's no crime to escape
> There's still time, so escape

We are permitted to lay aside the rock and walk away—a political act if society is permanently flawed. We move from "escape is never the safest path" to escape becoming the only rational choice.

It is a remarkable conclusion to a record that began with the ramshackle optimism of "Brain of J" and the interpersonal commitments of "Faithful," "Given to Fly," and "Wishlist." The tension within *Yield* elevates it from a well-crafted, optimistic album about pausing to take a breath into something at war with itself, an attempt to grapple with the creeping fear that the challenges we face are beyond our ability to overcome. This fear, and the instinctive response to run from it, fully manifest in *Binaural*, Pearl Jam's darkest, most alienated record, a stunning thematic about-face from the space where *Yield* began.

"Hummus"

Uncredited Hidden Track

Lyrics:	Eddie Vedder
Music:	Stone Gossard
Live Debut:	None

A hidden track at the end of "All Those Yesterdays"—vaguely Middle Eastern, vaguely silly, featuring handclaps, and building to a triumphant conclusion as someone occasionally murmurs the word "hummus."

Selections from the Back Catalog: *Yield* Era

No Boundaries: A Benefit for the Kosovar Refugees

Released:	June 15, 1999
Musicians:	Eddie Vedder, vocals; Stone Gossard, guitar; Mike McCready, guitar; Jeff Ament, bass; Matt Cameron, drums
Producer:	Pearl Jam
Engineering:	Brett Eliason
Studio:	Constitution Hall in Washington, D.C., U.S.A.

"LAST KISS"

Also appears on the 1998 Fan Club/Holiday Single (September 19, 1998) and the *Lost Dogs* compilation album.

Lyrics:	Wayne Cochran
Music:	Wayne Cochran
Peak U.S. Chart Position:	#2 on U.S. *Billboard* Hot 100
Live Debut:	ARO.space in Seattle, Washington, U.S.A., May 7, 1998 (Pearl Jam performing as Harvey Dent and the Caped Crusaders)
Alternate Versions/ Notable Performances:	Riverport Amphitheatre in Maryland Heights, Missouri, U.S.A., October 11, 2000
	Touring Band 2000, MGM Grand in Las Vegas, Nevada, U.S.A., October 22, 2000
	Kosei Nenkin Kaikan in Osaka, Japan, March 4, 2003
	Rod Laver Arena in Melbourne, Victoria, Australia, November 14, 2006

"Last Kiss" has the distinction of being Pearl Jam's biggest hit, a feat that feels slightly incongruous and perfectly appropriate. Eddie found an old 45 of Wayne Cochran's "Last Kiss" at a garage sale, and Pearl Jam decided to record a cover for their 1998 fan club single. Radio stations began playing the song, and to capitalize on the buzz, it was given a more formal release on *No Boundaries: A Benefit for the Kosovar Refugees*. It peaked at No. 2 on the *Billboard* Hot 100 in 1999, raising over $10 million.

"Last Kiss" tells the story of a pair of young lovers who were in a terrible car crash, the woman dying in her boyfriend's arms. A minimalistic performance, it derives its power from Eddie's ability to highlight the youthful purity embedded in the tragedy, and make the grief feel beautiful, even enviable.

Binaural

Released: May 16, 2000
Musicians: Eddie Vedder, vocals, guitar
                       Stone Gossard, guitar
                       Mike McCready, guitar
                       Jeff Ament, bass
                       Matt Cameron, drums
                       Mitchell Froom, keyboard and harmonium
                       Pete Thomas, percussion
                       Wendy Melvoin, percussion
Producer: Tchad Blake and Pearl Jam
Engineering: Matt Bayles with Adam Samuels and Ashley Stubbert
Studio: Litho Studio in Seattle, Washington, U.S.A.
Art Direction: Eddie Vedder as Jerome Turner
Cover Art: Raghvendra Sahai and John Trauger
Peak Chart Position: No. 2 on the U.S. *Billboard* 200, No. 5 U.K. Top Albums

While all Pearl Jam albums are in conversation with each other, *Binaural* is particularly noteworthy for being the first record to feel simultaneously like an evolution and contradiction of its predecessor. *Yield* tried to slow down and be still. It aspired to a peace decoupled from other obligations. But Pearl Jam has always swam against the prevailing current—stubbornly fighting even when there is no chance of victory. Escape is never the safest path, and by embracing the opposite, *Yield*'s conclusions are unsustainable.

Binaural is both a negation of *Yield* and an expansion of its inherent tension. *Yield* is warm and inviting. *Binaural* is cold and isolating. *Yield* embraces. *Binaural* refuses. *Yield* is expansive. *Binaural* is claustrophobic. *Yield* reaches for fulfillment. *Binaural* is haunted by ghosts it cannot lay to rest. The unease is both personal and political, and it may still be a crime to escape, protestations of "All Those Yesterdays" to the contrary.

Binaural is more mood than narrative. Its songs are about a loss of personal agency and the haunted decline into powerlessness that follows. The album artwork features several nebulae, presented in a way as to emphasize insignificance and loneliness, as does the murky sound and texture of the recording. It is a dispiriting, disempowering warning of an album and lays the groundwork for the loss of power and purpose chronicled on *Riot Act*. These two albums constitute the spiritual low point of Pearl Jam's catalog, the exploration of the flight reflex from a band with fight encoded in its DNA, and they derive their power and complexity from that juxtaposition. Within the cold and the darkness is a refusal to let the light die.

"BREAKERFALL"

Lyrics:	Eddie Vedder
Music:	Eddie Vedder
Live Debut:	Mt. Baker Theatre in Bellingham, Washington, U.S.A., May 10, 2000
Alternate Versions/ Notable Performances:	*Live at the Showbox*, The Showbox in Seattle, Washington, U.S.A., December 6, 2002 Verizon Wireless Amphitheatre Kansas in Bonner Springs, Kansas, U.S.A., June 12, 2003

"Breakerfall" storms out the gate with shades of The Who's "I Can See for Miles"— the strong, playful, build a stark contrast to the exploration of a mind on the verge of a mental breakdown. "Breakerfall" seems frustrated with, rather than sympathetic to, its main character's almost willful misery. That frustration comes from a place of concern, but it is surprisingly cavalier, almost mocking in tone, a marked contrast to how other characters in crisis are treated ("Jeremy," "Daughter," "Better Man").

The opening lyrics cry out for an intervention ("there's a girl on a ledge she's got nowhere to turn") whose "life is on fire." The music is almost diffident, the lyrics accusatory and dismissive, as "the love that she had was just wood that she burned." She is the architect of her own decline, "standing outside hating everyone in here." This carries into the chorus, from the dismissive repetition of the word "fall" at the end of the first verse to the taunting outro. The double-tracked vocals add to the effect, with a slight sneer in the lower range. This is reinforced by the rollicking music's refusal to provide sympathetic emotional cues.

There is an obvious solution to the subject's alienation, as "only love can break her fall," but she pointedly ignores it. And this sets the tone of the album, as most of the characters on *Binaural* find their choices reproduce the root cause of their powerlessness.

"Gods' Dice"

Lyrics:	Jeff Ament
Music:	Jeff Ament
Live Debut:	Mt. Baker Theatre in Bellingham, Washington, U.S.A., May 10, 2000
Alternate Versions/ Notable Performances:	*Touring Band 2000*, Shoreline Amphitheatre in Mountain View, California, U.S.A., October 31, 2000 Adelaide Entertainment Centre in Adelaide, South Australia, Australia, November 21, 2006

"Gods' Dice" is not Pearl Jam's first song to deal explicitly with the relationship between God and man, but there are significant differences between "Gods' Dice" and its thematic predecessors "Sometimes" and "Faithfull." In each song, the subject is overwhelmed by the gulf between the human and the divine, and each time, the singer attempts to negate rather than bridge that gap.

"Gods' Dice" has us surrender to our own insignificance. The opening lyrics recognize the singer's basic powerlessness ("it's out of my hands, making your hands meet"), which he returns to in each verse. The chorus makes it clear our lives are completely out of our own hands—someone else designates our opportunities, desires, and expectations with an arbitrary roll of the dice. The singer resigns himself to his circumstances, culminating in an overwhelmed third verse and the declaration, "why fight forget it, cannot spend it after I go." Struggling against odds like this, a power this totalizing, is exhausting.

"Gods' Dice" feels sarcastic, and its argument may be a straw man. Certainly, this is a curiously energetic, almost festive celebration of passivity. Another possibility is that "Gods' Dice" documents another breakdown, a person collapsing under the weight of their own irrelevance, which would explain the frantic pace of the song and the way the tightly controlled performance feels about to fall apart. Perhaps the best way to make sense of these seeming contradictions is to treat "Gods' Dice," like much of *Binaural*, as a cautionary tale written by a band struggling to internalize *Yield*'s message.

"Evacuation"

Lyrics:	Eddie Vedder
Music:	Matt Cameron
Live Debut:	Mt. Baker Theatre in Bellingham, Washington, U.S.A., May 10, 2000
Alternate Versions/ Notable Performances:	*Touring Band 2000*, Ice Palace in Tampa, Florida, U.S.A., August 12, 2000

Tweeter Center in Mansfield, Massachusetts, U.S.A.,
August 30, 2000

"Evacuation" is the muted blaring of a siren broadcast through a fading PA,
its weary pleading a byproduct of being ignored for too long. The song
prophesizes imminent collapse and urges us to act. It is time "to take heed
and change direction," "to plant seeds of reconstruction," because there "is no
time this time to feign reluctance." Something must be done, and we cannot
wait to act until that perfect moment where everything aligns "like you're
waiting for a diamond shore to wash your way." This is nicely encapsulated in
the bridge:

> There was a solemn man who watched his twilight disappear (in the sand)
> Altered by a fallen eagle, a warning sign
> He sensed that worry could be strength with a plan

The song's artwork is revealing. There is a head surrounded by two bullhorns,
their blaring too close and too loud to be understood. The song is a call to arms,
but against an unnamed and unknowable enemy with no strategy or cause to
rally behind. It is a protest song directed against a formless, disquieting feeling.
In the end, "Evacuation" wants to be urgent, to take to the streets, but does not
know how or why or if anyone will even show, and so it counsels retreat and
abandonment. "Time for evacuation."

"Light Years"

Lyrics:	Eddie Vedder
Music:	Stone Gossard and Mike McCready
Single Release Date:	July 10, 2000
Peak U.S. Chart Position:	17
Live Debut:	Mt. Baker Theatre in Bellingham, Washington, U.S.A., May 10, 2000
Alternate Versions/ Notable Performances:	*Puzzles and Games* demo Pinkpop Festival: Megaland Park in Landgraaf, Netherlands, June 12, 2000 Tweeter Center in Mansfield, Massachusetts, U.S.A., August 30, 2000

Pearl Jam has written about death before, but "Light Years" takes a different
approach. If it were focused on reconciling with loss, it would sound quite
different.[1] There is something unsettled and jarring about the music even in its

beautiful moments. Eddie's voice is even a little pleading, railing against the base unfairness of loss while he longingly eulogizes the departed.

Eddie begins the song shaken—skill and mastery are irrelevant in the face of death, incapable of undoing the enormity of its permanence. The second verse is equally personal and honest, tinged with the regret and guilt that follows an irreversible loss. Did I spend all the time I was given? Did I take everything I could? Did I give everything I had? The answer is no. It must be. But, knowing the truth and feeling the truth are two quite different things, and where "Long Road" makes its peace with that tension, "Light Years" is trapped by guilt, haunted by opportunities not taken. It is hard to fully appreciate how much someone illuminates our life until we must learn to see without them. "Light Years" leaves us wondering if we will have to spend forever in the dark.

Light years are a measure of distance between stars, a unit of time and distance beyond human experience. Something light years away may as well not exist. At the same time, we discover who we are and what shines best and brightest in us through our bonds with others (echoes of "Faithfull"): "We were but stones. Your light made us stars." Our own light originates within them. Can that light reach us when the distance is impossibly vast?

There are moments of promise in "Light Years," a plea to share your life with the ones you love while you can, but this advice is offered too late, delivered with a plaintive sadness that comes from knowing you have missed your chance. It is followed by a bridge whose soaring notes and transcendent moments are strangely discordant, a revelation arriving too late. Like the songs that precede it, "Light Years" is a cautionary tale, offering salvation and redemption in its warning. One light is gone. We must preserve the ones that remain.

"NOTHING AS IT SEEMS"

Lyrics:	Jeff Ament
Music:	Jeff Ament
Single Release Date:	April 25, 2000
Peak U.S. Chart Position:	3
Live Debut:	Bridge School Benefit: Shoreline Amphitheatre in Mountain View, California, U.S.A., October 31, 1999
Alternate Versions/ Notable Performances:	*Pearl Jam Twenty: Original Motion Picture Soundtrack*, demo (1999) *Live at Benaroya Hall*, Benaroya Hall in Seattle, Washington, U.S.A., October 22, 2003 *Live on Ten Legs*, Adelaide Entertainment Centre in Adelaide, South Australia, Australia, November 22, 2006

Binaural's lead single encapsulates its essence. It is cold, lonely, and expansive. Stone and Jeff create a bleak, isolated landscape, and Mike spends the song in an endlessly frustrated oppositional search for something. There is no journey, just an ever-present and desolate now.

"Nothing As It Seems" possesses a suffocating beauty with surprisingly little movement, given its vast open space and sorrowful solos. There is a period during the bridge when you imagine, just for a moment, that some catharsis or confrontation is coming before the song retreats into the void rather than collapsing under its own weight. It is an impressive soundscape.

Eddie is distant, worn down, and strangely empty. This is not a song about losing faith. Instead, it explores how long you can sustain yourself without it. Jeff's lyrics are a scattershot collection of images, each a snapshot of the same enervating moment in time. They describe someone completely alienated from their own life. Everything that should mean something means nothing, everything that should be rewarding feels empty, and every sweeping gesture is devoid of significance, a "whisper through a megaphone." The lyrics have the same spacey feeling as the music—immeasurable, dark, and distant. He has not quite given up. There is still a part of him that demands more, that recognizes he is being cheated of something—but it is getting increasingly hard to care.

"THIN AIR"

Lyrics:	Stone Gossard
Music:	Stone Gossard
Live Debut:	Bridge School Benefit: Shoreline Amphitheatre in Mountain View, California, U.S.A., October 30, 1999
Alternate Versions/ Notable Performances:	Forum Milan in Assago, Italy, June 22, 2000
	Dom Sportova in Zagreb, Croatia, September 26, 2006

"Thin Air" is a reprieve, one of *Binaural*'s counterpoint moments whose inclusion draws attention to the miasma enveloping the rest of the album. It has the same sense of distance and space but is experienced without anxiety. There is a smoky quality to Eddie's vocals, dark and delicate. Even the song's outro, its most energetic moment, sounds a little fragile—like something of substance slowly dissipating into thin air.

And that is its purpose—to remind the listener, at the halfway point of *Binaural*, that there is still someone or something at the core of that emptiness worth preserving, a reminder that human connection is the font of meaning. *Binaural* is an intensely lonely album. And, when "Thin Air" informs us "how to be happy and true is the quest we're taking on together", the significant word is "together," recalling "Breath" and "Leash."[2] "Light Years" is a song about struggling to see when the light dies. "Thin Air" reminds us that love is how we create it.

"INSIGNIFICANCE"

Lyrics:	Eddie Vedder
Music:	Eddie Vedder
Live Debut:	Mt. Baker Theatre in Bellingham, Washington, U.S.A., May 10, 2000
Alternate Versions/ Notable Performances:	Arena di Verona in Verona, Italy, June 20, 2000
	Adams Field House in Missoula, Montana, U.S.A., August 29, 2005

"Insignificance" is a glowing ember of resistance, confronting our own alleged powerlessness in opposition to forces beyond our control. It faces the enormity of the challenge laid out in "Do the Evolution," and while it does not offer much in the way of immediate hope, it does not surrender, either. Instead, in the darkest of spaces and in the most stressful of times, it reasserts our fundamental humanity—the desire to live, to be seen, to have a voice.

"Insignificance" is one of Eddie's more sophisticated musical compositions, a destructive soundscape of "bombs dropping down," buildings collapsing, and people dying. Even the quieter moments impart a feeling of impending doom—the guitar is nervous, the bass foreboding, the urgent build into the final chorus ringing with the mad truth of prophecy.

Like the music, Eddie's vocal performance encapsulates the essence of the song. The natural move would be to swing for the fences and defy the lyrics throughout the performance. Instead, Eddie's voice is subdued. He sings underneath the music. His plea for forgiveness cannot be heard over the dropping bombs, and it would ring false if it had—that is the essence of this song's absurd tragedy. Even its most important lyric, "it's instilled to want to live," has a tough time registering over the firestorm transition into the last chorus.

Lyrically, "Insignificance" offers a compelling mixture of mysterious, provocative images and simple truths made profound by the empathy and conviction in his voice. Almost every line is a highlight. "The swallowed seeds of arrogance, breeding in the thoughts of ten thousand fools who fight irrelevance" sounds like an accusation, and the listener's first instinct is to think he is talking about those whose ambition or greed make the lives of others disposable. But it refers to the victims themselves, a celebration of their "arrogance"—the sense of self-worth and basic human dignity that leads to people asserting their humanity in impossible conditions.

When Eddie sings, "Please forgive our hometown in our insignificance" he offers two meanings. He references the people dying—innocent victims of another's violent dream—but he is also singing about those like himself who must take responsibility for what they have so far failed (or refused) to stop. Lyrics like "I was alone and far away when I heard the band start playing" remind us that despite our powerlessness, others have given voice to our shared humanity. We are not alone.

"Insignificance" does not have a happy ending, and, unlike most anti-war songs, it does not accuse, at least not directly, as the ability to accuse is the act of an agent, and this is a song about the loss of agency. Instead, "Insignificance" tells us that being powerless together is better than being powerless alone, but it is a chilling reminder of the odds against us if we want to assert control over our lives and hold those in power responsible for the damage they have done.

"OF THE GIRL"

Lyrics:	Stone Gossard
Music:	Stone Gossard
Live Debut:	Mt. Baker Theatre in Bellingham, Washington, U.S.A., May 10, 2000
Alternate Versions/ Notable Performances:	*Pearl Jam Twenty: Original Motion Picture Soundtrack*, Instrumental Demo (2000)
	The Pyramid in Memphis, Tennessee, U.S.A., August 15, 2000
	Live at Benaroya Hall, Benaroya Hall in Seattle, Washington, U.S.A., October 22, 2003

The atmosphere of "Of the Girl" is hazy and seductive, full of mystery and forbidden promise. And, it spends its time firmly planted in that space, sitting at the bar, fantasizing about the girl at the other end, never making the move. The swells during the chorus reinforce this—pushing something away instead of drawing it close. Mike's leads and fills give "Of the Girl" an air of frustrated indecision—someone repeating the same mistake because they cannot imagine making another choice.

Stone's lyrics are simple and understated, but the sentiment fits the music, as does Eddie's unhurried delivery. "Of the Girl" does not tell a story and offers minimal detail. Instead, like so much of *Binaural*, it is an abstract warning from someone looking for a human connection but unable to bridge that gap between themselves and others. Through ignorance, self-sabotage, or both, they are trapped in a pattern they refuse to escape. "Of the Girl" offers no grand conclusion. The music does not quite fade out as much as trail off inconclusively. There is no need for resolution when this will all play out again the next day, and the day after that, looped into a wearying and perpetual now.

"GRIEVANCE"

Lyrics:	Eddie Vedder
Music:	Eddie Vedder
Live Debut:	Mt. Baker Theatre in Bellingham, Washington, U.S.A., May 10, 2000
Alternate Versions/ Notable Performances:	*Late Show with David Letterman*: Ed Sullivan Theatre in New York, New York, U.S.A., April 12, 2000 *Touring Band 2000*, Cynthia Woods Mitchell Pavilion in The Woodlands, Texas, U.S.A. October 15, 2000 Verizon Wireless Amphitheatre in Charlotte, North Carolina, U.S.A., April 16, 2003

"Grievance" is one of Pearl Jam's finest political songs. Despite being inspired by the 1999 "Battle of Seattle" World Trade Organization (WTO) protests, it is not specifically tied to that moment. There are details in the lyrics, "progress laced with ramifications," "progress, taste it, invest it all," and "for every tool they lend us, a loss of independence," that ground "Grievance" in the dawn of the internet age. Eddie called out tech companies in particular. But they are also describing dynamics that transcend the WTO and the World Bank. "Grievance" is a call for frustrated underdogs to rally around something larger than themselves and demand recognition of their worth—a response to the moral charge laid down by "Insignificance."

"Grievance" is a war cry, an attempt to remind the listener of their agency, to reassert the power of mass, and with it a restoration of democracy. Like "Insignificance," "Grievance" requires us to first recognize our current powerlessness. It urges us to confront the world as it is, stripped of illusion. There is no immediate space for action when bombs are dropping, the enemy distant, and your life an abstraction. But the great promise of democracy is the possibility that people will awaken to their strength, the great fear of those with power is what happens when that mass realizes "we're all deserving something more." They can "raise the sticks and bring 'em down," but only when we divide ourselves, and only for as long as we let them. The music and vocals get frustrated more than angry. "Grievance" does not punch its enemy in the face. It grabs its allies by the shoulders and demands their focus.

The song culminates with its statement of principles. Meaning is derived from action. We are not free unless we are agents, and we become agents when we embrace the desire to live with meaning. "Grievance" urges us to remember that the assertion of self makes everything possible. That no matter what obstacles lie before us, "I will feel alive as long as I am free."

If *Binaural* ended here, we would be left with an ultimately optimistic album. Instead, "Grievance" becomes an outlier—a reminder of what once was and might be again.

"Rival"

Lyrics:	Stone Gossard
Music:	Stone Gossard
Additional Musicians:	Dakota, canine vocals
Live Debut:	Pinkpop Festival: Megaland Park in Landgraaf, Netherlands, June 12, 2000
Alternate Versions/ Notable Performances:	Tweeter Center in Mansfield, Massachusetts, U.S.A., August 29, 2000
	Pacifico Yokohama in Yokohama, Japan, March 1, 2003

From the song's first growling moments there is a pervading, ominous sense that something has gone very wrong, that the world is not as it should be. The music has a demonic carnival quality, festive if not for the prickly, discordant notes that drive the song—especially the bridge and outro. Eddie's double-tracked vocals (especially his higher/strained notes) add to the song's coiled insanity. This is probably the most menacing song in their catalog.

"Rival" grapples with the Columbine shootings of the prior year. Stone "tried to think about what those guys may have been thinking the night before," and his lyrics to "Rival" are full of apocalyptic intent ("I've been harboring fleets in this reservoir").[3] "Rival" is light on specific details, offering snapshots of a cracking mind—its hateful rebellion against a diseased society. Though its subjects feel powerless, "Rival" is not passive and instead explores the nihilistic agency of those convinced we are damned. We would rather lie to each other than confront our sickness. ("How's our father supposed to be told?" and "This nation's about to explode.") But no one seems to care. We are fiddling while America burns, hence the festive undertones to the music. The plea at the end of "Grievance" has fallen on deaf ears. Instead of solidarity, we are all rivals to each other, with no way to move forward once we've divided. "Rival" makes it clear that "Grievance," in the context of *Binaural,* is a temporary resurgence of principles that no longer govern.

"Sleight of Hand"

Lyrics:	Eddie Vedder
Music:	Jeff Ament
Live Debut:	Paegas Arena in Prague, Czech Republic, June 14, 2000
Alternate Versions/ Notable Performances:	Allstate Arena in Des Plaines, Illinois, U.S.A., October 9, 2000
	Adams Field House in Missoula, Montana, U.S.A., August 29, 2005

A "sleight of hand" is a misdirection of the subject's focus. While they are looking at what they think is significant, someone is acting upon them without their knowledge or consent. A victim of sleight of hand is no longer in control of their own story and does not recognize it until it is too late.

The music captures this perfectly—a great soundscape on an album full of them. The scratched and mournful crystalline guitar and the thrumming uncertainty underneath; the lost, wistful fills; the crazed feedback of the chorus; and the distant sadness in Eddie's voice. "Sleight of Hand" works best at this elemental level as it cuts to the heart of *Binaural*—cold, lonely, and lost.

"Sleight of Hand" offers the story of someone trapped in the same dull, repetitive, monochromatic life. "Routine was the theme." Hopes, dreams, and ambitions surrendered to the daily grind of living—the years of commute, meaningless work, and empty rituals. It presents a character trying to escape who he was, not knowing who he is, and fearful of who he has become. "Not remembering the change. Not recalling the plan." He has lost himself, and what remains is a shell devoid of substance and meaning. "Sleight of Hand" explores the themes of "Small Town" or "I'm Open" without their promise of rebirth. The dreams of the life he never got to live are both a warning and a call to action for others. It is too late for him. There is still a tiny spark left, the part of him that was capable of dreaming. But it is so small, so insignificant, he might have been better off without remembering it. Empty, still, but not so haunted.

"Soon Forget"

Lyrics:	Eddie Vedder
Music:	Eddie Vedder
Additional Musicians:	Eddie Vedder, ukulele
Live Debut:	Mt. Baker Theatre in Bellingham, Washington, U.S.A., May 10, 2000
Alternate Versions/ Notable Performances:	Riverbend Music Center in Cincinnati, Ohio, U.S.A., August 20, 2000
	Warner Theatre in Washington, D.C., U.S.A., August 16, 2008 (Eddie Vedder solo performance)

"Soon Forget," performed on a ukulele and borrowing heavily from The Who's "Blue, Red, and Gray," is an exercise in campfire songwriting Eddie credits with breaking the writer's block he felt during *Binaural*. It is the most mean-spirited song on *Binaural*, lacking the subtlety and empathy found elsewhere on the album. The narrator taunts the singer over poor choices and personal failings made in service of "living a day he'll soon forget." He dies alone, unloved, forgotten, as we sing and dance away the memory of "a man we'll soon forget."

There is a smug bitterness to "Soon Forget," out of step with Pearl Jam's humanism. But it was never presented that way live. In concert it is a moment of connection, not critique. And so perhaps "Soon Forget" is a warning from Eddie to himself. To not lose sight of what matters as his journey takes him farther and farther from where he began.

"Parting Ways"

Lyrics:	Eddie Vedder
Music:	Eddie Vedder
Additional Musicians:	April Cameron, viola; Justine Foy, cello
Live Debut:	The Palace of Auburn Hills in Auburn Hills, Michigan, U.S.A., October 7, 2000
Alternate Versions/ Notable Performances:	*Touring Band 2000*, United Spirit Arena in Lubbock, Texas, U.S.A., October 18, 2000 Wachovia Spectrum Arena in Philadelphia, Pennsylvania, U.S.A., October 30, 2009

"Parting Ways" chronicles the final moments of a dying relationship, the moment of detachment when you realize it's ending, and you lack the will to try to save it. It is one of the more atmospheric love songs in the catalog. The guitars manage to feel fuzzy (warm) and distant (cold) at the same time. There is a gentle, drifting melody harshly punctuated at the mention of "parting ways." Eddie walks a careful line between disengagement and the memory of passion. There is a wistful remembrance to the delivery of lyrics like "behind her eyes there's curtains, and they've been closed to hide the flame"—something recalled but not felt. Too distant to stop it from drifting away, but close enough to quietly grieve the loss.

The lyrics match the delivery. There is a superficial sense that everything is fine, but only because the subjects refuse to confront the reality that something is wrong. Maybe they do not know how to fix it—easier to smile and pretend everything is fine. But the costs of self-deception are real. Curtains are closed so neither person must confront the unmet need and desire hidden behind them.

"Parting Ways" is a song about the costs of lying. We cannot be there for someone else unless we are open and honest with them, and that requires us to first be honest with ourselves. The subjects of the song are not just drifting away from each other; they are drifting away from themselves, lost in the barren expanse of their lives.

In a world defined by alienation, it is easier to die a slow death than fight to get it back again. "Parting Ways," and *Binaural,* want to remind us that gradual decay is not an escape. It is not life, just a muted death. *Binaural*, more than any other album in the band's catalog, is a cautionary tale. Its answers are negative, its anthems warnings. That is the source of its power.

"WRITER'S BLOCK"
Uncredited Hidden Track
Music: Eddie Vedder
Additional Musicians: Eddie Vedder, typewriter
Live Debut: None

Eddie suffered from writer's block during the *Binaural* sessions, and to document his struggle *Binaural* concludes with the sound of furious typing.

Riot Act

Released:	November 12, 2002
Musicians:	Eddie Vedder, vocals, guitar
	Stone Gossard, guitar
	Mike McCready, guitar
	Jeff Ament, bass
	Matt Cameron, drums
	Boom Gaspar, Hammond B3, Fender Rhodes
	Adam Kasper, piano
Producer:	Adam Kasper and Pearl Jam
Engineering:	Sam Hofstedt with John Burton
Studio:	Studio X in Seattle, Washington, U.S.A.
Art Direction:	Jeff Ament as Al Nostreet
Cover Art:	Jeff Ament and Kelly Gilliam
Peak Chart Position:	No. 5 on the U.S. *Billboard* 200, No. 34 U.K. Top Albums

Binaural and *Riot Act* are the thematic nadir of Pearl Jam's journey, a deep, probing skepticism of their core commitments. Their validity and sustainability are aggressively called into question. *Binaural* ended in a lost and lonely place, and a series of external events pushed the band even further into a space of existential uncertainty.

The Roskilde festival tragedy occurred on June 30, 2000. Playing to over 100,000 people, nine fans were killed in a crowd surge during Pearl Jam's set and under circumstances where they did not have oversight over safety and security protocols. For a band that had always prioritized the health and welfare of its fans, checking in on them throughout live shows and stopping performances when crowds looked unsafe, Roskilde was a nightmare made real. Pearl Jam considered breaking up in its aftermath, and the experience casts an explicit shadow over *Riot Act*—a reminder of the arbitrariness of life and our inability to master or control it. The impact of the Roskilde tragedy was explored in Henrik Tuxen's *Pearl Jam: The More You Need the Less You Get,* so, while this chapter will not lean too heavily into that history, its influence looms large.

Riot Act is also Pearl Jam's response to the early years of the Bush presidency and the 9/11 terrorist attacks. Like many progressives, they were not only blindsided by the enormity of 9/11 but also by the reactionary wave that followed. It stood in especially stark contrast to the surging optimism of the 2000 Ralph Nader presidential candidacy, of which Eddie was a vocal supporter and active campaigner.

Any engaged artist trying to respond (musically or politically) found themselves muted by a suddenly incomprehensible world. Pearl Jam found itself alienated and isolated, failing to recognize its world, country, and fellow citizens. Progressive solidarity felt almost performative, an unsolicited tribute to a shattered view of the world. The band found itself in opposition to power and the people. It is not surprising that *Riot Act* was the lowest charting album in Pearl Jam's history.

The cover art reflects *Riot Act*'s despondency. It features two crowned skeletons (Bush and Cheney?) looming over the smoldering remains of their kingdom, nothing left but ashes and bone, no base from which to rebuild. The title *Riot Act* sounds like a call to arms, but instead of outrage and engagement, we find defeat and reflection. An assertive title for an introspective album, it asks whether solidarity and progress are possible in a post-9/11 world. The anger and confrontation that animates the self-titled follow-up are not possible until the band first surveys the wreckage and discovers what remains after conviction and certainty are ground to dust. Is Sisyphus out there in that bleak and empty landscape, still pushing his rock, and what meaning infuses the gesture?

While there are few overtly political songs on *Riot Act*, the entire personal journey grapples with the possibility that the world has become a fundamentally hostile place. *Riot Act* is not a cynical record, but it struggles to be hopeful in toxic times.

Through our journey, we have learned that freedom takes work and cannot be experienced in isolation, and *Riot Act* is an exhausted, lonesome album. It is not defeatist, and never quite gives up. But it goes to dark and difficult places, and it does not fight as much as it endures, with Eddie's voice taking on a weary resonance.

Not surprisingly, we see the final pivot into an ultimately healthier place during the 2003 *Riot Act* tour. Here modern Pearl Jam is truly born, openly and actively affirming its values not just despite but because of everything conspiring against them, leaning fully into the live experience as a revival—celebrating and serving a community of like-minded seekers united in their love of music, and, through that, each other. There are moments on *Riot Act* that point to that destination, but they are tentative flames—guttering, but still alive.

"Can't Keep"

Lyrics:	Eddie Vedder
Music:	Eddie Vedder
Live Debut:	Wiltern Theatre in Los Angeles, California, U.S.A., February 26, 2002 (Eddie Vedder solo performance)

Alternate Versions/
Notable Performances: *Ukulele Songs*, solo album by Eddie Vedder (2011)
Budokan in Chiyoda-Ku, Japan, March 3, 2003
Rupp Arena in Lexington, Kentucky, U.S.A., April 21, 2003

"Can't Keep" is wistful rather than forceful. It is not a strident song—it offers cautious hope, with a delicate certainty that crests at the end of each verse without ever fully committing. A tentative song, it tests and explores rather than asserts, and yet underneath is a current of suppressed, expansive power searching for a way out: "I've lived all these lives like an ocean in disguise."

There is a desire to say goodbye, to move on to something better, unencumbered by the past. There are some fond recollections of what will be left behind ("it's been wonderful at night"), and no hard feelings ("forgive every being"), but home is slowly suffocating, and attachments are fading. We only have one life, and we owe it to ourselves to move on when what we have is not healthy: "I don't live forever/I won't wait for answers/you can't keep me here." Like much of *Riot Act*, these reflections are both personal and political, though the politics are subtle, unfolding throughout the rest of the album. Eddie is singing to his country, saying farewell to a people and a place no longer recognizable. There is no confrontation, no attempt at reconciliation. Instead, he turns inward and elsewhere.

"Can't Keep" has a restless, stifled energy and the emancipatory promise of lyrics like "I wanna race with the sundown. I want a last breath I don't let out" are unrealized in the performance, smothered by time and place. The percussion in "Can't Keep" tries to move us forward, but we get lost in the music's swirling currents. When everything has turned against you, when there are no safe harbors, you have no choice but to retreat into yourself. "Can't Keep" becomes about an internal battle to maintain and preserve a sense of self in a world that has called all the old values and certainties into question. A world we would leave behind if only there was somewhere else to go.

"Save You"

Lyrics:	Eddie Vedder
Music:	Jeff Ament, Matt Cameron, Stone Gossard, Mike McCready, and Eddie Vedder
Single Release Date:	December 9, 2002

Peak U.S. Chart Position: 23
Live Debut: *Late Show with David Letterman*: Ed Sullivan
                                     Theatre in New York, New York, U.S.A., November
                                     14, 2002
Alternate Versions/
Notable Performances: *Live at Chop Suey*, Chop Suey in Seattle, Washington,
                                     U.S.A., September 6, 2002 (rehearsal filmed by Danny
                                     Clinch)
                                     Live at Easy Street, East Street Records in Seattle,
                                     Washington, U.S.A., April 29, 2005
                                     QSAC Stadium in Brisbane, Queensland, Australia,
                                     November 25, 2009

"Save You" is partly a refutation of "Habit." As Eddie described:

> One thing I've learned about addiction in the last few years is that having seen
> other folk go through it ... I didn't have a complete understanding and a lot of
> times it was easy to come to the conclusion that you place blame on the person
> or accuse them of weakness.... What I've learned is there really isn't any blame.
> It has happened to some folks I cared about so much and had it so together, so
> it really isn't a blame thing. I think the song is expressing how badly you want
> to help.[1]

"Save You" is a song about addiction—quite possibly Mike's struggles, given
the timing—and the lyrics are about the singer's assertion of power, the driving
need to do and control something. The focus is on the person doing the saving, as
opposed to the person being saved. This is a subtle but important distinction: It's
okay to fall because I'm going to save you. I (later we) need you. I'm not leaving
until it's done.

But it is not just about wanting to help. When Eddie screams "please help me to
help you help yourself"—the only scream on the album—we get a window into
how this is also about the singer's needs. They are trying to convince themselves
that they are still a subject capable of acting rather than an object being acted
on. Their doubt causes the disparity between the forceful nature of the lyrics
and their subdued, hesitant delivery, at least up until that final, explosive
"help yourself." But even that leaves them exhausted rather than empowered,
overtaken by the music and by events.

"Save You" is *Riot Act*'s heaviest song, and it leans into the weight but lacks
the triumphant, cathartic solo we might expect to find. Instead, it lingers on its
main riff, waiting for a breakthrough that never comes. One of the most striking
elements of *Riot Act* is the absent climax that speaks to the experience of being
trapped in, but not quite surrendering to, this unhealthy, enervated moment.

Given the lack of specificity in the lyrics and the larger context of the record, "Save You" can also be read as a political song with Eddie speaking to a nation that surrendered its spirit, its principles, and its identity to avoid processing its grief. "Save You" is a call to arms, a demand that his fellow citizens do not use the shock and trauma of 9/11 to abdicate their public responsibilities and retreat into a narrow, private sphere that allows us to block out the rest of the world. Even if no one is listening now, you must keep speaking in anticipation of the moment when others are finally ready to hear.

"LOVE BOAT CAPTAIN"

Lyrics: Eddie Vedder
Music: Eddie Vedder and Boom Gaspar
Single Release Date: February 24, 2003 (Europe, Australia, and Canada)
Peak U.S. Chart Position: N/A
Live Debut: House of Blues Chicago in Chicago, Illinois, U.S.A., September 23, 2002

Alternate Versions/
Notable Performances: *Live at Chop Suey*, Chop Suey in Seattle, Washington, U.S.A., September 6, 2002 (rehearsal filmed by Danny Clinch)
                            General Motors Place in Vancouver, British Columbia, Canada, May 30, 2003
                            Live at the Garden, Madison Square Garden in New York, New York, U.S.A., July 8, 2003
                            The Molo Sessions (Eddie Vedder with the Walmer High School Choir), Recorded at Studio Litho, Seattle Washington, U.S.A., September 8–9, 2004

"Love Boat Captain" offers one of the most direct presentations of Pearl Jam's thesis statement when Eddie sings "once you hold the hand of love it's all surmountable." As usual, Eddie is not just (or even primarily) thinking about romantic love, and "Love Boat Captain" is an offering of love and friendship from the band to its fans. Perspective matters here, and there is a generational dynamic that will become more prevalent on subsequent records. "Love Boat Captain" explicitly celebrates the wisdom of experience. ("The young they can lose hope because they can't see beyond today, the wisdom that the old can't give away.") It is easy to get trapped in dark places, and we need those who have survived their own tragedy to remind us of the existence of light and love. The reference to Pearl Jam's own immediate experience of Roskilde ("lost nine friends we'll never know … two years ago today") marks them as survivors of life's "constant recoil"— willing to be a guide for others and confident enough to accept the responsibility.

These ambitions are successful in the song itself—in live performances, especially, where audience interplay gives "Love Boat Captain" a lift that helps it fully realize its aspirations. However, *Riot Act*, with a few exceptions, challenges this message. Eddie rushes past his realization that "to the universe I don't mean a thing," but the universe is not done with us yet, and love is fragile, delicate, and needs protection from the world as much as it protects us from it.

"CROPDUSTER"

Lyrics:	Eddie Vedder
Music:	Matt Cameron
Live Debut:	The Showbox in Seattle, Washington, U.S.A., December 5, 2002
Alternate Versions/ Notable Performances:	Sydney Entertainment Centre in Haymarket, New South Wales, Australia, February 14, 2003 *Live at the Garden*, Madison Square Garden in New York, New York, U.S.A., July 8, 2003

"Cropduster," another song heavily indebted to Daniel Quinn, is a curiously upbeat celebration of our insignificance as an opportunity. Impermanence becomes a precondition of renewal, certainly on a planetary timeline, but a human one as well. It celebrates the limits of our mastery and the existence of cycles offering the possibility of starting over.

The song's imagery, and Quinn's influence, make "Cropduster" at least partly about the environment, starting with the title—crop dusting is the process of spreading pesticides over a wide area, using technology and science to assert control over nature for the benefit of man. "Cropduster" begins with the cycle of life, recognizing death as a condition of rebirth, a beginning as much as an ending. ("Every life is falling down. Dies to be part of the ground.") Death is inevitable, but we can hope that something better than who and what we are rises from our rot.

When Eddie sings, "I was a fool because I thought I thought the world. Turns out the world thought me" we are reminded that control is illusory, our lives contingent. We live at the mercy of structural forces, natural and manmade, and arbitrary power we did not consent to. We are the object rather than the subject of the system, characters in a story authored by someone else.

This leaves us in a complex place. On the one hand, it offers a thinly veiled critique of the conservative politics of the moment, a reminder that they will not endure even if we cannot imagine their end. But impermanence transcends ideology, and progressive values require, on some level, an assertion of mastery. Structural forces can be overcome, harm mitigated, and safe and authentic spaces created and defended. Pearl Jam's music is an assertion of agency in the name of fighting the fights that seem unwinnable.

"Cropduster" ends on a potentially uplifting note—a reminder that if the cycle continues ("the moon is rolling 'round") we have the chance to begin again ("there's an upside of down"). Human beings have the potential to do great harm and great good, and we must not surrender the possibilities of the latter in the face of the former. Earlier (and later) incarnations of Pearl Jam have leaned into this realization, and while "Cropduster" does not abandon hope for the future, the rest of the album is not overly optimistic for the present.

"Ghost"

Lyrics:	Jeff Ament and Eddie Vedder
Music:	Jeff Ament
Live Debut:	The Showbox in Seattle, Washington, U.S.A., December 5, 2002
Alternate Versions/ Notable Performances:	Sydney Entertainment Centre in Haymarket, New South Wales, Australia, February 14, 2003 *Live at the Garden*, Madison Square Garden in New York, New York, U.S.A., July 8, 2003

"Ghost" is the sound of freedom stuck in gear. Eddie sounds exhausted from his running, and what he flees is too expansive to escape and so much more powerful than him. Aptly named, "Ghost" features some of the gloomier lyrics in PJ's catalog, images of failing hope in the face of accelerated decline ("The mind is grey … like the city"). The struggle is internal and external, the two trapped in a negatively reinforcing feedback loop as the world loses its vibrancy—fading to gray rather than black. "Ghost" is a song about shrinking vitality rather than destruction or annihilation. The subject looks for love to pull them through, but it, and they, are too far gone. They are willing to give up, to accept the false peace that comes from hiding, but even this avenue is closed to them.

The chorus plays off the tension between these hopes and failures. Eddie declares that he is going to escape (driving and flying references calling back to "Rearviewmirror" and "Given to Fly"), looking for something he missed before, something to guide his way back. But the vocal performance reveals he is trying to convince himself of something he no longer believes.

The song's climax tries to put a brave face on powerlessness. Eddie sings, "It doesn't hurt when I bleed, but my memories they eat me. Seen it all before. Bring it on, 'cuz I'm no victim," the bravado in the lyrics matched by the stubborn grind of the outro solo. Still, the psychological torment and sense of isolation (punishing for someone who equates freedom with love) are destroying him.

"Ghost" ends with the repetition of "dying," suffering a spiritual death as his world, his potential, and his self fades away, a phantom trapped outside the process of renewal.

"I AM MINE"

Lyrics: Eddie Vedder
Music: Eddie Vedder
Single Release Date: September 23, 2002
Peak U.S. Chart Position: 43
Live Debut: Bridge School Benefit: Shoreline Amphitheatre in
                                    Mountain View, California, U.S.A., October 21, 2001
Alternate Versions/
Notable Performances: *Late Show with David Letterman*: Ed Sullivan Theatre
                                    in New York, New York, U.S.A., November 14, 2002
                                    Live at the Garden, Madison Square Garden in New
                                    York, New York, U.S.A., July 8, 2003
                                    Brisbane Entertainment Centre in Brisbane, Queensland,
                                    Australia, November 10, 2006

"I Am Mine," *Riot Act*'s lead single, is a stubborn ray of tarnished light in an otherwise shadowy collection of songs. It was written before Pearl Jam's first post-Roskilde show, an attempt by Eddie to "reassure myself that it is going to be all right."[2] It is introspective but questing rather than questioning, as if trying to recover, rather than discover some foundational truth. It gives the music and performance confidence. While *Riot Act* vocals typically feel withdrawn, "I Am Mine" sounds as though Eddie is advancing rather than retreating—ascending out of the darkness instead of descending from the light. The song is not exactly a call to arms, at least, not until the very end. Instead, it marshals the strength needed to fight the battles to come. "I Am Mine" is the journey one must take to defend the convictions articulated in "Love Boat Captain."

The first two verses convey the powerlessness that characterizes our lives, how much is beyond our capacity to understand, let alone control. You can read the senseless tragedy of Roskilde or the paralysis of a dissenter in Bush's post-9/11 America in the lyrics. We confront a world too big and impersonal, seemingly without justice or meaning. Too often, the best we can do is surrender and hope for mercy: "The selfish, they're all standing in line, faithing and hoping to buy themselves time." A selfishness born of powerlessness, of being forced to live in a world where we must hope for privilege because we cannot rely on justice. "The ocean is full because everyone's crying," and in our misery we turn away rather than toward each other, trapped by our isolation in a world where justice is impossible, and our lives remain incomplete.

"I Am Mine," like most of Pearl Jam's best music, is about trying to build solidarity. And, as always, that fight begins by mastering ourselves, our sense of irrelevance, and a twinned fear of our powerlessness and our power. By declaring ourselves willing to fight and take responsibility for our own lives, we have the chance and obligation to begin again. We do not need the certainty of victory—the meaning comes from our struggle: "I know I was born and I know that I'll die, the in-between is mine." Our sense of self can be surrendered, but it cannot be taken without our consent, and it offers a powerful base from which we can rebuild our capacity to love others.

This plays out through the magnificent chorus, with its subtle shifts in meaning and allusions to Roskilde and 9/11. "I Am Mine" urges us to look deep into ourselves and find the strength we need to endure. "There's no need to hide;" we are safe and in control if we can tap that strength.

As the song approaches its climax, Eddie brings "I Am Mine" back down into the gloom but does so to prove that we will survive in the face of our lost innocence. We will refuse to let the world break what is most human within us. We may want to hide, but we do not have to if we protect each other. "I Am Mine" ends with a glorious release, Mike's gorgeous solo rising from the depths and reaching toward the promise of that distant, better world, an album's worth of catharsis in eighteen seconds.

"I Am Mine" leaves *Riot Act* at a crossroads, striving for what it cannot have. Not yet.

"Thumbing My Way"

Lyrics: Eddie Vedder
Music: Eddie Vedder
Live Debut: *Live at the Showbox*, The Showbox in Seattle, Washington, U.S.A., December 6, 2002
Alternate Versions/
Notable Performances: General Motors Place in Vancouver, British Columbia, Canada, May 30, 2003
Waldbühne in Berlin, Germany, July 5, 2018

Eddie described "Thumbing My Way" as "hitchhiking your way through a broken heart."[3] The narrator has done his best, and his best is just not good enough. "Thumbing My Way" is a song about aimlessly stumbling through a dark, empty world with only the thinnest of hopes that things will get better. This is not a political song, but it fits in with the theme of succumbing to totalizing desolation that runs through *Riot Act*. The music is stark and unadorned, the accents hijacked by a lack of faith. Eddie sounds lost and beaten. There is no joy or anger, transcendence or rebirth, confrontation or healing. Just a cold, shuffling, perpetual now.

When Eddie sings "I let go of a rope thinking that's what held me back, and in time I've realized it's now wrapped around my neck," we return to the now familiar theme that true independence and freedom are found in love and solidarity. Without it, we are lost, alone, and strangled by our superficial freedom. The image of the hitchhiker is inverted. Free and unencumbered, yes, but also powerless and alone. Stripped of all but the self and wanting for everything.

The music paints a picture of a solitary, insignificant man walking alone along a vast empty stretch of highway, shivering in the chill, hoping for a ride that isn't coming and he doesn't deserve. Part of the song's darkness is that the narrator does not think he is worth loving or saving. He endures because he does not know what else to do, but he has no destination, and with no place to go, no hope for the future. There are brief moments of possibility: "no matter how cold the winter there's a springtime ahead" but they are negated by sentiments like "I smile, but who am I kidding," turned into cliches no one expects to believe. "Thumbing My Way" joins the ranks of Pearl Jam's cautionary tales, a warning to cherish the love we have because we are lost without it.

"YOU ARE"

Lyrics: Matt Cameron and Eddie Vedder
Music: Matt Cameron
Studio: Space Studio in Aurora, Colorado, U.S.A.
Live Debut: "Live at the Showbox," The Showbox in Seattle, Washington, U.S.A., December 6, 2002
Alternate Versions/
Notable Performances: Instrumental demo (2002), by Matt Cameron
                        MGM Grand, Las Vegas, Nevada, U.S.A., June 6, 2003
                        Nassau Veterans Memorial Coliseum in East Garden City, New York, U.S.A., April 30, 2003

"You Are" is one of Pearl Jam's more grinding, muscular songs—the music is a stormy, cluttered night where you travel at your own peril. The opening lyric "This broken wheel is coming undone and the road's exploded" is a striking summation of the space where *Riot Act* begins.

"You Are" was originally titled "Undone," and the original title is suggestive, highlighting the contradiction embedded in its central metaphor of love as a tower—the strength of the tower and the permanent fragility of its foundation. "You Are" is simultaneously about love's power to keep us grounded, granting us the fortitude to endure, and love's tenuous vulnerability. Eddie captures this tension in the soaring restraint of his delivery of lyrics like "I am the shoreline, but you're the sea." The shoreline is at the mercy of the sea, which can either embrace or destroy. "You Are" is worn down, struggling to hold on but unable to let go. Exhausted but surviving, sustained by the sea, and weathering the storm for as long as it can.

"GET RIGHT"

Lyrics:	Matt Cameron
Music:	Matt Cameron
Live Debut:	The Showbox in Seattle, Washington, U.S.A., December 5, 2002
Alternate Versions/ Notable Performances:	Demo (2002), with Matt Cameron on vocals Nassau Veterans Memorial Coliseum, East Garden City, New York, U.S.A., April 30, 2003 Hersheypark Stadium in Hershey, Pennsylvania, U.S.A., July 12, 2003

"Get Right" inaugurates what will become a Pearl Jam standard—a comparatively low-stakes song that signals the transition into the album's final sequence. It is an unassuming highlight, a crunchy, catchy song about getting high. The liner notes feature a picture of a joint, one of only three margin doodles in the whole booklet. It feels strangely out of place on what is otherwise a consistently serious, humorless album, but its handclaps, throbbing bassline, celebratory solo, and sing-along choruses do provide a brief respite from *Riot Act*'s weight. With aspirations that do not move beyond wanting to have a disposable good time, its inclusion over "Down" or "Undone" (both songs with weightier themes that still feel relatively light and airy) is itself a statement. With the world as it is, perhaps that is the best we can hope for while we ride out this moment.

"GREEN DISEASE"

Lyrics:	Eddie Vedder
Music:	Eddie Vedder
Live Debut:	House of Blues Chicago in Chicago, Illinois, U.S.A., September 23, 2002
Alternate Versions/ Notable Performances:	Smirnoff Music Centre in Dallas, Texas, June 9, 2003 Leeds Festival in Leeds, U.K., August 25, 2006

There is an interesting juxtaposition between the music and lyrics of "Green Disease." The music is lighthearted, if not quite danceable, as if the only way to respond to the mess we have made of our world is a playful shrug. But it is a knowingly disingenuous dismissal, as there is a bright urgency to the performance, and the lyrics mark the first (and rather late) effort on *Riot Act* to explicitly unpack why we feel so alienated.

The unambiguous title, as well as the opening ("G-R-E-E-D"), is a bit on the nose. When Eddie believes something passionately, he can fall back on superficial declarations that feel like vibrant truths to him. Sometimes, the simple ideas are the right ones, but Eddie's lyrical talents as a social commentator lie with misdirection and making emotional abstractions accessible and immediate. Diagnostic directness is not always one of his strengths.

"Green Disease" is about the toxicity of greed and the harm caused by stripping the value from goods that cannot be quantified, especially among the elite: love, community, solidarity, and sustainability. But that is only part of the problem. Attached to this worldview is a ruthlessly destructive belief that collective action is doomed to fail, and that care and empathy are private concerns. We are isolated and alone. That is the real tragedy of "Green Disease"—not that we have a world full of greedy people, but that they actively work to stifle, if not eliminate, our capacity to envision a world defined by compassion and cooperation. We are left struggling against each other in day-to-day battles for survival. We need to "tell the captain the boat's not safe and we're drowning," but we are conditioned to keep quiet and just save ourselves.

"Help Help"

Lyrics:	Jeff Ament
Music:	Jeff Ament
Live Debut:	Adelaide Entertainment Centre in Adelaide, South Australia, Australia, February 16, 2003
Alternate Versions/ Notable Performances:	DTE Energy Music Theatre in Village of Clarkston, Michigan, U.S.A., June 25, 2003
	O2 Arena in Prague, Czech Republic, July 1, 2018

"Help Help" is an impending breakdown—the collapse of everything familiar and dependable into a swirling, sinister existence devoid of grounding touchstones. It begins peacefully enough, but everything is slightly off-kilter as if its serene façade is about to shatter. The guitar effects coloring the verses play like demented birdsong intruding on a staged pastoral scene. The whole composition feels imbalanced by design. Eddie's vocals feature the same basic distortion as the music, a veneer of calm built on unstable foundations.

Jeff's lyrics capture the complete and total alienation of the subject. He no longer wants to fight. He no longer wants to resist. He wants the storybook. He wants the pleasant lies, easy answers, and attractive illusions that the rest of his country has embraced. Far better to surrender than to resist alone.

This gives us two ways to interpret the "help me" cry of the chorus. He is asking to be saved from himself (help me embrace the story; help me embrace the lie) or to be saved from the illusions (help me resist the story; help me resist the lie). The bridge offers a moment of clarity—a recognition of the dangerously seductive power of that story, grounded as it is in hate and fear, easier emotions to embrace than love and courage: "Reservoir of hate and fear, invisible, in repair, a hundred thieves cast a spell. This is hell." "Help Help" builds to a frantic conclusion as it tries to claw its way out of the pervasive illusions of a post-9/11 world ("the more you read, we've been deceived. Every day it becomes clearer"), while rejecting the frightened politics of division ("the man they call my enemy I've seen his eyes he looks just like me ... a mirror"). Division and difference are weapons deployed by people in power to prevent those they would rule from forging bonds of solidarity capable of resisting.

"Help Help" culminates with a desperate attempt to grasp that truth ("clearer ... clearer ... not my enemy ... not my enemy...") but sometimes knowing the truth is not enough. The clarity cannot overcome our totalizing alienation, and its catharsis cannot fit our fractured pieces back together.

"Bu$hleaguer"

Lyrics:	Stone Gossard and Eddie Vedder
Music:	Stone Gossard
Live Debut:	*Live at the Showbox*, The Showbox in Seattle, Washington, U.S.A., December 6, 2002
Alternate Versions/ Notable Performances:	Nassau Veterans Memorial Coliseum in East Garden City, New York, U.S.A., April 301, 2003
	Bill Graham Civic Auditorium, San Francisco, California, U.S.A., July 15, 2006

In 2002, President George W. Bush embodied everything *Riot Act* rebelled against. He was the man partially responsible for the attendant fear, cruelty, and confusion tearing the world apart. And, musically, "Bu$hleaguer" is among the most sinister pieces in the catalog—it looms and threatens, stalking the listener. Although a recording with fully sung vocals allegedly exists, *Riot Act*'s version features spoken word verses, and the performance lacks gravity. This may be deliberate—a casualness matching the banality of the evil—but it does not do enough to raise the stakes of the composition. The pre-chorus and chorus are more effective at conveying the bottom dropping out of the world, calling back to "Help Help." There is a plaintive quality to the chorus itself, with distorted vocals begging for answers rather than accountability—which requires more assertiveness and confidence than "Bu$hleaguer" can muster. He finds himself overwhelmed by the object of his contemplation. The Bush phenomenon too big and destructive to grasp.

The music pulls this off, but outside of the chorus, the lyrics are a collection of minor taunts and abstract metaphors that talk around the subject. The grand sweeping moments of outrage will have to wait for *Pearl Jam*. The chorus is more effective. "Blackout weaves its way through the city" captures a creeping decline, a darkening world, both literally and figuratively. We are powerless to resist the encroaching and unaccountable night. At best, we can condemn Bush's character, but in the face of the social, political, and human costs of his administration, this comes across as underwhelming.

The song's most enduring legacy may be its live performances during the Riot Act tour, where Eddie would wear and then serenade a Bush mask. It was a minor bit of Bono-style theatricality but did provoke several fan backlash moments, given Bush's soaring popularity. Of note was the performance on April 30 at Uniondale, New York, where "Bu$hleaguer" was met with boos from a notable percentage of the audience and led to an uncomfortable and awkward extended exchange with the audience that demonstrated band/audience interactions are designed for community, not dialogue.

"1/2 Full"

Lyrics:	Eddie Vedder
Music:	Jeff Ament
Live Debut:	The Showbox in Seattle, Washington, U.S.A., December 5, 2002
Alternate Versions/ Notable Performances:	*Live at Easy Street*, East Street Records in Seattle, Washington, U.S.A., April 29, 2005
	Bercy in Paris, France, September 11, 2006

The brawny playfulness of "1/2 Full" taps into something akin to a fierce joy at being alive, especially after the paranoia of the tracks preceding it—a willingness to stay up all night to greet the dawn. But the lyrical content speaks to a darker reality that undermines the music's dismissive abandon. This is not a song about the self, the community, or even the nation. "1/2 Full" is about the state of the world, the smoldering domain of kings Bush and Cheney, filtered through Daniel Quinn in his final appearance as a lyrical muse.

"1/2 Full" returns to themes in "Cropduster"—affirming our own comparative inconsequence. Neither we nor the politics of our moment matter all that much. "Whispering that life existed long before greed … balancing the world on its knee." There is an indictment of our hubris in having forgotten this, especially the powerful and their insatiable, destructive desire for more.

At the same time, "1/2 Full" is a fight song. There is no middle anymore. Given the great and disruptive harm that we are capable of, you must commit to a side. You must be willing to take responsibility for the world we have made and the world we want. In this respect, "1/2 Full" is more a call to arms than to apathy that is so tempting in dark times.

However, the final lyrics undermine both the optimism in the music and the engagement in the words. The world needs to be saved, but the task is beyond the singer. Someone else needs to do it ("Won't someone save the world?"). "1/2 Full" becomes less about action and more about faith—a hope that an external savior will come along and do what must be done because we have lost the confidence to do it ourselves.

"ARC"

Lyrics:	Eddie Vedder
Music:	Eddie Vedder
Live Debut:	San Diego Sports Arena in San Diego, California, U.S.A., June 5, 2003
Alternate Versions/ Notable Performances:	Palacio de los Deportes, Distrito Federal, Mexico, July 18, 2003
	Water on the Road: Eddie Vedder Live, Warner Theatre in Washington, D.C., U.S.A., August 16, 2008

"Arc" is an intensely personal song, a mournful, wordless, looping chant Eddie sings unaccompanied. It was dedicated to the nine lives lost at Roskilde and performed nine times during the 2003 tour. But Eddie is releasing more than their memories in his performance. "Arc" tries to encapsulate what words cannot—the bewilderment, the absence of hope, the alienation, and the nearly totalizing loss of faith carried across the album.

"ALL OR NONE"

Lyrics:	Eddie Vedder and Stone Gossard
Music:	Stone Gossard
Live Debut:	The Showbox in Seattle, Washington, U.S.A., December 5, 2002
Alternate Versions/ Notable Performances:	*Live at Benaroya Hall*, Benaroya Hall in Seattle, Washington, U.S.A., October 22, 2003
	The Vic Theatre in Chicago, Illinois, U.S.A., August 2, 2007

"All or None" is a stark, despondent song that embodies the spirit of *Riot Act*'s cover art. It surveys a broken, defeated planet, country, and self, and wonders what, if anything, we can do next. There is no answer other than survive until we stumble upon a way forward. Other than "Parting Ways" and "Stupid Mop," there is no darker conclusion to a Pearl Jam album.

A richness lurks underneath Stone's mournful performance, but even more than "Thumbing My Way," it highlights the desolation of the soundscape. Each strum rings out heavy against the silence. The guitar fills alternately sound like sighs and tears, and Mike's outro solo is weighted down with despair. There is emotion, but no real catharsis, because there is no next step.

Eddie again sounds exhausted, but here he finally admits what he had been denying throughout the rest of the record: "It's a hopeless situation and I'm starting to believe that this hopeless situation is what I'm trying to achieve." The lyrics and performance lack the strength that emerges from confrontation and fails to empower the way the dark revelations of songs like "Better Man" or "Rearviewmirror" do. Sometimes, the bars on our cage are solid, the locks are strong, and there really is no way out. We are left not with a prelude to redemption but a confirmation of failure. The baggage of an entire record, fourteen prior songs, is nicely summarized in that one lyric.

"That this hopeless situation is what I'm trying to achieve" is a self-recriminating sentiment. He is clearly chastising himself for being on the verge of giving up and accepting the dismal wreckage of his world. The second verse is meant to steel his nerves ("Here's the selfless confession leading me back to war") even though he doubts it will make a difference: "Can we help that our destinations are the ones we've been before?" If he is going to surrender, he vows (weakly, a tired vow coming from a solitary place) that it will be to himself and his own grim defiance. Better to be miserable and faithful to himself than coexist in benign acceptance of a world anathema to his values—a grim moment of existential freedom.

The chorus, therefore, is meant to be an affirmation—a call to arms despite the odds, but the lack of belief is apparent. That he sings, "I still try to run on" rather than the more determined "I will run on" highlights his paralyzing doubt. Even the emotional climax grounds his voice before it can take flight, and the wordless vocalizations that are his final contribution to the album are deflated, far too burdened by what he has seen and experienced to be inspirational.

Riot Act closes with Mike's solo, one of his most despairing pieces to date, gradually fading off into silence, with no end in sight. Just a primal sadness directed at how far we have fallen, and the impossible heights we must climb to see light again. We can see that sparks of resistance are there, buried deep but still alive, ready to come roaring back to life with the explosive beginning of the self-titled album, a reaffirmation of their core commitments in the aftermath of *Riot Act*'s crisis of faith.

We are not alone, and the darkness is not as permanent and all-encompassing as it may appear. It was not an easy journey back, but it had begun.

Selections from the Back Catalog: *Riot Act* Era

"I Am Mine" Single

Released:	September 23, 2002
Musicians:	Eddie Vedder, vocals, guitar; Stone Gossard, guitar; Mike McCready, guitar; Jeff Ament, bass; Matt Cameron, drums; Boom Gaspar, Hammond B3, Fender Rhodes; Adam Kasper, piano
Producer:	Adam Kaspar
Engineering:	Adam Kaspar
Studio:	Studio X in Seattle, Washington, U.S.A.

"DOWN"
Also appears on the *Lost Dogs* compilation album

Lyrics:	Eddie Vedder
Music:	Mike McCready and Stone Gossard
Live Debut:	The Showbox in Seattle, Washington, U.S.A., December 5, 2002
Alternate Versions/ Notable Performances:	Nassau Veterans Memorial Coliseum, East Garden City, New York, U.S.A., April 30, 2003
	TD Garden in Boston, Massachusetts, U.S.A., May 24, 2006

Riot Act was the last Pearl Jam record whose singles featured new songs as B-sides. "Down" and "Undone" arrived as companion pieces to the lead single "I Am Mine." Inspired by historian Howard Zinn, whose *A People's History of the United States* charts the often-untold history of social resistance, "Down" is an unabashedly optimistic moment of light. The riff is infectious, the sound is rich, and Eddie's performance has an energy often absent from *Riot Act*.

He acknowledges the depths to which he had fallen while demanding we rise and accept responsibility for changing the world. Engagement is the best cure for powerlessness, and Eddie insists that anyone can ascend from their darkness before concluding with Mike's celebratory solo—more playful than cathartic, but the sound of a person unbowed by the world around them.

"UNDONE"

Also appears on the *Lost Dogs* compilation album

Lyrics:	Eddie Vedder
Music:	Eddie Vedder
Live Debut:	Gorge Amphitheatre in George, Washington, U.S.A., September 1, 2005
Alternate Versions/ Notable Performances:	Newcastle Entertainment Centre in Newcastle, New South Wales, Australia, November 19, 2006
	TD Garden in Boston, Massachusetts, U.S.A., May 17, 2010

"Undone" takes a step back from the churning optimism of "Down." It is a less assertive song, its groove more reflective and patient. It begins with an overdue homecoming, and "Undone" beautifully conveys the feeling of exhaling after a long, tense, moment.

While his homeland is occupied (exactly the right word to use), he affirms his conviction that having lost a battle does not mean surrendering the field ("Well you know the pendulum throws, farther out to the one side swinging, has to sweep back the other way"). He has sloughed off the hopeless depression that left him paralyzed, summarizing "Down" in the bridge couplet "all this hope and nowhere to go. This is how I used to feel but no more." Eddie's use of the word "undone" is well chosen. The world has been picked apart piece by piece, but we can replace those pieces one a time—"like a wave building before it breaks."

Together "Down" and "Undone" represent the road not taken, and their inclusion on the record would have re-contextualized *Riot Act*, making it a wounded series of songs still fighting despite it all, as opposed to the story of a person, a band, a country, and a world utterly lost but too stubborn to quit, with no immediate plan other than to hold on.

Big Fish: Original Motion Picture Soundtrack

Released:	November 26, 2003
Musicians:	Eddie Vedder, vocals, guitar; Stone Gossard, guitar; Mike McCready, guitar; Jeff Ament, bass; Matt Cameron, drums
Producer:	Adam Kaspar
Engineering:	Sam Hofstedt
Studio:	Studio X in Seattle, Washington, U.S.A.

"MAN OF THE HOUR"

Also appears as a single (with a B-side demo) and on *Rearviewmirror (Greatest Hits 1991–2003)*

Lyrics:	Eddie Vedder
Music:	Eddie Vedder

Live Debut: *Live at Benaroya Hall*, Benaroya Hall in Seattle, Washington, U.S.A., October 22, 2003

Alternate Versions/
Notable Performances: Forum Milan in Assago, Italy, September 17, 2006
                          Unimed Hall in São Paulo, Brazil, March 30, 2018
                          (Eddie Vedder solo performance)

The Golden Globe-nominated "Man of the Hour" was written for Tim Burton's *Big Fish*, playing over the closing credits. It explores the oversized mystery of fathers, and the larger-than-life impact they have on the development of their children. Unlike "Release," where he cries out for his unknown father to fill the void inside of him, "Man of the Hour" reflects on the unknowable distance between parent and child. It reflects on how, for better or worse, we are shaped within that space. An aching, wistful performance, it mourns the opportunities for understanding and reconciliation lost to death. Yet, it is simultaneously warm and healing, making peace with what he did not understand during his father's life ("tidal waves don't beg forgiveness. Crash, then on their way") and swelling with gratitude for gifts that took a lifetime to appreciate.

Above: Pearl Jam. *Left to right*: Mike McCready, lead guitar; Jeff Ament, bass; Matt Cameron, percussion; Eddie Vedder, vocals and guitar; Stone Gossard, rhythm guitar. (*Photo: Danny Clinch*)

Right: Pearl Jam's first album *Ten* (1991) is considered critical in the rise of "grunge" and alternative music which dominated popular music in the 1990s. The album was certified RIAA Diamond (10 million+ copies sold) status in 2009, boosted, in part, by a remastered and remixed release that same year. (*Photo: PearlJam.com*)

Vs. (1993) set the record for most copies of an album sold in its first week despite a concerted effort by the band to scale back promotional efforts and refusing to produce any videos for the album's singles. (*Photo: PearlJam.com*)

Pearl Jam's third album, *Vitalogy* (1994), was released on vinyl two weeks prior to its CD release, setting a record for the most vinyl sales in one week (which stood until 2014). It was also the fastest-selling album of all time behind *Vs.* (*Photo: PearlJam.com*)

No Code (1996) represented a tonal shift away from the aggressive rock sound Pearl Jam was known for. Though it was the third consecutive number one album, it was the first of their albums to not reach multi-platinum status. (*Photo: PearlJam.com*)

With their fifth album, *Yield* (1998), Pearl Jam began a more collaborative approach to song writing and eased up on their promotional blackout, releasing the album as well as a book, *Place/Date* by Charles Peterson and Lance Mercer; a DVD, *Single Video Theory*; and their first video since "Jeremy" for the song "Do the Evolution." (*Photo: PearlJam.com*)

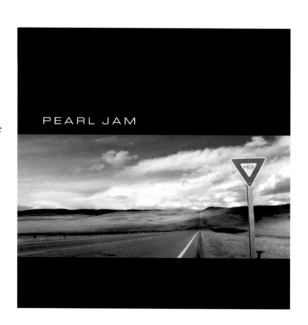

Pearl Jam were notorious for providing minimal and incomplete lyrics in their liner notes, telling fans in each Fan Club newsletter, "The only available lyrics are already published in the albums. Headphones are recommended." (*Photo:* Ten, 1991)

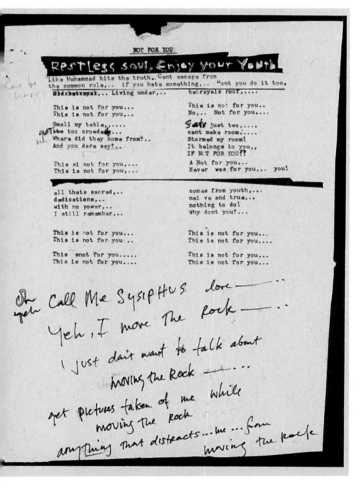

In the early albums, lyrics were often Vedder's handwritten notes from his ever-present composition books (or typewritten by Vedder on a 1946 Smith-Corona Sterling typewriter), giving fans some unexpected insight into his thoughts. (*Photo:* Vitalogy, 1994)

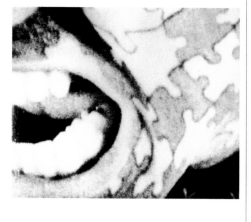
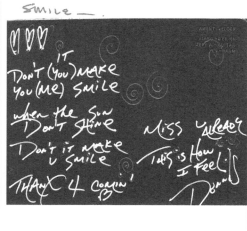

Since the release of *Vs.*, Pearl Jam has experimented with packaging (shunning the ubiquitous CD "jewel" cases) by releasing *No Code* in a 4-fold cardboard sleeve featuring one of four different sets of Polaroids with lyrics on the back. (*Photo:* No Code, 1996)

Liner notes and lyrics began to take a more traditional look with the release of *Yield*, but Pearl Jam still created added value for fans by hiding a "yield" sign in each photo, making a game of the packaging. (*Photo:* Yield, 1998)

PEARL JAM *LIVE*
ON TWO LEGS

Above: For a band of their size, Pearl Jam maintains a minimalist stage set, choosing to focus on their relationship with their fans. O2 World in Berlin, Germany, July 5, 2012. (*Photo: Alive87, flic.kr/p/cvdgLo*)

Left: In 1998, Pearl Jam began to focus on the fans trading and collecting tapes of live shows and inconsistently compiled bootlegs of their music, hoping to address it with the release of *Live on Two Legs* (1998), featuring live performances from throughout the band's 1998 North American tour. (*Photo: PearlJam.com*)

Above: Time Warner
Cable Arena in Charlotte,
North Carolina, U.S.A.,
October 30, 2013.
(*Photo: Brandon Rector*)

Right: Pearl Jam kicked off
a year-long celebration of
their twentieth anniversary
with *Live on Ten Legs*
(2011), a companion to
1998's *Live on Two Legs*, a
compilation of performances
ranging from 2003–2010.
(*Photo: PearlJam.com*)

PEARL JAM *LIVE*
ON TEN LEGS

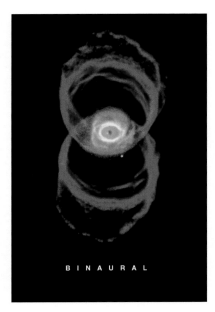

BINAURAL

Left: Pearl Jam's sixth album, *Binaural* (2000), was the first album with a producer other than Brendan O'Brien since *Vs.* The title references a recording technique in which two microphones are arranged to create a more directional sensation, which lends itself to the more atmospheric sound of the album. (*Photo: PearlJam.com*)

Below: *Riot Act* (2002) was Pearl Jam's first post-9/11 album and their first since the accidental death of nine fans during their 2000 performance at the Roskilde Festival in Denmark. Both events heavily influenced the album and the 2003 tour. (*Photo: PearlJam.com*)

PEARL JAM RIOT ACT

Right: Pearl Jam's 2006 eponymous album (commonly called "Avocado") was their first release following the completion of their contract with Sony Records, but was released by their subsidiary, J Records. "Let's throw an avocado on the cover"—Eddie Vedder. (*Photo: PearlJam.com*)

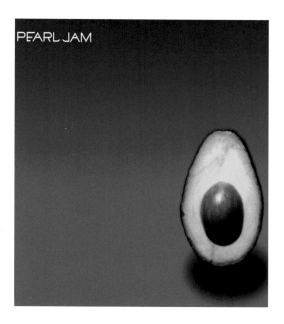

Below: Backspacer (2009) was Pearl Jam's first album released under their own label, Monkeywrench Records. This album marks the band's first major effort to promote their album via social media, releasing previews of the artwork and a scavenger hunt allowing fans to earn giveaways by members of the Coalition of Independent Music Stores. (*Photo: PearlJam.com*)

VINYL FILMS presents a MONKEYWRENCH, INC. and TREMOLO PRODUCTIONS production A CAMERON CROWE film "PEARL JAM TWENTY"
JEFF AMENT MATT CAMERON STONE GOSSARD MIKE McCREADY EDDIE VEDDER edited by NICOLA B. MARSH music by CHRIS PERKEL KEVIN KLAUBER
producer BARBARA McDONOUGH producer MICHELE ANTHONY executive producers KELLY CURTIS CAMERON CROWE MORGAN NEVILLE ANDY FISCHER
written and directed by CAMERON CROWE

Pearl Jam Twenty (2011), a documentary filmed by Cameron Crowe in celebration of Pearl Jam's twentieth anniversary, was their theatrical debut. The film featured footage edited from 1,200 hours of video spanning the band's career. It was also released as a DVD or Blu-Ray package including *The Kids are Twenty*, a collection of full song performances featured in the film, and *The Fans Are Alright*, a ninety-minute documentary focusing on the band's relationship with their fans. (*Photo: PearlJam.com*)

Right: Following Pearl Jam's two-night stand at Wrigley Stadium in Chicago, the band returned to theaters with the release of *Let's Play Two* (2017), a film directed by Danny Clinch, chronicling the band's performances, Eddie's history with the city of his birth, and the 2016 World Series victory by the Chicago Cubs over the Cleveland Indians. (*Photo: PearlJam.com*)

Below left: The third single from the album *Ten*, "Jeremy," for better or for worse, launched Pearl Jam's fame with an MTV video directed by Mark Pellington which went on to win MTV's Best Video of the Year. The CD single, originally released only overseas, introduced fans to the *Ten* outtakes, "Footsteps" and "Yellow Ledbetter." (*Photo: discogs.com*)

Below right: A companion piece to Neil Young's Mirrorball (which features Pearl Jam, credited only as "The Band," due to label disputes), *Merkinball* (1995) introduced fans to "I Got Id" (also known as "I Got Shit") and "Long Road." (*Photo: PearlJam.com*)

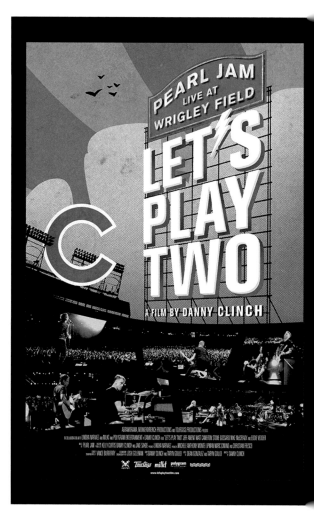

Left: The compilation album *Lost Dogs* (2003) brings together thirty-one B-sides, promotional releases, covers, and never-before-heard outtakes spanning the breadth of Pearl Jam's first twelve years. (*Photo: PearlJam.com*)

Below: To date, Pearl Jam's only greatest hits compilation, *Rearviewmirror (Greatest Hits 1991–2003)* (2004) consists of thirty-three of Pearl Jam's most commercially successful songs, including some alternative takes, new lyrics, and remixes that have resulted in endless debates amongst fans as to which versions are superior. (*Photo: PearlJam.com*)

In the writing of this book, several shows have made repeated appearances in our Notable Performances. Luckily, since 2000, Pearl Jam has made a habit of releasing high-quality recordings ("bootlegs") of their shows and, later, annual "Vault" releases to combat the proliferation of poorly recorded or sloppily compiled bootlegs.

Above: Fox Theater in Atlanta, Georgia, April 3, 1994. (*Photo: Pearljam.com*)

Orpheum Theater in Boston, Massachusetts, U.S.A., April 12, 1994. (*Photo: PearlJam.com*)

Pearl Jam's practice of allowing fans to openly tape and trade their shows resulted in an active community of tape traders throughout the 1990s, and in an age of easily available bootlegs, that community now collects the best performances and recordings by the band, repackaging them into fan-friendly collections that are freely distributed to grow and strengthen the band's fanbase. (*Photo: ridleybradout*)

Fans are also known for hunting down songs scattered across various releases, such as Pearl Jam's Fan Club/Holiday Singles (1991–2018), and compiling them into collections for friends to enjoy. (*Photo: ridleybradout*)

Pearl Jam's tenth album, *Lightning Bolt* (2013), was released with what was possibly the band's most personal promotion to date, coming out alongside hours of interviews by friends of the band. The artwork, consisting of multiple paintings by skateboard artist, Don Pendleton, won a 2015 Grammy for Best Recording Package. (*Photo: PearlJam.com*)

Gigaton (2020) was released following a promotional run of augmented reality puzzles, allowing fans to use their smart phones to view moving avatars tied to the album and the cover art, a photo by Paul Nicklen. However, the release date (March 27) fell just as the COVID-19 pandemic was causing the world to close all large public events, forcing Pearl Jam to postpone their supporting tour for over two years. (*Photo: PearlJam.com*)

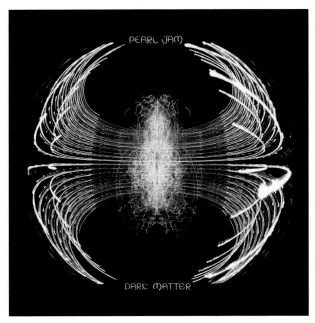

Dark Matter (2024) was preceded by a series of listening parties at music stores and in movie theaters where it was paired with visualizations created by cover artist, Alexandr Gnezdilov. This album was written over approximately three weeks as an in-studio collaboration with producer Andrew Watt, who had previously worked with Eddie Vedder on his solo album, *Earthling* (2022). (*Photo: PearlJam.com*)

The Dark Matter World Tour features the most expansive stage shows Pearl Jam has ever undertaken. Visuals, created by Rob and Stephanie Sheridan of Sheridan Productions, are projected behind the band. Sheridan posted to his blog shortly after the start of the tour that to make the video he "followed paths of inspiration through elements and states of matter: Light refractions, chemical reactions, fluid dynamics, incandescent projections, and other experimental setups tracing the connective tissue of the universe." (*Photo: Travis Hay / GuerrillaCandy.com*)

Pearl Jam

Released:	May 2, 2006
Musicians:	Eddie Vedder, vocals, guitar
	Stone Gossard, guitar
	Mike McCready, guitar
	Jeff Ament, bass
	Matt Cameron, drums
	Boom Gaspar, Hammond B3, piano, pump organ
	Gary Westlake, Optigan
Producer:	Adam Kasper and Pearl Jam
Engineering:	Sam Hofstedt and John Burton
Remixed and re-released on November 11, 2017, with production by Brendan O'Brien
Studio:	Studio X in Seattle, Washington, U.S.A.
Art Direction:	Eddie Vedder as Jerome Turner
Cover Art:	Brad Klausen
Peak Chart Position:	No. 2 on the U.S. *Billboard* 200, No. 5 U.K. Top Albums

The self-titled *Pearl Jam* (often dubbed "Avocado" for its cover art) is Pearl Jam's most reactionary album, a direct sonic and thematic response to *Riot Act*. Whereas *Riot Act* was a tentative album, cautious and richly textured, *Pearl Jam* is an explosive burst of sandpaper energy—and there is a lot *Pearl Jam* wants to scour away. It is loud and abrasive, with an immediacy lacking on the exceedingly introspective *Riot Act*. *Pearl Jam* features some of Eddie's most full-throated vocals in the entire catalog.

Why the direct refutation of *Riot Act*? Some of this reflects the times. *Riot Act* was recorded and released during the early days of the Bush Administration and the War on Terror. It was a time when progressive values were in retreat and even voicing a critique came with profound consequences. *Riot Act* grapples with the experience of doubting your own values and being unable to reinforce them through your engagement with others—undermining a core philosophic tenant of their music.

By 2006, the public turned against President Bush. The premature declaration of "Mission Accomplished in Iraq," the burgeoning recognition that these wars might last a generation, and the fatally flawed response to Hurricane Katrina combined to create a space where the band's political instincts could be shouted from the rooftop, confident their voice would be heard, affirmed, and shared.

The experience of two incredible tours in the interim (2003 and 2005) set the template for the modern revivalist feel of a Pearl Jam concert and influenced the album that followed. *Pearl Jam,* more than any other of their records, was written to be played live, and with a clarity and intensity that could be directly translated into a concert performance in a way unmatched since *Vitalogy.*

The result was a record where Pearl Jam could finally read (or scream) the riot act to America, as each song either directly engages with the politics of the War on Terror/Iraq or emerges from the existential dislocation of the early Bush years, giving even the personal songs a political edge. *Pearl Jam* saw more promotion than any Pearl Jam album since *Ten* or *Vs.* Multiple televised live performances were an opportunity to share politicized songs as "it seem[ed] like a critical time to participate in our democracy."[1] And, although this will become much more prominent on later records, the birth of Eddie's first daughter lent a sense of urgency to his writing: "Now that I see it as my daughter's planet, I'm even more [angry]."[2]

But it is also an album about processing grief and trauma: 9/11, the War in Iraq, the Bush administration, and overwhelming personal loss, all told through political stories of the war's dead while referencing more intimate personal tragedies. As Eddie told *Rolling Stone* years later, "Half the record is based on the loss of the guy who turned out to be the best friend I ever had on the planet [Johnny Ramone]."[3]

Pearl Jam is also noteworthy for being their first album as an "independent band," their contract with Epic Records having ended in 2003. And there are subtle shades of Pearl Jam struggling to define itself as it embarks on the next stage in its career. Despite a self-titled release declaring "this is Pearl Jam," the cover artwork is just a picture of a halved avocado. The interior art features sculptures by Fernando Apodaca depicting the band as zombies, representations of fragility and decay, oddly out of synch on a record celebrating the re-emergence of strength. It is as if each musical moment is being asked to speak for itself, and the overall meaning will be given coherence by the larger Pearl Jam community once they process the songs with the band—that Pearl Jam is to be defined collectively through the live experience.

"Life Wasted"

Lyrics:	Eddie Vedder
Music:	Stone Gossard
Single Release Date:	August 28, 2006
Peak U.S. Chart Position:	13
Live Debut:	Astoria in London, U.K., April 20, 2006
Alternate Versions/	
Notable Performances:	*Late Show with David Letterman*: Ed Sullivan Theatre in New York, New York, U.S.A., May 4, 2006
	Xcel Energy Center in Woodbury, Minnesota, U.S.A., June 26, 2006
	Blue Room at Third Man Records in Nashville, Tennessee, U.S.A., June 9, 2016

Pearl Jam's music has always struggled with alienation—learning to cope with a world you cannot understand or control. But there was an experiential solidarity in the lyrics. Eddie was right there in the trenches. *Pearl Jam* is the band's first record since he crossed forty, and you cannot help but view the world differently than you did in your twenties. He embraces the role of elder statesman, offering "the wisdom that the old can't give away" with newfound assurance. The themes in "Life Wasted" are not appreciably different from a song like "Present Tense," but there is a greater confidence in the message, amplified by a gritty, slashing riff, an explosive solo, and a vocal performance combining the intensity of "Habit" and the empathy of "Save You." Eddie has called it "funeral energy," but survivor's energy may be the better description.[4] It celebrates letting go of what eats you inside as the precursor to fully living, and it does so with the confidence of one who has made it through and is ready to guide others on their own journey. Earlier records floated the possibility that things could get better. "Life Wasted" confirms that they will, if we let them, and revels in the freedom that follows from having that choice: "I have faced it, a life wasted. I am never going back again."

"Life Wasted" introduces a few recurring thematic elements, in particular the idea of home: "I've seen the home inside your head, all locked doors and unmade beds." Home is a source of security—a safe and grounding space. From its foundation, we build our lives. The object of "Life Wasted" (Eddie is the subject) has lost that sense of security. It is easier to revel in feeling disaffected and to be "one with negativity" (see *Riot Act*), but not without consequence.

Also, central to *Pearl Jam* is the idea of movement, which manifests in the dominant images on "Life Wasted," and throughout the record. Movement carries with it a sense of possibility—the chance to change the direction of our lives, our culture, our country, and our world. *Riot Act* was unsure of where to go. The songs on *Pearl Jam*, almost without exception, steer away from a life wasted.

"WORLD WIDE SUICIDE"

Lyrics:	Eddie Vedder
Music:	Eddie Vedder
Single Release Date:	March 14, 2006
Peak U.S. Chart Position:	41
Live Debut:	Astoria in London, U.K., April 20, 2006
Alternate Versions/	
Notable Performances:	*Saturday Night Live*: Studio 8H, NBC Studios in New York, New York, U.S.A., April 15, 2006
	Live on Ten Legs, Sazka Arena in Prague, Czech Republic, September 22, 2006
	Lollapalooza, Grant Park in Chicago, Illinois, U.S.A., August 5, 2007

There is more narrative on *Pearl Jam* than on any of their other albums, and "World Wide Suicide," the first single, contains the most explicit political commentary on any Pearl Jam single, arguably any song, to date.[5] It explores the family of a dead soldier coping with the experience of loss, the senselessness of the death, and the lack of accountability. It strikes a calibrated balance for such a loose song. The main character is lashing out in bewildered rage at the war, at those responsible, and the rest of us for allowing it to happen, while grappling with a sense of overwhelming futility ("the wave won't break"). And yet, "World Wide Suicide" is one of Pearl Jam's most upbeat and curiously danceable numbers, refusing to stop so the pain cannot define it.

Other songs on *Pearl Jam* will explore the loss. "World Wide Suicide" does not linger in that space. Instead, it tries to process an overpowering frustration and anger, captured in Eddie's raw and shredded chorus vocals. The hell is man-made, artificial, and appalling. Equally maddening is the recognition that countless others will be subjected to the same emotional devastation until we are willing to name the cause. War is the destruction of love, security, and happiness. It consumes everything. A worldwide suicide.

The second verse specifically condemns President Bush and the lack of accountability gifted to our masters of war: "Medals on a wooden mantle next to a handsome face that the President took for granted. Writing checks that others pay." Then it is quickly back to the hypocrisy of invoking God in the cause of partisan murder, the never-ending madness of wartime hysteria.

"World Wide Suicide" is a protest song and recognizes that only righteous anger at the way things are and the conviction that they can be better can stand before the incoming wave. This is best captured in the bridge's desperate plea: "looking in the eyes of the fallen you've got to know there's another, another, another, another, another way." We must stare down at the overwhelming forces in our lives and refuse to blink. Anger is a font of power when focused on the right people. And the twitchy, scratching energy of "World Wide Suicide" knows how to pull that anger out of grief and exactly where to aim it.

"Comatose"

Lyrics:	Eddie Vedder
Music:	Mike McCready and Stone Gossard
Live Debut:	Paramount Theater in Seattle, Washington, U.S.A., March 18, 2005 (called "Crapshoot Rapture")
Alternate Versions/ Notable Performances:	Palace of Auburn Hills in Auburn Hills, Michigan, U.S.A., May 22, 2006 *Immagine in Cornice*, Duomo Square in Pistoia, Italy, September 20, 2006 The Vic Theatre in Chicago, Illinois, U.S.A., August 2, 2007

"Comatose" is a dirty, strident, punk-inflected howl, a totalizing critique that transcends specificity. The verse and chorus are sung from the perspective of a "typical" American, lost in his vacuum, oblivious to the friction of the outside world, and unaware of how his actions affect those around him. The lyric about hanging upside down attests to the inversion of priorities and values—the celebration of hatred and selfishness instead of love and community.

The chorus introduces the image of falling, crucial to the next three songs. Falling implies a mistake, an imperfection. We fall when we are not careful, or when the ground becomes unstable. Down also implies damnation, and our trajectory is unmistakably down. Yet, here we are, happy in our vacuum, with no comprehension of the danger we are in and, therefore, no fear of it. After all, we are Americans (or humans more generally), and problems are for other people. We are oblivious, unaware of the "blood on all the pistons," and "comatose with no fear of falling."

While the bridge is a critique of conservative opposition to LGBTQ+ equality ("high above I'll break the law if it's illegal to be in love"), it is also a prelude to the themes of "Marker in the Sand." Its perspective is infused with love, compassion, and understanding instead of hate, vengeance, and judgment. Those are seductive values. Hate is less demanding than love. As a society, and as individuals, we are so self-absorbed that it is difficult to love one another, and in some cases, even ourselves. When Jesus was crucified, he was supposed to die for our sins, to grant us a new beginning, and unless we "leave the hatred on the cross," he would have died in vain. And, "Comatose" closes with a general sense of righteous incomprehension. How did things get this way, what part did I play, and how do I change it? *Pearl Jam* is a working through of these questions, familiar stakes given fresh urgency.

"Comatose" caps off an explosive start to the album, the most aggressive run of songs in the catalog. Moving forward, *Pearl Jam* shifts its focus to processing and directing its anger—embracing the hurt behind it and looking for a way to heal so the driving energy for change that moves us forward is not stumbling over its own furious grief.

"Severed Hand"

Lyrics: Eddie Vedder
Music: Eddie Vedder
Alternate Versions/
Notable Performances: *Saturday Night Live*: Studio 8H, NBC Studios in New York, New York, U.S.A., April 15, 2006
                           Rod Laver Arena in Melbourne, Victoria, Australia, November 13, 2006
                           Tauron Arena Kraków in Kraków, Poland, July 3, 2018

"Severed Hand" is about the experience of psychedelic drugs (articulated in the bridge), but the most interesting idea explored centers around their use—to what end and purpose. "Severed Hand" begins with an explosive build transitioning into a staccato corkscrew riff, and Eddie's vocals hint at danger. The subject sees too clearly and knows too much, armed with dangerous knowledge but not the means to process it. The singer confronts a gatekeeper holding the secrets to the clarity he craves. Made clear is the fact that this is a journey the singer must make on his own. Loved ones are left behind in his desperation to escape—a risky choice, as salvation and peace are rarely achievable alone.

The crucial lyric "have no fear but for falling down" is a callback and rejection of the narcissistic naivety of "Comatose." But the knowledge that leads him to reject it is equally paralyzing—a fear of falling is a fear of everything since nothing worthwhile comes without attendant risk. And the singer is overwhelmed with reality and everything in it, personal and political. Other lyrics intimate this may be a veteran traumatized by wartime experiences. Either way, he needs a way home, back to a grounded sense of safety and serenity.

Are drugs the answer? They offer an escape, the chance to "explore and not explode." You can see dragons instead of war. His room is larger, and there is more space for him within it. It buys him time to process, but the questions have not gone away. Reality will be waiting and must be confronted before he can decide how he can live in, and hopefully transcend, the world of pain outside our vacuum.

"MARKER IN THE SAND"

Lyrics:	Eddie Vedder
Music:	Mike McCready
Live Debut:	Astoria in London, U.K., April 20, 2006
Alternate Versions/	
Notable Performances:	Van Andel Arena in Grand Rapids, Michigan, U.S.A., May 19, 2006
	Sazka Arena in Prague, Czech Republic, September 22, 2006

"Marker in the Sand" contains Eddie's most mature and sophisticated exploration of faith, laying out a spiritual journey—its verses mirroring the chopped-up state of our world, juxtaposed against a contemplative, almost transcendent, sense of hope and promise in a chorus that illuminates what is best in ourselves.

It begins with a reference to a marker, lost because "the sand has covered over the messages it kept misunderstanding," evoking both wars in the Middle East and mysteries hidden by the passage of time. Either way, we have lost track of the marker's original message, that the core of faith is love and forgiveness, its truth buried in the desert.

Faith is dangerous because of its power. It can defy reason and compromise, and presumes infallibility. The appeal to God is the ultimate, unanswerable justification for any act, and Eddie argues that the faithful are more concerned with damnation than redemption, superiority over salvation, and judgment over love: "What went wrong walking tightrope high over moral ground, seeing visions of falling up somehow?" The falling imagery returns. Despite our imperfections, we believe we can stumble our way up to heaven. But, as imperfect beings, salvation is a consequence of grace and forgiveness, unknowable, but somehow earned through the recognition of our shared humanity.

This speaks to one of the central tenets of "Marker," the reminder that dogmatic certainty is not necessary to be worthy of love: "Those undecided needn't have faith to be free and those misguided, there was a plan for them to be." That we hate what we cannot understand is a monstrous and inexplicable perversion of God's love.

Where the first chorus asked us to be humble and recognize our limits as human beings, the second chorus highlights the plea for acceptance—a stronger, more demanding idea than tolerance. Eddie asks us to understand one another, to "walk the bridges before you burn them down." But he knows that his message is not being heard by the faithful and so "Marker" ends with a challenge to God: "God, what do you say?" The calling out is not a cry of despair or uncertainty. Instead, Eddie demands that God take some responsibility for the mess people have made in its name. But, if God refuses, we will have to do it ourselves.

"Parachutes"

Lyrics:	Eddie Vedder
Music:	Stone Gossard
Live Debut:	TD Garden in Boston, Massachusetts, U.S.A., May 25, 2006

Alternate Versions/
Notable Performances: Palaisozaki in Torino, Italy, September 19, 2006
The Vic Theatre in Chicago, Illinois, U.S.A., August 2, 2007

Pearl Jam's second Beatles-infused composition, also written by Stone, "Parachutes" floats effortlessly along, keeping its wearer safe and secure as they fall through the world. It is wistful and off-kilter but still melodic, appropriate for an optimistic and mature celebration of a love that saves, and whose legacy lingers beyond loss.

The song's lyrics center on both halves of a relationship. It begins with the person left behind. The first verse returns to the grounding imagery of the home, offering the love and stability through which we find the strength to engage and endure. And, in the lover's absence, the home is failing: "All the dreams we shared and lights we turned on, but the house is getting dark." And yet, "Parachutes" refuses to remain in that space and pivots to gratitude for the life they shared: "I won't need nothing else 'cause when we're dead we would've had it all." Love is experienced as salvation: "I would have fallen from the sky 'til you. Parachutes have opened now." Destined to fall but descending together.

There is a subtle pivot in the song's second half as the perspective shifts to the other lover, far from home. It is likely a soldier, both contextually from the rest of the album and some of the lyrics. It is not clear if the singer is dying or just in a melancholy mood, but instead of panic, or anger, they too are filled with gratitude. Their last thoughts dwell not on what is lost, but on how thankful they are for what they had. Their life meant something because they "found this love with you."

"Unemployable"

Lyrics:	Eddie Vedder
Music:	Matt Cameron and Mike McCready
Live Debut:	Astoria in London, U.K., April 20, 2006

Alternate Versions/
Notable Performances: Bill Graham Civic Auditorium in San Francisco, California, U.S.A., July 15, 2006
Palaisozaki in Torino, Italy, September 19, 2006

"Unemployable" grapples with the death of the "American Dream," the enduring belief that honest work and sacrifice are always rewarded with a secure future. It is an article of deeply felt faith as every aspect of mainstream American society indoctrinates this belief. But there is an insidious corollary to the American dream, that economic struggle is a result of personal failure rather than external obstacles. This is the backdrop for "Unemployable." The subject was laid off because employees are expendable costs of production, not human beings with families, hopes, and dreams. Although it is not directly textual, it is easy to imagine the main character as a veteran, adding a new dimension to their sacrifice.

The Jesus ring detail is a bit of heavy-handed characterization. But it also sets up the multiple meaning behind the lyric "this life is sacrifice." It references both the sacrifice of his time and labor, as well as the literal sacrifice of his livelihood on the altar of someone else's profit. It also recalls Jesus's sacrifice, dying for the possibility of redeeming humankind, spotlighting our misplaced priorities.

"Unemployable" evokes the working-class stories Bruce Springsteen effortlessly tells, and Springsteen will be an increasingly prominent influence in Eddie's writing. The jumping trains lyric references displaced people during the Great Depression, hopping on freight trains and traveling the country, desperate for work. Other details highlight the existential/psychic trauma that comes from losing your job in the absence of a strong safety net. What if he can no longer support his family, a responsibility also bound up in certain images of masculinity the subject is coded as believing? The unknown future no longer represents possibilities but a creeping dread too terrifying to contemplate. Living in fear strips us of our power to imagine a better world, and the subject is mocked by the pop stylings of the chorus.

But there are cautiously hopeful notes in the song. When he sings "I've seen the light ... I'm scared alive," he is speaking of a growing class consciousness. He is seeing clearly for the first time. He may still be trapped in a cage, sentenced to die within it, but the bars are no longer invisible. The enormity of the realization is terrifying, but it makes it possible to plot an escape.

"BIG WAVE"

Lyrics:	Eddie Vedder
Music:	Jeff Ament
Live Debut:	Viejas Arena in San Diego, California, U.S.A., July 7, 2006
Alternate Versions/ Notable Performances:	Bill Graham Civic Auditorium in San Francisco, California, U.S.A., July 16, 2006
	Members Equity Stadium in Perth, Western Australia, November 14, 2009

"Big Wave" is a light, tension-breaking moment of frantic guitar interplay before the thematic heaviness of *Pearl Jam*'s final sequence. It is a celebration of surfing, reveling in its freedom, the experience of oneness with nature and "exceeding limitations," performed with frenzied abandon. There is not much more going on, nor does there have to be. It is important to find a healthy avenue of escape rather than stay locked in a cluttered home inside your head.

"Gone"

Lyrics:	Eddie Vedder
Music:	Eddie Vedder
Single Release Date:	October 7, 2006
Peak U.S. Chart Position:	40
Live Debut:	Borgata Events Center, Atlantic City, New Jersey, U.S.A., October 1, 2005
Alternate Versions/ Notable Performances:	Demo (2005), appears on the 2005 Fan Club/Holiday Single
	VH1 Storytellers, The Avalon in New York, New York, U.S.A., May 31, 2006
	Acer Arena in Sydney, New South Wales, Australia, November 18, 2006

"Gone" is about trying to escape from the idea of America—narratively, the unnamed city is Atlantic City, where Eddie wrote the song. It begins as a static acoustic dirge in which he is sick of "upset mornings" and "trying evenings," ready to embrace his own disaffection. Disbelieving the American dream does not mean he rejects it as an ideal as much as he recognizes how far we have fallen from it. He is trapped, unable to sleep, let alone dream.

The car imagery is quintessentially American, and its use in "Gone" owes another debt to Springsteen. The United States is a stifling, unsympathetic place when you need help, but there is freedom and clarity to be found on the road. The music quickens, the vocals soar, and for a moment, he is free. His head is clear. He can let go of the weight limiting his imagination and understanding.

It is a minor, personal act of rebellion. "No one thinks to witness," but as the American dream continues to fail, more people will have their own epiphany. He has not failed. His country has failed him. The promise of American life will not be realized until we overcome its nightmarish perversion. That is what needs to be left behind. We are not encouraged to dream beyond ourselves. Outside, there is nothing. But this nothing is where the reclamation of our lives will have to begin.

"Wasted Reprise"

Lyrics:	Eddie Vedder
Music:	Stone Gossard
Live Debut:	Air Canada Centre in Toronto, Ontario, Canada, May 10, 2006
Alternate Versions/	
Notable Performances:	Rod Laver Arena in Melbourne, Victoria, Australia, November 16, 2006
	Blue Room at Third Man Records in Nashville, Tennessee, U.S.A., June 9, 2016

"Wasted Reprise" returns to the chorus of "Life Wasted," the thesis of the record, featuring a pump organ rather than rough guitars. But the reprise also centers on a different message. "Life Wasted" was an exhortation by someone who had freed themselves for others to do the same. The subject of the reprise is more cautious and tentative, lacking that confidence. It is a quiet, dignified effort to bolster a resolve about to be sorely tested.

"Army Reserve"

Lyrics:	Eddie Vedder and Damien Echols
Music:	Jeff Ament
Live Debut:	Astoria in London, U.K., April 20, 2006
Alternate Versions/	
Notable Performances:	Pepsi Arena in Albany, New York, U.S.A., May 12, 2006
	Dom Sportova in Zagreb, Croatia, September 26, 2006

"Army Reserve" tells a story from two perspectives—a family coping with a father off at war, and the father's fear of not making it back home. The music is almost beautiful, almost comforting, but slightly off its axis, a picture of discordant tranquility. It begins with the mother, ground down by the stress of the father's absence, her constant fear of his death, the brave mask she is forced to wear for her family. The possibility of losing him to war, of having to raise their children and go through life without him, completely uproots her: "How long must she stand until the ground gives way into an endless fall?" The verse ends with a powerful image of her "folding in darkness, begging for slumber."

The children resent their father's absence and fear he will not come home. Their home is more mausoleum than sanctuary, a fragile shrine to a man who may never return. She hardly believes her own reassurance, and the kids can tell. She is trying to justify her husband's sacrifice with the declaration that he is fighting and dying for their freedom—the standard line fed to anyone sent to war. But she knows her husband was not taken away for any noble purpose. He was transformed into a tool, stripped of his humanity, dying for nothing.

The chorus was written in prison by Damien Echols, one of the West Memphis Three.[6] The lyrics imagine the moments before an execution, repurposed to apply to either parent. From the mother's standpoint, there is the acknowledgment that he may be lost, accepted with grim a determination to weather the storm about to engulf her. But they are also meant for the father about to die, using his last moments to accept the inevitable and think about his family, hoping they will find the resolve to endure lives about to shatter.

"COME BACK"

Lyrics:	Eddie Vedder
Music:	Eddie Vedder and Mike McCready
Live Debut:	Irving Plaza in New York, New York, U.S.A., May 5, 2006
Alternate Versions/	
Notable Performances:	Xcel Energy Center, St. Paul, Minnesota, U.S.A., June 26, 2006
	Wuhlheide in Berlin, Germany, June 30, 2010

"Come Back" begins with the familiar home imagery, but it is a home in even worse shape than the locked doors and unmade beds of "Life Wasted": "If I keep holding out, will the light shine through? Under this broken roof, it's only rain that I feel."

Rather than move on, the subject stays trapped in their memories, "wishing out" their days, but failing to live them. Anticipating sleep so they can be together in dreams—for as long as they can still hold onto their memories. They indulge in fantasies of their loved ones' return. It may be a sad comfort, but it is no life.

What is worse, it prevents them from moving on. They leave the door open so their lost love can return, but refuse to step through it, to travel beyond the confines of this failing home. As the song builds to its powerful conclusion, they stand there crying in the rain, pleading, "I'll be here, come back," as the mourning tension between the forlorn lyrics and the soulful music breaks and Mike's solo grieves on their behalf.

"INSIDE JOB"

Lyrics:	Mike McCready
Music:	Mike McCready
Live Debut:	Air Canada Centre in Toronto, Ontario, Canada, May 9, 2006

Alternate Versions/
Notable Performances: *Let's Play Two: Original Motion Picture Soundtrack*,
Wrigley Field in Chicago, Illinois, U.S.A., August 20, 2016
MGM Grand in Las Vegas, Nevada, U.S.A., July 6, 2006

"Inside Job" features the only lyrics written by Mike McCready to appear on a Pearl Jam album, chronicling his ultimately triumphant struggles with addiction.[7] But that journey also offers a microcosm of *Pearl Jam*, a moment of hope and redemption at the end of a long and bitter struggle. It reaffirms the subject's humanity and, through that, their chance to be a fully realized human being for themselves and others. It is the journey taken by the singer of "Life Wasted" and gives the record an appropriately cyclical structure. There will always be new challenges and, with them, the need to rediscover your strength.

"Inside Job" begins in a quiet space, though there is a gasping tension within it, an internal grappling with loss and failure. The first step is realizing we must confront the demons we carry if we wish to be free of them, and while we need to do this ourselves (an inside job) we cannot do it alone. Love is more powerful than fear and death, but also scarier for the ways it leaves us exposed. When we invest ourselves in others, we become dependent on them, and the subject used to run from that dependency. But they have finally accepted that a life running away from love, from the human light that creates it, is not a life worth living. They are not sure they can "rise and fix my broken soul, again," but they have faith, and are willing to accept the risk. There is light in the distance, faint, but there to guide them, and as the music quickens, they know that this time will be different. This time there is forgiveness and strength.

They emerge into the light, and there is rain, but it is not the cold, dark rain of "Come Back." These are not tears of loss and suffering. This rain is cleansing. It washes away the darkness, but not the past, and the light that remains is clear, strengthened by what has come before. They can love and use the light they find in others to guide themselves, offering their own light to guide in return. There may never be a world without war, death, fear, and hardship, but anything better must begin with the need to love one another, even if those connections make us vulnerable. Without it, there are no open doors, only a life wasted.

Backspacer

Released:	September 20, 2009
Musicians:	Eddie Vedder, vocals, guitar
	Stone Gossard, guitar
	Mike McCready, guitar
	Jeff Ament, bass
	Matt Cameron, drums
Producer:	Brendan O'Brien and Pearl Jam
Engineering:	Nick DiDia with Billy Bowers, Tom Tapley, and John Burton
Studio:	Henson Recording Studios in Hollywood, California, U.S.A., and Southern Tracks Recording in Atlanta, Georgia, U.S.A.
Art Direction:	Eddie Vedder as Jerome Turner and Tom Tomorrow (Dan Perkins)
Cover Art:	Tom Tomorrow
Peak Chart Position:	No. 1 on the U.S. *Billboard* 200, No. 9 U.K. Top Albums

Backspacer is Pearl Jam's lightest record. Its songs are leaner, quicker, less adorned. But that simplicity is deceptive. *Backspacer* is the first time Pearl Jam ever truly sounded unburdened and dwelled for an extended period on how it feels to be free— freedom as something experiential rather than aspirational. Seventeen years prior, Eddie sang on "Breath," "If I knew where it was, I would take you there. There's much more than this." *Backspacer* inhabits the place he was searching for and celebrates both the experience of arriving and not having arrived alone. If *Pearl Jam* captures the sound of a Pearl Jam concert, *Backspacer* embodies the feeling.

It also marks the pivot into the second major thematic trajectory of their career, exploring familiar questions from the vantage of the middle-aged, alongside new concerns about the legacy being left for those still on their own journey. For the first time, Pearl Jam celebrates life as much as they glorify struggle. We fight not simply because resistance imbues meaning, but because something precious needs defending. There is no narrative arc to *Backspacer*. It does not tell a story or work through an idea. Instead, it revels in the realization that you are blessed when you have something to give and something to lose.

Although it is their least politically engaged album outside of *No Code*, it must be understood in the context of the election of Barack Obama, the formal repudiation of George Bush's America, and the lived experience of hope. *Backspacer*'s politics are found in the choice not to be political. We see this reflected in the backspace key referenced in the title—a backspacer would be someone ready to delete their past and start a new story on a clean white page. Only this brief window of time could have produced *Backspacer*.

"GONNA SEE MY FRIEND"

Lyrics: Eddie Vedder
Music: Eddie Vedder
Live Debut: Key Arena in Seattle, Washington, U.S.A., September 21, 2009
Alternate Versions/
Notable Performances: Wachovia Spectrum Arena in Philadelphia, Pennsylvania, U.S.A., October 30, 2009
Adelaide Oval in Adelaide, South Australia, Australia, November 17, 2009

"Gonna See My Friend" can be understood as a companion to "Breakerfall." But, while "Breakerfall" is about pushing someone away, "Gonna See My Friend" is about the catharsis found in drawing them close. It rockets out of the gate with a joyful and exuberant riff, full of celebration and rediscovery. Eddie's ragged vocals match the fearless energy of the music. He sounds exhausted, but it is a satisfied exhaustion—simultaneously bone tired and fully charged.

Much of "Gonna See My Friend" is mildly satirical. The lyrics sound heavy and freighted, the singer struggling with a heavy burden ("do you wanna hear something sick, we are all victims of desire?") but the delivery is playful and enthusiastic. It explores familiar feelings in a new way, focusing on the release rather than the burden.

The chorus's start/stop cadence and growling vocals offer some of the grungiest moments in their catalog, and lyrics like "I'm sick of everything, I'm gonna see my friend make it go away" typically conjure images of alcohol, drugs, and suicide. Yet, this is a song about finding strength in healthier places than your own misery. There is a rejection of the near-nihilism prominent in so much of grunge music, inverting familiar sounds and language into a victory cry. This is especially true of the bridge, with its sloppy, wild determination and statement of purpose: "Wanna be there, hard as a statue, black as a tattoo, never to wash away." Unlike previous songs that dwelt in darkness and cried out for help, "Gonna See My Friend" celebrates strength and permanence—a safe harbor in a sea of uncertainty. There is no need to retreat to dark places when things are rough. We finally have somewhere better to go, and someone waiting for us there.

"Got Some"

Lyrics:	Eddie Vedder
Music:	Jeff Ament
Live Debut:	Canada Olympic Park in Calgary, Alberta, Canada, August 8, 2009
Alternate Versions/ Notable Performances:	*The Tonight Show with Conan O'Brien*: Universal Studios, Stage 1, in Hollywood, California, U.S.A., June 1, 2009 *Live on Ten Legs*, Viejas Arena in San Diego, California, U.S.A., October 9, 2009 TD Garden in Boston, Massachusetts, U.S.A., May 17, 2010

"Got Some" makes public what was, for all its energy and intensity, the private moment documented in "Gonna See My Friend." When Eddie sings he has "got some if you need it," he references the recharged sense of purpose discovered at the start of the record, and his compulsion to share it.

The music does the primary storytelling. It does not begin so much as detonates, its fanfare guitars sounding the alarm. Urgent declarations across three separate bridge/chorus sequences urge the listener to lean on the singer, to find within him the strength to carry on through the interconnected series of highs and lows that define our lives. After the initial burst of energy, an understated quality to the performance creates intimacy juxtaposed against an explosive climax. "Got Some" helps set the mood and tone of *Backspacer*—the need to take the peace and power within us and turn that energy outward.

"The Fixer"

Lyrics:	Eddie Vedder
Music:	Matt Cameron, Mike McCready, and Stone Gossard
Single Release Date:	August 24, 2009
Peak U.S. Chart Position:	56
Live Debut:	Canada Olympic Park in Calgary, Alberta, Canada, August 8, 2009

Alternate Versions/
Notable Performances: *Pearl Jam Twenty: Original Motion Picture Soundtrack*, *Need To Know* (Matt Cameron Demo), 2007
QSAC Stadium in Brisbane, Queensland, Australia, November 25, 2009
Live on Ten Legs, TD Garden in Boston, Massachusetts, U.S.A., May 17, 2010
United Center in Chicago, Illinois, U.S.A., August 23, 2009

"The Fixer" is a pure and unaffected instance of joy that makes it the ideal lead single for *Backspacer*. It possesses a compelling immediacy, existing purely in the moment like no other Pearl Jam song does. Pearl Jam's music is usually burdened by its past and struggles to overcome it. "The Fixer" embraces that history, as the freedom it celebrates is earned in the eight records preceding it, not within this perfect moment.

The music of "The Fixer" manages to feel comforting, even innocent, without being naive or syrupy sweet. Its circular movement is too energized to sit still, but too drawn in to drift away. Eddie's vocals are just weathered enough to offer a spark of hard-won triumph. There is a slight sense of wonder—not only at the gift of freedom but also at the shock of finding it after searching for so long. The performance welcomes the listener in and asks them to sing along, achieving the typical live metamorphosis within the studio track itself.

The overall composition conveys a sense of new beginnings and new possibilities, of a bright, clear dawn emerging from a long, dark night. The ten lyrical couplets present a desire to repent the past, to look ahead, and an overpowering celebration of the need to act, all culminating with the declaration that when something is gone or lost, we need to "fight to get it back again."

We have seen variations of this message throughout the catalog but never articulated so casually. There is a restless urgency in its desire to do something. In an interview with the *Global and Mail*, Eddie acknowledged that there is a mild critique of that mindset embedded in the song—that, sometimes, it is less important to fix what is wrong than it is to own and experience it. That sentiment will appear elsewhere on the album and those that follow—that you cannot rush someone through their journey, just support them on it, and that fixing your mistake does not absolve you of the harm it may have caused.

"The Fixer" culminates with its bridge, and its ringing promise to do whatever is needed to help us lay down our burdens and embrace the possibilities of the moment ("I'll say your prayers, I'll take your side. I'll find us a way to make light. I'll dig your grave. We'll dance and sing. What say, could be one last lifetime?"). "The Fixer" holds onto the singular instant of discovery when we realize that, right now, if we own our power, we can do anything.

"Johnny Guitar"

Lyrics:	Eddie Vedder
Music:	Matt Cameron and Stone Gossard
Live Debut:	Key Arena in Seattle, Washington, U.S.A., September 21, 2009
Alternate Versions/	
Notable Performances:	Mt. Smart Stadium in Auckland, New Zealand, November 27, 2009
	XL Arena in Hartford, Connecticut, U.S.A., May 15, 2010

"Johnny Guitar" celebrates not taking yourself so seriously, and its crude lyrics and low stakes are critical to *Backspacer*'s overall message. It tells the story of a lifelong obsession with a girl on a poster for the flamboyant funk and blues musician Johnny Guitar Watson. The song focuses on her innocence and how the singer plans to awaken her sexuality. The muscular, slightly filthy swagger of the guitars affirms the subject's image of himself, the sound of a guy trying but failing to strut.

He is jealous of "Johnny Guitar," who attracts women with such casual ease. He maintains a stubborn faith he will someday possess her for himself, pining for that future in a present that extends for decades. He lives for his dreams since they are the one place his need is answered. And his moment finally comes after thirty years of patient devotion. She slinks over to the bed in her red dress, leans over, and asks if he has seen Johnny Guitar. Even in his fantasy, he cannot win.

The lack of judgment is the key to "Johnny Guitar." It is full of playful double entendres and grubby innuendo delivered in a rapid-fire, accomplished vocal melody that does not give us time to take any of this very seriously. The faux desperation in Eddie's voice creates a self-aware sense of self-importance that is intentionally deflating.

It is not clear that "Johnny Guitar" would be written today, in an era where incels are hopelessly bound up with misogyny, violence, and male supremacy— its critique of the male gaze would certainly have more teeth. But, in 2008, "Johnny Guitar" was written in celebration of silly dreams and nonsensical ambitions. Pearl Jam knew how to take life seriously, but on *Backspacer*, they are comfortable enough in their own skin to laugh at themselves too.

"Just Breathe"

Lyrics:	Eddie Vedder
Music:	Eddie Vedder and Eddie Horst
Additional Musicians:	Justin Bruns, violin; Christopher Pulgram, violin; Cathy Lynn, viola; Danny Laufer, cello
Single Release Date:	October 31, 2009
Peak U.S. Chart Position:	78
Live Debut:	Key Arena in Seattle, Washington, U.S.A., September 21, 2009

Alternate Versions/
Notable Performances: Austin City Limits in Austin, Texas, U.S.A., October
3, 2009
*Pearl Jam Twenty: Original Motion Picture
Soundtrack*, Studio 8H, NBC Studios in New York,
New York, U.S.A., March 13, 2010
Live on Ten Legs, Madison Square Garden in New
York, New York, U.S.A., May 21, 2010

"Just Breathe" is the purest love song in the catalog, possessing a sense of spiritual calm and rooted certainty derived from a long-standing, healthy relationship. When we settle into the foundations of a shared life, we realize that love is as much the small quiet moments as it is white-hot fire. It is easy to miss those moments, but when we stop and notice, they can still take our breath away.

Musically, the gentle, *Into the Wild*-inspired playing transports the listener somewhere secure and still, the fingerpicking conveying a whispering peace juxtaposed against a chorus bursting with gratitude.[1] Eddie takes the time to consciously remind himself of how fortunate he is to have the gifts he has been given, and how empty he would be without them: "I'm a lucky man to count on both hands the ones I love." There is a sense of peace, and a willingness to live in a moment outside of time, grateful for the vulnerability and dependency that flow from love. There are undercurrents of death serving as a reminder that this cannot last forever, and that it must not be taken for granted. It is clear the person he sings to his refuge in an uncertain world, the most precious thing she can be for him. So, the most romantic line in the whole piece may be "stay with me, let's just breathe," a perfect distillation of what it means to live in the present tense. There may not be a purer expression of love than the desire for that person to just be there, asking nothing more of them than their continued participation in a shared existence.

"Amongst the Waves"

Lyrics: Eddie Vedder
Music: Stone Gossard
Single Release Date: June 21, 2010
Peak U.S. Chart Position: 27
Live Debut: Key Arena in Seattle, Washington, U.S.A., September
21, 2009

Alternate Versions/
Notable Performances: Wachovia Spectrum Arena in Philadelphia, Pennsylvania,
U.S.A., October 31, 2009
Members Equity Stadium in Perth, Western Australia,
November 14, 2009

"Amongst the Waves" is one of the more evocative compositions on *Backspacer*. The misty buzzing and quiet electricity of the melody, the bright coloration, enveloping bass, and gentle drumming create the perfect backdrop for appreciating the gift of a hard-won life and sharing it with the person who helped you create it. The music sounds like a living memory, past and present coming together and lifting you up in the process.

"Amongst the Waves" celebrates how love and commitment have finally granted the subject the peace and stability they have spent so long trying to achieve: "What used to be a house of cards has turned into a reservoir." Theirs is a peace earned through stubborn struggle ("you've bled yourself, the wounds are gone"), surviving nameless violence, and lost innocence. The chorus features now familiar wave and water imagery—at this point, Eddie's shorthand for release, possibility, and transcendence. The juxtaposition in "gotta say it now, better loud than too late" recognizes that life is not only about seizing its necessary moments but doing so with a totalizing commitment. Freedom and salvation (for Pearl Jam these are usually the same) are achieved through active surrender, but by surrendering to someone else, not the world, and dictating the terms of your submission to someone who submits to you in turn. Shared power kept honest and accountable through shared vulnerability.

"Unthought Known"

Lyrics:	Eddie Vedder
Music:	Eddie Vedder
Live Debut:	Key Arena in Seattle, Washington, U.S.A., September 21, 2009
Alternate Versions/ Notable Performances:	*Saturday Night Live*: Studio 8H, NBC Studios in New York, New York, U.S.A., March 13, 2010
	Live on Ten Legs, Wuhlheide in Berlin, Germany, June 30, 2010
	Rock Werchter Festival in Werchter, Belgium, July 30, 2022

The phrase "unthought known" refers to experiences known and understood without conscious processing. "Unthought Known" is about appreciating the world for what it is—a stage upon which we act, and, through those actions, fulfill potential and create ourselves. There is a sense of wide-eyed awe and cosmic liberation, celebrating the possibilities inherent in existence.

Eddie commits with a childlike sense of wonder filtered through the experiences of an older, wiser man returning to a place of innocence and asking us to share that moment with him. The call to "look for love and evidence that you're worth keeping" captures the music's faith that everyone is worthy of love and, through love, salvation—a welcome reminder in a world that alienates us from each other and ourselves.

The images throughout "Unthought Known" are pregnant with an empowering sense of hope and gratitude for being a part of creation—the beauty of "a pool of blue sky," love's capacity to fill a void with light, and the sense of perfect oneness with the world that allows you to "see the path cut by the moon for you to walk on."

"Feel the sky blanket you with gems and rhinestones" offers a powerful juxtaposition—the world gives us tokens of objective value and moments we can make priceless by assigning our own limitless significance.

When Eddie sings "dream the dreams of other men, you'll be no one's rival" we are challenged to bind ourselves to each other and commit to the lives of the people around us. If we are prepared to love them and learn from them, the artificial barriers between us fall. We can finally discover who we are through this sense of communion with the world, with each other, and with ourselves.

"SUPERSONIC"

Lyrics:	Eddie Vedder
Music:	Stone Gossard
Live Debut:	O2 Arena in London, U.K., August 18, 2009
Alternate Versions/ Notable Performances:	Key Arena in Seattle, Washington, U.S.A., September 22, 2009
	New Orleans Jazz and Heritage Festival in New Orleans, Louisiana, U.S.A., May 1, 2010

"Supersonic" is *Backspacer*'s late album cooldown song, a punk-pop celebration of their love of music featuring an incongruously muscular solo from Mike. There is a brightness to the music and performance, self-deprecation in the lyrics "I catch a break, then a punch to the head. I smile big with a toothless grin" or "I've been thinking, I already know nothing 'bout nothing, or so I have been told," and a childlike giddiness to Eddie's vocals, all in celebration of its now familiar but still deeply felt commandment to "live your life with the volume full."

"SPEED OF SOUND"

Lyrics:	Eddie Vedder
Music:	Eddie Vedder
Live Debut:	Wachovia Spectrum Arena in Philadelphia, Pennsylvania, U.S.A., October 28, 2010

Alternate Versions/
Notable Performances: Demo (2009), released digitally via PearlJam.com
                     Viejas Arena in San Diego, California, U.S.A., November
                     21, 2013
                     Canadian Tire Centre in Ottawa, Ontario, Canada, May
                     8, 2016

Inverting its name, the measured cacophony of "Speed of Sound" tries to slow us
down, warning us not to lose sight of our immediate lived experience as we rush past
in pursuit of dreams we may never achieve. It begins by contemplating the delicate
fragility of the past and the difficulty of achieving permanence in a world in constant
motion. The chorus is both hopeful and regretful. The singer keeps his dream of
"distant light" fixed in his mind. But this is offset by a grim awareness of just how long
we spend floating through dark, empty spaces "waiting on a sun that just don't come."

The lyrics are increasingly urgent as he struggles to halt his momentum, to stop
striving for perfection. For right now to be enough. "Speed of Sound" assures us we
can make peace with a flawed world without abandoning the commitment to change
it. "Can I forgive what I cannot forget and live a lie? I could give it one more try." But
he still feels guilty, as if moments of serenity are betrayals of a life-long struggle.

The gravity of his situation catches up with him in the final verses. He hears a voice
and reaches for its promise of something better than now but cannot tell if what he
reaches for is real. Trapped by his doubts, his fear of missing his chance leaves him
unable to commit to the world he actually lives in. "It's gone so quiet now. Can't you
see I'm farther out, moving faster than the speed of sound?"

"Speed of Sound" urges us to make our peace with what we cannot change even as
we work to transform the limitations of what is possible. But the perfect cannot be the
enemy of good. The speed of sound is not sustainable, and the speed of light is beyond
us. Ours is an imperfect world, but not lacking in moments of light made brighter
contrasted against the surrounding darkness.

"FORCE OF NATURE"

Lyrics: Eddie Vedder
Music: Mike McCready
Live Debut: Gibson Amphitheater in Universal City, California,
                       U.S.A., September 30, 2009
Alternate Versions/
Notable Performances: Etihad Stadium in Docklands, Victoria, Australia,
                       November 20, 2009
                       TD Garden in Boston, Massachusetts, U.S.A., May 17,
                       2010

"Force of Nature" best embodies the weathered, emancipatory optimism of *Backspacer,* celebrating a stubborn, unwavering belief that, evidence to the contrary, people can change if we refuse to give up on them.

"Force of Nature" is a deceptively evocative composition for a stolid song about endurance: "One man stands on the edge of the ocean, a beacon of dry land. Eyes upon the horizon in the dark before the dawn." It is the sound of one person's willingness to stare across unbridgeable distances without blinking, leaning into howling winds and bend but never break—an act of devotion to an elemental commitment. "Force of Nature" is full of flourishes buried deep in the mix that fade in and out of hearing. The brighter guitar parts push through the wind and rain right before the chorus—rays of light peeking through a storm, moments of hope that sustain a lonely vigil. They become more prominent with each chorus as the singer renews their strength. Mike's bridge leads play like flashes of lightning, and his outro sounds like a long-promised new beginning.

This is a song about determination and defiance, but also faith. It celebrates refusing to give in when confronted by uncertainty and never wavering in the face of hostile doubt, when there are no guarantees of victory or mile markers to confirm you're on the right path. This is the essence of faith.

The central phrase "force of nature" evokes something wild, uncontrollable, and eternal—impossible to stand against. It is this impossibility that makes his vigil so moving, his refusal to back down in the face of something beyond mastery: "A silhouette in the black light, full moon glow. In the sand there he stands upon the shore forevermore." "Force of Nature" documents his determination not to give up on someone deeply flawed and wounded. They will never make it back unless he acts as their beacon. Someone must make sure the light does not go out. Someone must have faith even when the source that sustains it is beyond our capacity to justify: "Somewhere there's a siren singing a song only he hears."

There are moments of doubt, and the crashing bridge witnesses his crisis of faith as he cries out to a cold and indifferent world, "is it so wrong to think that love can keep us safe?" Love is more than caring for another person. Love is safety. Love is shelter against a storm. The baseline that makes all futures possible. Without it, we are alone, trapped in a hostile, disenchanted universe. Should we give up on it, even when all we have is a vulnerable faith in the possibility of love? Love is risk. The world does not reply. The world never does. But its silence demands a response, and his enduring faith is his answer: "Eyes are closed, you cannot know. But his heart don't seem to roam."

"THE END"

Lyrics:	Eddie Vedder
Music:	Eddie Vedder and Eddie Horst

Additional Musicians:	Justin Bruns, violin; Christopher Pulgram, violin; Cathy Lynn, viola; Danny Laufer, cello; Brice Andrus, horn; Susan Welty, horn; Richard Deane, horn
Live Debut:	Shepherd's Bush Empire in London, U.K., August 11, 2009
Alternate Versions/ Notable Performances:	Gibson Amphitheater in Universal City, California, U.S.A., October 7, 2009 Madison Square Garden in New York, New York, May 21, 2010

Despite its simplicity, "The End" feels like the heaviest song on the record. It carries the intimated weight of shared history, giving "The End" an understated depth that enables Eddie's emotive performance (and the string accompaniment) to avoid descending into melodrama. The music offers a quiet celebration of a life that, against long odds, found serenity and joy. It is the sound of salvation juxtaposed against one of Eddie's most vulnerable vocals, rich with the quiet wisdom of experience and the delicate vulnerability and subtle strength of age.

"The End" is tinged with fear and regret, but they come from finally winning something priceless and realizing it will be taken from you someday. The lyrics are full of frustration and self-recrimination, but the subject's haunted guilt stems from an inability to fully embrace and experience the gifts they have been given, that no matter what they do, no matter how much they commit, it is simply impossible to ever drink it all in.

"The End" mourns the impossible finality of death because, for the first time, there is something too precious to contemplate losing. Pearl Jam's music has always clung to the possibility of love as the one light that could stand against the darkness. Now, they have it, and with it comes a whole new set of fears—the terror of losing it, the remorse of not fully embracing it, the desperate need to take it with them. "Before I disappear, whisper in my ear, give me something to echo in my unknown future's ear". What happens when the light dims for the last time? How can we ensure that the one thing we carry forward is not regret? We need to make space for this fear and hold onto the enormity of what we must lose so we never take it for granted. We need those reminders sometimes, that even a dark world is full of impossibly precious things. We need to make time for the past and clear space for the future, but the end draws near, and now is all we have. We had better make the most of it. *Backspacer* celebrates our chance to do so.

Lightning Bolt

Released:	September 20, 2009
Musicians:	Eddie Vedder, vocals, guitar
	Stone Gossard, guitar
	Mike McCready, guitar
	Jeff Ament, bass
	Matt Cameron, drums
	Brendan O'Brien, keyboards, guitars
	Boom Gaspar, keyboards
	Ann Marie Simpson [Calhoun], violin
Producer:	Brendan O'Brien and Pearl Jam
Engineering:	Tom Syrowski, Martin Cooke, Billy Joe Bowers, Lowell Reynolds, Nick DiDia, John Burton, Tom Tapley, Floyd Reitsma
Studio:	Henson Recording Studios in Hollywood, California, U.S.A.; Studio X in Seattle, Washington, U.S.A.; and Studio Litho in Seattle, Washington, U.S.A.
Art Direction:	Jeff Ament and Don Pendleton
Cover Art:	Don Pendleton
Peak Chart Position:	No. 1 on the U.S. *Billboard* 200, No. 2 U.K. Top Albums

Much of *Lightning Bolt* is inspired by the band members' children, and everyone who will inherit a mess not of their making. Given how much of *Ten* was colored by a sense of intergenerational betrayal, *Lightning Bolt*'s songs are as much about accepting responsibility for failing to be better as they are about the obligation to finally be better.

Pearl Jam is no longer a band of scrappy underdogs, unlikely spokespersons, or disaffected seekers. *Lightning Bolt* was written by seasoned, enormously successful musicians with families of their own. The result is a middle-aged record that struggles with the significance of life being closer to its end than its beginning. It takes its cues from the outlier moments on *Backspacer* that interjected notes of anxiety, even fear, into an otherwise joyful proceeding. The music (and Don Pendleton's Grammy Award-winning artwork) grapples with guilt, redemption, and apocalyptic fears rooted in natural imagery that recontextualizes the size and scope of our human experiences. And the elemental power of love as a vehicle for charting an enduring path forward is asserted with an explicit, sustained commitment. The result is a record about legacy, the relationship between past, present, and future, the challenge of renewal, and the fragility, insecurity, and drive that comes from having something, finally, to lose.

"Getaway"

Lyrics:	Eddie Vedder
Music:	Eddie Vedder
Live Debut:	Time Warner Cable Arena in Charlotte, North Carolina, U.S.A., October 30, 2013
Alternate Versions/ Notable Performances:	Big Day Out, Sydney Fairgrounds, in Sydney, New South Wales, Australia, January 26, 2014
	Wrigley Field in Chicago, Illinois, U.S.A., August 18, 2018

"Getaway" begins *Lightning Bolt*'s discussion about generating and sustaining the social and political optimism needed to confront the challenges facing our world. The music is bouncy and playful, its sharp edges sanded down, yet the lightweight presentation is punctuated by mounting frustration and rising urgency.

While "Getaway" expresses some anti-religious sentiments, its religious language serves as a stand-in for a non-reflective and self-satisfied conservatism, fundamentalism, or sense of powerlessness and futility—all we can do in the face of injustice and disaster is hope and pray. Eddie condemns inaction justified through faith in our own righteousness as a society, or how surrendering to our own powerlessness and placing the future in God's hands absolves us of responsibility for our actions. The world is on fire, and our priority is finding people to blame ("Everyone's a critic looking back up the river. Every boat is leaking in this town"). But "Getaway," *Lightning Bolt*, and Pearl Jam never stop embracing the possibility of recovery and transformation. Religion provides the cultural vocabulary necessary to talk about redemption and salvation. No one is going to save us. We are going to have to save ourselves.

That is the message of the chorus. "I've got my own way to believe" or "Sometimes you've got to put your faith in no faith" are not anti-religious sentiments. They are larger statements about our own power and capacity to drive change, placing our faith in the unrealized potential of humanity. We just need the people who say it cannot be done to stand down, and the current generation to give way to the rising potential and limitless possibility of the next.

"Mind Your Manners"

Lyrics:	Eddie Vedder
Music:	Mike McCready
Single Release Date:	July 11, 2013
Peak U.S. Chart Position:	2
Live Debut:	Budweiser Gardens in London, Ontario, Canada, July 16, 2013
Alternate Versions/ Notable Performances:	Big Day Out, Western Springs Stadium in Auckland, New Zealand, January 17, 2014
	Late Show with Stephen Colbert: Ed Sullivan Theatre in New York, New York, U.S.A., September 13, 2015
	Oakland Arena in Oakland, California, U.S.A., May 13, 2022 (fan Kai Neukerman is brought on stage to play drums)

The lead single "Mind Your Manners" is an attack on passivity, not religion—whether it comes from a smug confidence in the rightness of the world, a loss of personal agency, or simply ceasing to care. Our civilization is failing, drowning in unnecessary tragedies of our own creation, as the stylized apocalypse of the "Mind Your Manners" video makes clear. So, why aren't we doing anything about everything?

Perhaps the forces arrayed against dramatic social, economic, and political change are too strong—that resistance is futile. But that is certainly not the position of "Mind Your Manners," or of a band whose catalog always celebrated struggle as inherently worthwhile even in the face of uncertainty.

The music starts off heavy, throbbing, like a tension headache after a long day of bad news, but it lifts as soon as the singer openly confronts the reality that our world is failing. Eddie's confident performance, angry but measured, matches the music's clipped and focused energy. . The front page of every major newspaper in the country should be screaming with headlines about impending environmental catastrophe, oligarchy, social injustice, and democratic backsliding, but they don't, and it is strangely liberating to finally admit everything is fucked ("I got an unfortunate feeling. I been beaten down. I feel that I'm done believing. Now the truth is coming out"). The intergenerational consequences are immediately named: "They're taking young innocents and then they throw 'em on a burning pile." The focus on the "young innocents" is significant. Not just because the young are innocent, trapped by a world they did not make. There is also the concern about the kind of world future generations will inherit. Looking around, he concludes "this world's a long love letter that makes me want to cry." There is so much to love, so much to protect that we are overcome by the intensity of our blessings, and our failure to be worthy of them.

The "mind your manners" chorus is the status quo's response to challenge. Don't disrupt the way things are. Don't force me to confront ugly truths I would rather ignore. This refrain has been repeated throughout history and shoved in the face of anyone speaking truth to power. The conservative backlash against Black Lives Matters and LGBTQ+ rights has only made "Mind Your Manners" more prescient. The mind your manners phrasing transforms a legitimate grievance into a violation of social norms.

It would be wonderful if someone could snap their fingers and save the world. But that person's not coming, and we cannot afford to wait.

> Self-realized and metaphysically redeemed.
> May not live another life. May not solve our mystery.
> Right round the corner could be bigger than ourselves.
> We could will it to the sky or we could something else.

We are going to have to be our own saviors.

The music tracks the journey, becoming less intense and taking on a questing coloration during the chorus—asking important questions and seeking significant answers. A second guitar under the main riff becomes more prominent as the chorus progresses—a rising optimism. It is followed by an excellent information overload solo by Mike, a mixture of new ideas, insights, and maybe answers. It is not clear how they all fit together, but something is there. We just need time and the will to make sense of it.

"My Father's Son"

Lyrics:	Eddie Vedder
Music:	Jeff Ament
Additional Musicians:	Mike McCready, six-string bass
Live Debut:	First Niagara Center in Buffalo, New York, U.S.A., October 12, 2013
Alternate Versions/ Notable Performances:	Big Day Out, Bonython Park in Adelaide, South Australia, Australia, January 31, 2014
	Pepsi Center in Denver, Colorado, U.S.A., October 22, 2014

"My Father's Son" is miserable and haunted, full of ghosts. Eddie explores the fear and tragedy of reproducing destructive relationships with rising generations, appropriate for a record grappling with legacy. When Eddie sings "Now father you're dead and gone and I'm finally free to be me," he is terrified. What if the past is something we cannot escape, something that prevents us from becoming the person we want or need to be for our own children? Shaped by those experiences, we risk reproducing the worst elements of our past in our individual and collective lives. What if we cannot escape this cycle? The lyrics fixate on genetics—the one thing we cannot change in ourselves and, metaphorically, in society.

The music is nasty and insecure, the bass line angry and self-recriminating like the morning after the familiar repetition of a terrible mistake. The guitar hovers just behind—a shiver up the spine, intimations of broken promises, past failures, and the specters of those we disappointed. The bridge offers a twisted carnival celebrating a tainted, poisoned future—a fresh start forever in view but permanently out of reach. It would be nice if we could cut off our past, and start over, a "volunteer amputee." But we cannot run from what has happened. There is no getaway. We can only confront and learn from it.

"Sirens"

Lyrics: Eddie Vedder
Music: Mike McCready
Single Release Date: September 18, 2013
Peak U.S. Chart Position: 76
Live Debut: Consol Energy Center in Pittsburgh, Pennsylvania, U.S.A., October 11, 2013
Alternate Versions/
Notable Performances: *Late Night with Jimmy Fallon*: NBC Studio 6B in New York, New York, U.S.A., October 24, 2013
                                 Moda Center in Portland, Oregon, U.S.A., November 29, 2013

"Sirens" explores the moment after waking from a nightmare—lying in the dark, heart pounding, savoring the gradual realization that it was all a dream. The sirens are heading elsewhere. Everything you care about is here beside you, peaceful but vulnerable, the terrible dream bringing the fragility of our lives into stark relief. Every moment of doubt and desolation on *Lightning Bolt* inevitably returns to "Sirens," and the things in our life that ensure "the fear goes away"—if we can keep them safe and make ourselves worthy of them.

The music is the beating heart in the gentle aftermath of a violent awakening. So much of "Sirens" feels alternately muted or distant even as it swells—images rapidly receding in the way dreams do, a refusal to voice delicate sentiments too loudly for fear of disturbing a fragile peace. The terror must be kept private, and it gives "Sirens" a disarming but curiously melancholy tone. Eddie sings his heart out, but he is singing to himself. Stone's subtle flourishes punctuate sentences that cannot be spoken, delicate background harmonies acting as whispered sentiments.

It is a middle-aged song concerned with appreciating and preserving what you have as opposed to what you hope to find.

> It's a fragile thing, this life we lead
> If I think too much I can get over
> Whelmed by the grace by which we live
> Our lives with death over our shoulder.

The lyrics are simple and honest. They convey doubt, fear of loss, and above all gratitude for possessing a peace and a love you never thought you would have, one that ensures "the fear goes away."

"LIGHTNING BOLT"

Lyrics:	Eddie Vedder
Music:	Eddie Vedder
Live Debut:	Wrigley Field in Chicago, Illinois, U.S.A., July 19, 2013
Alternate Versions/ Notable Performances:	*Late Night with Jimmy Fallon*: NBC Studio 6B in New York, New York, U.S.A., October 24, 2013
	Chesapeake Energy Arena in Oklahoma City, Oklahoma, U.S.A., November 16, 2013
	Let's Play Two: Original Motion Picture Soundtrack, Wrigley Field in Chicago, Illinois, U.S.A., August 20, 2016

"Lightning Bolt" celebrates elemental manifestations of love that inspire, challenge, and reward us, but lie beyond our control—"the wild seeds she sows in your sleep." It plays with our sense of timing and motion. Breathless amid flashes of revelation that rise into the ether, it rushes forward with almost too much adrenaline. It explores vast open spaces and rushing wind, shot through with significance and possibility—all the self-confidence that "Sirens" was lacking, the music rising with Eddie's frantic energy into an orgasmic climax, a release of the fears that so easily trap us in prisons of our own making. Mike's little bursts of drifting inspiration transform into fireworks. We even get a hint of church bells ringing in the background,

A lightning bolt is powerful, unpredictable, and brief. It is a fine if slightly obvious metaphor for how inspiration cannot be controlled, captured, or manufactured. It is something you simply must be open to—benevolent surrender is a theme that runs through much of the song. Continuing to equate nature with unencumbered freedom, there are references to seeds, beaches, waves, animals, and birds. Elsewhere, inspiration is presented as a meteor descending from the heavens—dangerous, destructive, and indifferent.

Life is defined by impermanence. "The crashing stormy waves erode her shoreline every day," and the ocean will always reclaim a castle made of sand. The people and experiences we love will not always be with us. The next great idea may not come when called. But it is out there, waiting for its time, and the song's dominant emotion is effusive gratitude. There is no way to systematize or control the things in your life that matter, and you cannot hold onto them forever. But we must celebrate them anyway, despite and because of this.

"INFALLIBLE"

Lyrics:	Eddie Vedder
Music:	Jeff Ament and Stone Gossard
Live Debut:	Consol Energy Center in Pittsburgh, Pennsylvania, U.S.A., October 11, 2013
Alternate Versions/ Notable Performances:	Rogers Arena in Vancouver, British Columbia, Canada, December 4, 2013
	American Airlines Arena in Miami, Florida, U.S.A., April 9, 2016

"Infallible" offers *Lightning Bolt*'s most systematic exploration of our ability to challenge and change a fracturing world, provided we embrace our capacity for imagination. Our collective potential for transformation is one of Pearl Jam's oldest themes, and the music scrambles to contain an impending collapse with nothing more than optimism and will.

"Infallible" understands we must change something in ourselves before we will be receptive to the possibility of a better world. To be infallible is to have faith in the absolute truth of your belief. The assumption of infallibility cuts off dialogue, making you answerable to nothing but your own prior conviction. What besets the world are not problems lacking solutions, but rather, our own sense of infallibility. Rather than a specific challenge, "Infallible" grapples with the resistance to change produced by the limits of our imagination: "Pay disasters no mind. Didn't get you this time. No prints left at the crime. Our ship's come in and it's sinking."

The diagnostic pessimism of the verses is offset by the optimistic, metamorphosing confidence of the chorus. Eddie's phrasing is simple, declarative, and powerful—the reclamation of a forgotten truth:

Of everything that's possible in the hearts and minds of men
Somehow it is the biggest things that keep on slipping right through our hands
By thinking we're infallible we are tempting faith instead.
Time to best begin, here at the ending.

We must challenge the twin infallible claims that the status quo is sustainable and nothing we do can change it. We can do better, and be better, but we are running out of time.

It is very much a post-*Backspacer*, post-2008 election sentiment. No savior is coming, we must roll up our sleeves and save ourselves. The bridge's background chanting invites the listener to add their voice in a small but meaningful way rather than passively witness an expansive, larger-than-life gesture. But that window is fast closing and doing nothing is so tempting. It is not surprising that "Infallible" fades out with a reproachful warning, "Keep on locking your doors. Keep on building your floors. Keep on just as before…"

"PENDULUM"

Lyrics:	Eddie Vedder
Music:	Jeff Ament and Stone Gossard
Additional Musicians:	Stone Gossard, bongo drums; Jeff Ament, bowed guitar and keyboard
Live Debut:	Consol Energy Center in Pittsburgh, Pennsylvania, U.S.A., October 11, 2013
Alternate Versions/ Notable Performances:	'Pendulumorphosis,' (instrumental), appears on the 2014 Fan Club/Holiday Single
	Wells Fargo Arena in Philadelphia, Pennsylvania, U.S.A., October 22, 2013
	Blue Room at Third Man Records in Nashville, Tennessee, U.S.A., June 9, 2016

"Pendulum" embodies the self-doubt and internal fears standing in the way of our better selves and a better world. The most atmospheric song on the record, the music conveys a haunted, creeping uncertainty, laced with recrimination, doubt, and fear. But rather than stemming from an external force that can be mastered, subjugated, or ignored, it rises from within, totalizing in its near paralysis and destructive in its impact. The album artwork envisions the pendulum as a bleeding, scything blade.

The pendulum metaphor is the key to understanding the song and the album. A pendulum's arc is cyclical, its forward momentum perpetually reversing itself. The image speaks to the inherent tension in finding everything you wanted while being acutely aware that not only will it not last, but its loss will have tremendous consequences—if not for you, then for the people left behind: "The future's bright, lit up with nowhere to go." We fear what lies before us and cannot find a pathway to something sustainable. The song's skulking doom highlights how little time we have (individually and as a people) to make it right "We are here, and then we go," and the maddening uncertainty of the future: "Understand what we don't know. This might pass. This might last. This may grow."

"Pendulum" does not despair but comes dangerously close to being paralyzed by the magnitude of our uncertainty, frustration, and powerlessness over the impermanence of a destination that was a lifetime in arriving. The struggle will never have an ending. We return to the core metaphor of Sisyphus pushing his rock toward an unreachable summit. No end, just waypoints where rest is possible, the act of movement continuously invested with significance, the struggle recontextualized as a search for the inspiration to keep pushing for someone else.

"Swallowed Whole"

Lyrics:	Eddie Vedder
Music:	Eddie Vedder
Live Debut:	First Niagara Center in Buffalo, New York, U.S.A., October 12, 2013
Alternate Versions/ Notable Performances:	John Paul Jones Arena in Charlottesville, Virginia, U.S.A., October 29, 2013
	Bon Secours Wellness Arena in Greenville, South Carolina, U.S.A., April 16, 2016

The *Into the Wild* inspired, R.E.M.-inflected "Swallowed Whole" seeks to reenergize the soul after the totalizing doubt of "Pendulum." It revels in the freedom of simply being alive, feeling present in something larger than ourselves, and embracing the emancipatory insight that all that is required of us is to do the best we can.

The lyrics and imagery celebrate the peace and purity of being able to step outside of the concerns and obligations that threaten to drown us, centered on the experience of the natural world: "Whispered songs inside the wind, breathing in forgiveness. Like vibrations with no end, hear the planet humming. What is clear far from the noise gets swallowed whole." Against the magnitude of the world, our burdens feel smaller, manageable, and contextualized. The challenge is holding onto that perspective when you reengage.

Fixing the world is beyond the power of any individual, but if life persists, we can do something to make the world better than it was before. "Swallowed

Whole" concludes with a quiet, muted sentiment, the experiential core of a temporary liberation, held tight and kept safe: "And the chapter I've not read. Turn the page."

"LET THE RECORDS PLAY"

Lyrics:	Eddie Vedder
Music:	Stone Gossard
Live Debut:	Consol Energy Center in Pittsburgh, Pennsylvania, U.S.A., October 11, 2013
Alternate Versions/	
Notable Performances:	Chesapeake Energy Arena in Oklahoma City, Oklahoma, U.S.A., November 16, 2013
	FedEx Forum in Memphis, Tennessee, U.S.A., October 14, 2014

"Let the Records Play" is *Lightning Bolt*'s cool-down track. It is a muscular, vaguely glam barroom blues song with a stomping groove, rough guitars, a tarnished shine to the vocals, and even some handclaps. There is an apocalyptic sheen to the lyrics ("when the Kingdom come…" and "should the future dim"), and the appropriate response is to find a way to indulge—a reminder that there are low-stakes pleasures in the world, and that if everything is a matter of life and death all the time, we will quickly burn ourselves out.

"Let the Records Play" understands the need for the occasional soothing, comforting numbness, one that cocoons without abandoning the core human commitments that are the source of pain and value: "Shaken, awakened, not one for faking. Kneeling, his healing, he lets the records play. There's wisdom in his ways." A nonjudgmental performance, it is playful, sympathetic, and willing to give people the ritualized space they need to process their grief and fear to face another day.

"SLEEPING BY MYSELF"

Lyrics:	Eddie Vedder
Music:	Eddie Vedder
Additional Musicians:	Eddie Vedder, ukulele
Live Debut:	QPAC Concert Hall in Brisbane, Queensland, Australia, March 10, 2011 (Eddie Vedder solo performance)
Alternate Versions/	
Notable Performances:	*Ukulele Songs*, solo album by Eddie Vedder (2011)
	LA Sports Arena in Pico Rivera, California, U.S.A., November 24, 2013
	Town Park in Telluride, Colorado, U.S.A., July 9, 2016

"Sleeping By Myself" was initially released as a solo Eddie composition on 2011's *Ukulele Songs*, but producer Brendan O'Brien was such a fan that he lobbied for a full band performance. The jaunty version on *Lightning Bolt* confronts desperate heartbreak and loneliness with wounded, smiling bravery.

The lyrics are among the most lovelorn in the catalog: "I believe in nothing, not today, as I move myself out of your sight." And later: "I believe in nothing but the pain, and I can't see this turning out right" before grappling with the brute reality that "I'll be sleeping by myself tonight." The song marches into a lonely, empty future, and yet the upbeat, even optimistic music cannot help but smile, not at the experience of his pain, but the recognition that heartache is a necessary byproduct of being open to the possibility of love: "I believe in love and disaster. Sometimes, the two are just the same." Alone perhaps, but not forever, and we will get through it one night at a time. It is a minor song in the face of a major tragedy, decisively human in its refusal to ignore or surrender to the ache.

"Yellow Moon"

Lyrics:	Eddie Vedder
Music:	Jeff Ament
Live Debut:	Consol Energy Center in Pittsburgh, Pennsylvania, U.S.A., October 11, 2013
Alternate Versions/ Notable Performances:	Barclays Center in Brooklyn, New York, U.S.A., October 19, 2013
	Telenor Arena in Oslo, Norway, June 29, 2014

"Yellow Moon" is perhaps the darkest song on *Lightning Bolt*. Stately in its composition, like musical portraiture, it is an elegy for a lost soul contemplating suicide as a response to their own insignificance in the face of an incomprehensible and uncaring world. The music creates a sense of vast expanse and distance. There is a childlike sense of awe invested throughout, both in the nursery rhyme structure of some of the lyrics and the mystical aura infused into the moon: "Moon, changing shape and shade, as we all do under its gaze." The moon has served as a metaphor for change before, eroding or restoring our innocence and acting as an impossibly distant, beckoning sanctuary—a place to escape from this world and recover what is lost. Reachable in death if not in life.

While previous Pearl Jam songs that intimated suicide stop before the execution, it is strongly implied that the subject follows through: "An echo that rings, a bullet unchained. One life, one grave joins the parade." The act is infused with empathetic dignity before Mike's solo carries their spirit away to the "yellow moon on the rise."

"Future Days"

Lyrics:	Eddie Vedder
Music:	Eddie Vedder
Live Debut:	Wrigley Field in Chicago, Illinois, U.S.A., July 19, 2013
Alternate Versions/	
Notable Performances:	Rock Werchter Festival in Werchter, Belgium, July 5, 2014
	2020 Game Awards (streaming performance), December 10, 2020 (Eddie Vedder solo performance)

There is a delicate, harvest-time beauty to "Future Days," *Lightning Bolt*'s concluding statement. An autumnal love letter that Eddie manages to address to both his family and a lost friend (Dennis Flemion of the band The Frogs—also the inspiration behind "Smile"), "Future Days" was the most nakedly sentimental song in the catalog to date. After a life of searching and struggle, of triumph and loss, "Future Days" makes clear that enduring victory is found in the love we share in the spaces we make safe.

"Future Days" recognizes love as an incalculable, unanswerable gift. It is not a question of whether you are worthy. You can't be, not all the time, but "try and sometimes you'll succeed." Love is a type of grace, and what matters most is that it is given. "Future Days" allows itself to receive and be grateful for it ("if I ever were to lose you, I'd surely lose myself"), the world love makes possible, ("everything I have found dear, I've not found by myself"), and its power to makes us whole ("all my stolen missing parts I've no need for any more"). In a violent, temperamental life, it offers solidity and stillness: "When hurricanes and cyclones raged, when winds turned dirt to dust, when floods they came or tides they raised, ever closer became us."

Love does not make the world simple. It does not make it easy. But, in the end, it is the only thing in this world that intrinsically justifies its own existence. And, from that love comes the compulsive need to struggle to preserve it, share it, hand it down, and be worthy of it.

Gigaton

Released:	March 27, 2020
Musicians:	Eddie Vedder, vocals, guitar
	Stone Gossard, guitar
	Mike McCready, guitar
	Jeff Ament, bass
	Matt Cameron, drums
Producer:	Josh Evans and Pearl Jam
Engineering:	John Burton and Josh Evans
Studio:	GT Studios in Seattle, Washington, U.S.A.; Jump Site Studios in Seattle, Washington, U.S.A.; Horseback Court in Blue Mountain, Montana, U.S.A.
Art Direction:	Jeff Ament as Al Nostreet and Eddie Vedder as Jerome Turner
Cover Art:	Paul Nicklen
Peak Chart Position:	No. 5 on the U.S. *Billboard* 200, No. 6 U.K. Top Albums

Gigaton was released in March 2020 just as the United States entered its first mass COVID-19 lockdown. Though written and recorded before COVID, it is a prescient album. It is the soundtrack for a moment of desolation that challenged many of our basic assumptions about the world and our place in it. *Gigaton* speaks to a time that laid bare the systematic failures of generations in power (including Pearl Jam's own), whose legacy is a barely functional world. *Gigaton* approaches its questions and themes from the lens of environmental collapse, the inexorable yet still contestable end of all things.

A gigaton is the unit of measurement that captures the glacier melt depicted on the album cover, and Pearl Jam appears in a red font, calling to mind a heartbeat or seismic monitor—forecasting imminent danger yet still holding on. *Gigaton* forces us into the reckoning promised since *Do the Evolution*—the long overdue recognition that the consequences of our actions echo beyond the immediacy of our lives, that we have become the villains of our story, the authorship of our destiny is more tentative than we realized, and that the next chapter will not be written by us.

Gigaton explores how to hold on when the world is on fire. The confused haze that suffocated *Riot Act* is absent, as is the personification of our ills in a singular person (Bush). *Gigaton*'s eyes are wide open, with no secrets to unlock. We know our problems, understand their cause, and can name their solution. Though he is referenced twice, Donald Trump is not regularly mentioned, and when he is, it is as a symptom or exemplar of our problems, not the cause.

While *Gigaton* is an incredibly present record, it is more reflective than urgent. Like *Lightning Bolt,* this is a middle-aged album, comfortable in its own skin, with nothing to prove and a great deal to share. But, if *Lightning Bolt* dealt with a fear of loss and was desperate to hold onto what it had, *Gigaton* confronts the end, aware of and prepared to take responsibility for the harm caused by our failures. An album authored by artists looking to exit gracefully, it is determined to be as useful as possible in the time that remains, armed with the faith that the next generation might succeed where this one failed.

Gigaton grapples with the responsibility the present owes to the future, increasingly aware that the time to make good on those debts is running out. It interrogates its own experiences, revisits its own assumptions, and finds the strength to fight for the future the next generation deserves. Nothing is romanticized, and for a band that has always privileged survival, there is the stark realization that fate cannot be outrun forever.

We have undeniably left the world in worse shape than we found it, making inevitable a terrible struggle the band always hoped the next generation would not need to fight. Yet, *Gigaton* remains an optimistic, even hopeful, album. It refuses to mire itself in anger or sadness even though these would be honest choices. It is Pearl Jam at its most humanistic, recognizing that any new beginning depends on forgiving the weakness and recognizing the humanity in ourselves and others. It has faith in our collective agency, believes in the promise of the next generation to craft a better story for themselves, and the power of this one to write a better ending to its own.

"Who Ever Said"

Lyrics:	Eddie Vedder
Music:	Eddie Vedder
Live Debut:	Doheny State Beach in Dana Point, California, U.S.A., October 1, 2021

Alternate Versions/
Notable Performances: Enterprise Center in St Louis, Missouri, U.S.A., September
                       18, 2022
                       United Centre in Chicago, Illinois, U.S.A., September 5,
                       2023

Gigaton begins with an ambient fade-in, the nagging, pulsating feeling that accompanies trying to remember a lucid dream. A pause, and then "Who Ever Said" rolls up its sleeves and churns out of the gate at a determined, rugged clip. It refuses to posture and features moments of play bursting through the serious proceedings until they are overtaken by the extended bridge that is the heart of the song.

"Who Ever Said" is reflective and self-interrogative, featuring lyrical content usually found in slower, more atmospheric compositions. It appears in a muscular, unadorned rock song as if acknowledging that the frantic doomscrolling urgency through which we experience the world refuses time for quiet reflection. Nor can we wait for the pace to slow down. We have lost the luxury of time and waiting for the perfect moment. An imperfect now is all we have.

"Who Ever Said" revolves around a slightly unwieldy, deceptively weighty statement: "whoever said it's all been said gave up on satisfaction." The first part of the clause continues to critique the narcissism of certainty, a common post-*Riot Act* theme. It is skeptical of anyone who tells you we cannot be better. And the word satisfaction is carefully chosen. To receive satisfaction is to acknowledge the payment of a debt and the righting of a wrong. To give up on satisfaction is to absolve yourself of your responsibilities to those you have harmed (directly or indirectly), and to deny others the opportunities and experiences you have enjoyed yourself.

The song's stunning bridge explores this idea with both deliberate care and rising urgency, recognizing time is running out (personally and collectively). Eddie reminds us that "all the answers will be found in the mistakes that we have made" and that moving forward requires finding the courage to reflect on our experiences and take responsibility for our actions. We know how to be better than we are. We wait for the application of will. *Gigaton* does not spend much time exploring the specificity of our mistakes but is clear our biggest is surrendering to the seductive myth of our own powerlessness and the absolution of responsibility that follows.

There are judgmental passages where Eddie vents his frustrations against the bad faith, ignorance, and mean-spirited cruelty that undermines solidarity: "Living forward in a backwards town, I feed 'em drinks just to watch 'em drown." He confesses to both a disconnected feeling of isolation and a heart-pounding awareness of the necessity of the present until the bridge makes its peace with the need to put all past certainties behind us and build something new: "A rubble of commandments in the road, step aside." "Who Ever Said" concludes with a breathless sense of empowerment, celebrating the possibilities of new horizons that open before us once we are no longer bound to the world we left behind.

"Superblood Wolfmoon"

Lyrics:	Eddie Vedder
Music:	Eddie Vedder
Additional Musicians:	Josh Evans, keys
Single Release Date:	February 18, 2020
Peak U.S. Chart Position:	4
Live Debut:	Asbury Park Waterfront in Asbury Park, New Jersey, U.S.A., September 18, 2021
Alternate Versions/ Notable Performances:	Viejas Arena, San Diego, California, U.S.A., May 3, 2022 Paycom Center in Oklahoma City, Oklahoma, U.S.A., September 20, 2022

"Superblood Wolfmoon" is a surprisingly inventive song hiding in a superficially straightforward pop/punk format. It eschews the traditional verse-chorus-bridge structure, using its chorus as an intro and bridge, and filling the rest of the song with frantic verses that tumble over each other. It is musically brash and plays like a self-aware tantrum as it rails against the unfairness of a world that gives and takes without rhyme or reason. The singer feels entitled to clarity they will never receive, sympathizing with the all-too-human frustration stemming from the denial of that all-too-human need.

"Superblood Wolfmoon" offers a series of epigrammatic insights into the root causes of and solutions to our existential dislocation. At its heart are a powerful loss, a haunted need, and a death during the solar phenomena of a superblood wolfmoon—a combination of a total lunar eclipse (supermoon or blood moon) and the common wolf moon nickname for January's full moon. But, beyond the singular loss is a larger awareness that time will cost us everything, that "this life I love is going way too fast." There is an inability to process this totalizing injustice ("I don't know anything, I question everything"), and a mounting fear that the world is beyond our ability to master and control. When Eddie sings, "The world kept a spinning, always felt like it was ending, and love notwithstanding, we are each of us fucked," he calls into question a central premise of much of the catalog—that our actions can make a difference.

And yet, "Superblood Wolfmoon," like *Gigaton*, remains fundamentally optimistic in orientation. There is a commitment to "focus on your focusness" and "hoping that our hope dies last." There is an indefatigable spirit to "Superblood

Wolfmoon" that manages to be powerful without fetishizing its own power, and a matter-of-fact willingness to carry on despite what life throws at us. It celebrates the act of refusing, of taking punches and getting back up, and recognizing that making it through today without surrendering offers us the chance to try again tomorrow. "Superblood Wolfmoon" reaches that conclusion through pig-headed stubbornness and a refusal to linger in its lost spaces.

"DANCE OF THE CLAIRVOYANTS"

Lyrics:	Eddie Vedder
Music:	Jeff Ament, Matt Cameron, Stone Gossard, Mike McCready, and Eddie Vedder
Additional Musicians:	Matt Cameron, drum program; Jeff Ament, keys and guitar; Stone Gossard, bass, Mike McCready, percussion
Single Release Date:	January 2, 2020
Peak U.S. Chart Position:	17
Live Debut:	Asbury Park Waterfront in Asbury Park, New Jersey, U.S.A., September 18, 2021
Alternate Versions/ Notable Performances:	*All In Washington: A Concert for COVID-19 Relief* (streaming performance), June 24, 2020 Moody Centre in Austin, Texas, U.S.A., September 19, 2023

"Dance of the Clairvoyants" is a singular moment in the catalog, leaning into untapped musical influences while still capturing the familiar yearning for authenticity at the heart of their best work. The Talking Heads are front and center, with Eddie doing a credible David Byrne pastiche during the verses. They are an appropriate touchstone for this song, serving as both a guide and influence.

Pearl Jam has always been at its best looking for answers rather than sharing them, and it has been a long time since a song spent so much time searching. The lyrics embrace how unknowable the world remains even after a lifetime of struggling to force meaning upon it. The patterns in the chaos need to be felt, rather than understood. "Dance of the Clairvoyants" embraces the constricting imperfection and confusion inherent in the world without surrendering to it. It is about learning to let go of the anger and release the tension we carry with us, and it counsels giving ourselves the grace to be a work in transition. It takes on faith that there is light at the end of a long darkness, and if we keep circling, we inch ever closer to it.

"Dance of the Clairvoyants" warns that our confusion, our commitments, and the love that grounds them are "imperceptibly big, big as the ocean, and equally hard to control," so you must "save your predictions and burn your assumptions." As we are warned in the chorus, "expecting perfection leaves a lot to ignore/endure." We expect perfection when we try to force a person, a relationship, an institution, or a world into a prescribed set of expectations. Life is too vast and unknowable to be quantified and schematized in that way. If perfection is our standard, we will find ourselves constantly disappointed, and disappointment becomes absolution.

There is a claustrophobic recognition of the world collapsing around us: time running out, options closing, and being overwhelmed by the vastness of what we are unable to control "when the past is the present and the future's no more. When every tomorrow is the same as before." The sense of disconnect builds throughout as we remain "stuck in our boxes, windows open no more collecting up the forget-me-nots, not recalling what they're for," until the song climaxes with a moment of spiritual surrender, a willingness to let go and let the world wash over you, allowing yourself to be reborn in each moment, and absolving yourself of the paralyzing need to control everything rather than simply live and act upon that one moment: "Stand back when the spirit comes."

"Dance of the Clairvoyants" promises that there are still mysteries out there, layers upon layers just below the surface waiting to be discovered. Our promise is not exhausted yet, and not being able to make everything right does not mean you have failed. The key is to find something and imbue it with all the meaning you can, while you can.

"QUICK ESCAPE"

Lyrics:	Eddie Vedder
Music:	Jeff Ament
Additional Musicians:	Jeff Ament, guitar, keys, and drum loop; Brendan O'Brien, keys
Single Release Date:	March 25, 2020
Peak U.S. Chart Position:	32
Live Debut:	Asbury Park Waterfront in Asbury Park, New Jersey, U.S.A., September 18, 2021
Alternate Versions/ Notable Performances:	Doheny State Beach in Dana Point, California, U.S.A., September 26, 2021
	Hyde Park in London, England, U.K., July 8, 2022

There is a dream-like quality to the oddly placid ferocity of "Quick Escape." Eddie's cautionary cries are softened and humanized by the warm harmonizing underneath them. Mike and Stone's air raid siren solos and Jeff's thundering bass draw attention to the impending apocalypse but are not the moment itself. Trump is explicitly referenced, but whereas prior references to George Bush were personal—references to the man himself—Trump himself is conceptualized as the personification of a particularly noxious idea: our basest, most self-destructive tendencies. In the face of what is worst in all of us, what else can we do but run away? Eddie spends the song fleeing, only to realize that there is no escape, the destination is empty, and we carry within us the seeds of our perpetual ruin ("And we think about the old days, of green grass, sky, and red wine. Should've known so fragile and avoided this one-way flight"). By trying to outrun or hide from what we hate and fear, we sacrifice the chance to change it.

Gigaton seeks peace and acceptance as a fulcrum for change. "Quick Escape" slaps you out of complacency and into focus, and then it's time to take a breath and get to work.

"ALRIGHT"

Lyrics:	Jeff Ament
Music:	Jeff Ament
Additional Musicians:	Matt Cameron, guitar; Jeff Ament, keys and kalimba; Josh Evans, drum program
Live Debut:	Doheny State Beach in Dana Point, California, U.S.A., September 26, 2021
Alternate Versions/ Notable Performances:	Ziggo Dome in Amsterdam, Netherlands, July 25, 2022 Paycom Center in Oklahoma City, Oklahoma, U.S.A., September 20, 2022

"Alright" is that breath, the aural equivalent of ethereal heat lightning on a warm summer night, illuminating and oddly calming in its quiet grandeur and understated drama. Eddie's performance is sympathetic and comforting. The music sustains a curious electric edge, enough to raise goosebumps but not enough to shock. When Eddie sings, "it's alright to shut it down, disappear in thin air," there is just enough magic and mystery to make you believe in the possibility.

Jeff's lyrics focus on finding peace within yourself, carving out a space to breathe within the swirling madness and failing certainty of our times: "If your heart still beats free, keep it for yourself." It absolves us of responsibility for everything ("when you want to run and leave some part unrevealed") so we can take responsibility for something. It is an anchoring sentiment, embedded in a dream, and segues into "Seven O'Clock"'s moment of awakening.

"Seven O'Clock"

Lyrics:	Eddie Vedder
Music:	Jeff Ament, Stone Gossard, Mike McCready, and Eddie Vedder
Additional Musicians:	Eddie Vedder, keys; Josh Evans, keys and drum program
Live Debut:	Asbury Park Waterfront in Asbury Park, New Jersey, U.S.A., September 18, 2021
Alternate Versions/ Notable Performances:	Oakland Arena in Oakland, California, U.S.A., May 13, 2022 (Richard Stuverud filling in on drums) United Centre in Chicago, Illinois, U.S.A., September 7, 2023

"Seven O'Clock" is Pearl Jam's longest song and *Gigaton*'s centerpiece, defining its stakes. Expansive and grounded, inspiring and practical, "Seven O'Clock" understands that a dream's power is found in the real-world footprints it leaves behind. A thematic callback to "Quick Escape," it reminds us that "all the lies we could have had" are distant illusions that distract us from the work at hand.

"Seven O'Clock" is a spiritual inversion of "Sleight of Hand." "Sleight of Hand" is a deeply claustrophobic song despite its expansive feel. Freedom is found in dreams because life is a prison. "Seven O'Clock" emphatically rejects this perspective, the singer waking with a perfect recollection of a beautiful dream of a better world and the will to carry it forward.

> Moved on from my despondency and left it in the bed.
> Do I leave it there still sleeping or maybe kill it better yet?
> For this is no time for depression or self-indulgent hesitance.
> This fucked up situation calls for all hands, hands on deck.

The verses flow with a gentle, steadfast confidence as they assess the mess we have made of the world, take ownership of our mistakes, and commit to doing something about it: "We saw the destination, got so close before it turned. Swim sideways from the undertow and do not be deterred." It is the most humanistic song on Pearl Jam's most humanist album. It does not flinch from the worst in us and loves us despite and maybe because of our failures—since they are what make us human. The singer takes responsibility for his own thoughtless and unintentional inhumanity, and it is hard not to read an environmental message into lyrics like:

> Caught the butterfly, broke its wings, and put it on display.
> Stripped of all its beauty once it could not fly high away.
> Still alive like a passerby overdosed on gamma rays
> Another God's creation destined to be thrown away.

Larger systemic problems are embodied once again in the personage of Trump. But, even here, there is sympathy and understanding, if not empathy—resistance to needed change manifesting in the clutching fear of losing one's place in the world and the inability to come to grips with our inevitable obsolescence. That could be any of us without someone to help us make peace with our own impermanence, and inspire us to leave something lasting behind.

Moving from the reality of the verses back to the dreamscape of the chorus, the music grapples with the juxtaposition as the singer draws comfort and inspiration from dreams to steel himself for the ugliness of our reality and to find the will to change it. To ensure "there's still a fire in the engine room."

"Seven O'Clock" ends with the repetitive charge, "Much to be done." It is less a call to arms than it is a call to punch your timecard and begin.

"Never Destination"

Lyrics:	Eddie Vedder
Music:	Eddie Vedder
Additional Musicians:	Josh Evans, keys
Live Debut:	Asbury Park Waterfront in Asbury Park, New Jersey, U.S.A., September 18, 2021
Alternate Versions/ Notable Performances:	Scotiabank Arena in Toronto, Ontario, Canada, September 8, 2022
	Moody Centre in Austin, Texas, U.S.A., September 19, 2023

Although "Never Destination" occupies the now familiar position of breather track, it is thematically integrated into *Gigaton* more explicitly than its peers. Eddie's rapid-fire lyrics and the breakneck pace of the music stand in defiant opposition to the exhaustion of the times: "Don't wanna believe it, these endless miles/lies, never destination, just more denial." "Never Destination" features some of Eddie's more successful uses of surfing as a metaphor for life's impossible challenges, the smallness of an individual facing down vast and overwhelming odds: "off in the distance, leviathans, 50 foot and breaking on our innocence." Victory is found in a brief coexistence with forces that cannot be mastered and the willingness to keep getting up every time a wave knocks you down. The singer is overwhelmed ("an angry sea, an ocean in my eyes, the waves are rolling, I'm becoming blind"), and yet the struggle to survive offers newfound clarity, an awareness of the illusions that impede our forward progress. And, in a winking Tom Petty-inspired outro, there is a recognition that we can draw strength to endure from the right kinds of illusions, the dreams that bridge the gaps between us and restore our faith in ourselves.

"Take the Long Way"

Lyrics:	Matt Cameron
Music:	Matt Cameron
Additional Musicians:	Matt Cameron, guitar, drum program, and vocals; Meagan Grandall, backing vocals
Studio:	Drums and backing vocals were recorded at the Ballad Baitshop in Seattle, Washington, U.S.A.
Live Debut:	Asbury Park Waterfront in Asbury Park, New Jersey, U.S.A., September 18, 2021
Alternate Versions/ Notable Performances:	Gärdet Park in Stockholm, Sweden, July 3, 2022 Xcel Energy Center in St. Paul, Minnesota, U.S.A., September 2, 2023

Matt Cameron's "Take the Long Way" is an outlier track on *Gigaton*, and is certainly the most Soundgarden-adjacent Pearl Jam has ever sounded. There are hints of danger, and a catchy chorus featuring the first female backing vocals on a Pearl Jam album (Lemolo's Megan Grandall). There is an intentionality to everyone's performance absent elsewhere on an imprecise album, and there is a hefty dramatic sweep to the bridge and outro.

Lyrically, "Take the Long Way" explores deep and enduring connections between people, though these are not always symbiotic. There are intimations of emotional abuse—not overtly hostile actions as much as hubristic certainty that the partner will always be there, waiting to take them back. "Take the Long Way" is written from the perspective of a person returning home, fully expecting to be welcomed with open arms. There are elements of possession in the lyrics ("plant a seed in your mind, what's yours is mine"), seconded by the music, which offers a warning of the implied toxicity in the relationship. "Take the Long Way" stands in sharp, possibly deliberate contrast to an album that specifically rejects entitlement and privilege, and it is easy to imagine it being about social or environmental relationships as surely as personal ones.

"Buckle Up"

Lyrics:	Stone Gossard
Music:	Stone Gossard
Additional Musicians:	Jeff Ament, piano; Stone Gossard, percussion and vocals; Josh Evans, piano
Live Debut:	Doheny State Beach in Dana Point, California, U.S.A., October 1, 2021
Alternate Versions/	

Notable Performances: Centre Vidéotron in Quebec City, Quebec, Canada,
                             September 1, 2022
                             Xcel Energy Center in St. Paul, Minnesota, U.S.A.,
                             September 2, 2023

The bubble bath dreamscape and recaptured childlike innocence infused into Eddie's vocals belie the complex emotional stakes of "Buckle Up." Despite the whimsy in the music and performance, "Buckle Up" grapples with generational transitions. It confronts the mortality of a parent and the discomfiting role reversal that accompanies aging. It is not surprising, then, that the music leans into the feel of childhood, grasping to hold on to something lost, never to return.

It is not simply that "Buckle Up" wrestles with loss and longing. It is a song of goodbyes, but it is not saying goodbye to the person as much as what they represent. When a parent can no longer be a source of benevolent authority, comforting assurance, and ancestral wisdom, those roles and responsibilities transition to the next generation regardless of whether they are prepared. The evocative chorus ("firstly do no harm, then put your seatbelt on. Buckle up") cycles between mundane and profound memories, lessons, and influences that comprise the legacy it now falls to the child to carry.

"COMES THEN GOES"

Lyrics: Eddie Vedder
Music: Eddie Vedder
Live Debut: None

The unadorned acoustic "Comes Then Goes" features a rich, enveloping fullness that feels surprisingly expansive for something intimate and confessional. Eddie's vocal performance centers on a melancholy sadness that accepts and understands rather than wallows in its pain. A quiet, lived-in authenticity lends "Comes Then Goes" its beauty and power.

"Comes Then Goes" contends with the death of someone profoundly important but distanced from them. Each verse explores how the singer imagines the unknowable state of the deceased's mind in their last moments, the complex relationship between the survivor and departed, and what it means to remain behind. The final couplet of each verse features some of Eddie's most powerful imagery, striking phrases attached to the epigrammatic truths that are the hallmark of his most effective writing.

When Eddie sings, "like images of angels in the snow, our courage melts away, it comes then goes," he recognizes that our best selves are not always in control at critical moments in our lives. We do not always have it in us to have that difficult conversation, to reach out and ask for or offer help. Retreating from the challenge of being there for others can have tragic consequences, but it is an altogether human response.

Elsewhere, the cold softness of snow is replaced by harder, calculating language: "Divisions came and troubles multiplied. Incisions made by scalpel blades of time." The cold logic of mathematical certainty. The clean cuts accrued as inevitable byproducts of living: "Thought you found a game where you could win. It's all vivisection in the end." To vivify something is to carve into it while it is still alive. It is typically a medical or scientific procedure and adds to the clinical, dehumanizing distance imposed by these lyrics. But that detached perspective transitions to something akin to guilt when he sings, "evidence in the echoes of your mind leads me to believe we missed the signs." It invests the song with a level of tragedy underneath the sadness and the loss. If only we had looked closer. Reached out earlier.

In its final reflection, "Comes Then Goes" embraces the selfishness behind death and loss—not simply the tragedy of a life ended, but the personal, reflected loss of their absence, things left unsaid, experiences never shared, and the haunting guilt at not having made the most of the time gifted to us: "The Queen of Collections took your time. Sadness comes 'cause some of it was mine." "Comes Then Goes" wants to explore and understand, rather than judge. It recognizes that people drift apart, that they fail, and hurt each other through their action and inaction. It does not make excuses, ask for forgiveness, or expect it. It just wants to name pain, loss, and imperfection as inextricably bound up in the reality of being human and share that common experience. One that, because of its inevitability, will allow us to do better next time.

"RETROGRADE"

Lyrics:	Eddie Vedder
Music:	Mike McCready
Additional Musicians:	Stone Gossard, Mike McCready, and Brendan O'Brien, keys
Live Debut:	Doheny State Beach in Dana Point, California, U.S.A., September 26, 2021
Alternate Versions/ Notable Performances:	Royal Arena in Copenhagen, Denmark, July 5, 2022 Enterprise Center in St. Louis, Missouri, U.S.A., September 18, 2022

"Retrograde," Mike's primary songwriting contribution to *Gigaton*, features the subdued lushness hiding within broad, sweeping gestures that define his writing. Its shuffling reluctance to fully embrace the grandeur of its message creates an understated contrast with the soaring, transcendent final minutes of the song, a moment of grand catharsis recognizing the tragedy of the world, the majesty of existence, and the possibilities found within.

After several songs exploring complex relationships, we return to larger social themes, reminded that "the more mistakes, the more resolve. It's gonna take much more than ordinary love to lift this up"—an effective encapsulation of *Gigaton*'s central message. There is mystical, astrological imagery running through the lyrics, and the idea of something being in retrograde, moving backward, calls to mind early scientific attempts to understand the seeming backward orbits of the planets. The difficult lesson *Gigaton* asks us to learn is that progress is not inevitable. But, while something in retrograde is in retreat, it is part of an orbit and will move forward again. Environmental themes and images are more prominent here than at any other moment on the album, and they offer a grounded juxtaposition to the earlier astral imagery, giving color and shape to the call for action. "Retrograde" never gives up on the possibility of change and maintains its faith in future generations to find answers to the mistakes we have made: "Shout, the echo returning back but now changed."

In its final minutes, the retrograde reverses, as Eddie sings, "hear the sound in the distance now. Could be thunder or a crowd." The theme of transformation running through the album makes the moment feel natural, almost inevitable. The music opens into something cleansing and triumphant, swelling as Eddie's elemental voice comes in from far away, soaring and majestic, convincing us a better world is possible if we can collectively hold on to that moment, lingering just long enough to plant a seed before fading out into the ethereal vastness of possibility. It feels like an appropriate moment to close the album, but also a little too clean. "Retrograde"'s message is too cyclical and passive for the depths of the challenges we face and the role we must play in rising to meet them.

"RIVER CROSS"

Lyrics:	Eddie Vedder
Music:	Eddie Vedder
Additional Musicians:	Eddie Vedder, pump organ; Jeff Ament, kalimba; Josh Evans, keys
Live Debut:	Doheny State Beach in Dana Point, California, U.S.A., September 9, 2017 (Eddie Vedder solo performance)
Alternate Versions/ Notable Performances:	*One Word: Together at Home* (streaming performance), April 18, 2020 (Eddie Vedder solo performance) American Express presents British Summer Time, Hyde Park in London, U.K., July 9, 2022

"River Cross" is Eddie's most naked and plaintive performance on *Gigaton*, the first song that allows him to truly wear his miles. Within that honesty lies the alchemy that transforms sentimentality into truth. It is a simple song, richly decorated and played with a quiet, enveloping dignity.

"River Cross" is the closest Pearl Jam has ever come to writing a prayer, and *Gigaton* is an atheist's prayer to humanity. Despite the world and the people in it letting us down time and time again, Pearl Jam's music has never abandoned the belief that we must not give up on ourselves, that we can be better than we are, and that our shared future depends on it.

The river in the metaphor is a barrier, and the song confronts the stark and awful reality that the other side—the dreams we have for ourselves, for our children, and our world—drifts farther and farther away. The struggle is harder. The challenges are greater. The world is scarier. The river is rising, widening: "Drifting in the undertow. Can't spot a figure on dry land. And afterthoughts of safety, when in truth, none to be had."

It names the powerlessness we all feel, "living beneath a lion's paw, knowing nothing can be tamed." And, later, "folded over, forced in a choke hold, outnumbered and held down." But, at the end of everything, the persistent refusal to give up endures. We still have all we need, if only we embrace our liminal power. When Eddie sings, "and all this talk of rapture, look around at the promise now. Here and now," we remain the promise he sings of. Every horror the world inflicts upon us, that we inflict on each other, is offset by acts of kindness and compassion and impossible love. They always have been. Absent any other touchstone, we have each other, and always will.

"River Cross" could have featured a soaring conclusion like "Retrograde," but its quiet mantra is more honest, a defiant call to "share the light" and stubborn insistence that the world "can't hold me down," before shifting to the collective "won't hold us down." Throughout Pearl Jam's thirty-year journey, for all the confessional, semi-autobiographical lyrics, it has never been about them. It is about us. It has always been about us. The water is rising, but we can cross the river.

There is still time.

Dark Matter

Released:	April 19, 2024
Musicians:	Eddie Vedder, vocals, guitar, piano, backing vocals
	Stone Gossard, guitar
	Mike McCready, guitar, piano
	Jeff Ament, bass, guitar, baritone guitar
	Matt Cameron, drums, percussion
	Josh Klinghoffer, piano, keyboards, guitar
	Andrew Watt, guitar, piano, keyboards
Producer:	Andrew Watt
Engineering:	Paul LaMalfa and Marco Sonzini with John Burton
Studio:	Shangri-La Studios in Malibu, California, U.S.A.; GT Studios, Seattle, Washington, U.S.A.; Henson Studios, Los Angeles, California, U.S.A.; and Jump Site Studios, Seattle, Washington, U.S.A.
Art Direction:	Eddie Vedder as Jerome Turner, Jeff Ament as Al Nostreet, and Stone Gossard as Carpenter Newton
Cover Art:	Alexandr Gnezdilov
Peak Chart Position:	No. 5 on the U.S. Billboard 200, No. 2 U.K. Top Albums

The 2024 *Dark Matter* tour has just begun at the time of publication, and we have declined to identify notable performances for most songs.

Gigaton recognized in its political, environmental, and personal themes that time is running out. The window for Pearl Jam's generation to leave a meaningful legacy, to be worthy of its potential and make good on its promise, is rapidly closing. It was an introspective record that sought to reawaken a fighting spirit within itself. A refusal to surrender to its collective failures, or to abandon the hope that things can get better.

Dark Matter is the validation of *Gigaton*'s questing spirit. It feels fresh and vital, achieving the fusion of wisdom borne of experience and transformative spirit of youth Pearl Jam has been searching for since *No Code*. In many ways, *Dark Matter* occupies a similar space to *Yield* and *Backspacer*. But while *Yield* has undercurrents of trepidation and guilt it tries to ignore, and *Backspacer* often forces a false dichotomy between reflection and immediate experience, *Dark Matter* can reflect within the moment. It is an incredibly open-hearted album that can hold two contradictory thoughts within itself at the same time. Every song owns its fear and embraces its joy. Each composition grapples with history and dreams of possibility. It understands the end is coming and the future is forever. More than any prior Pearl Jam album, *Dark Matter* embraces the totality of our lived experience.

Dark Matter is an album about time, connection, and purpose. It is about fearing the end before the work is finished. It is about renewal, and continuity, found and nurtured through the legacy we leave in the people whose lives intertwine with our own. It tries to resolve the contradiction between living fully in the present while recognizing that things must change. These are not new themes, but *Dark Matter* manifests them in a more visceral way than the cerebral *Gigaton*, and with a broader field of vision than *Backspacer* and *Lightning Bolt*. It strikes an impressive balance between emotional specificity and contextual generality, and like *Riot Act* and *Pearl Jam*, features songs about relationships that can be simultaneously personal and social/political.

This focus on connection, on relationships, is manifested in much of Eddie's post-*Pearl Jam* writing, as is the growing recognition that the greatest obstacle we face as individuals, and as a collective, is division. It understands that binding ourselves to each other is a necessary precondition of building something better. It is seen in the declining specificity of Eddie's political lyrics, and the increased emphasis on community and solidarity in his post-*Gigaton* concert speeches. Rather than fixate on who is right or wrong, or whose experience of oppression gets priority, *Dark Matter* focuses on challenges shared across all facets of human experience—our hopes and fears, our love and longing. Dark matter is the invisible substance of the universe, lacking discernable form and knowable only through its interaction with visible matter. Leaning into the metaphor, *Dark Matter* navigates the unseen and unsaid and undone things that define us so that we might strengthen our connections within the visible spaces where we consciously live.

It is a record that understands the generative force of a question and the fragile power of an answer. *Dark Matter* recognizes every moment holds within itself an ending and beginning, and that we get to choose. That we must choose. Our lives are a constant struggle to grasp that core truth. It is an idea Pearl Jam's music has instinctively grasped from the beginning, and always tried to articulate, but never with this much clarity and purpose.

This is partly because *Dark Matter* is the record that most successfully manifests the live energy of Pearl Jam. It allows each song to fully own an experience and see it through to the end, rather than edit itself along the way. Producer Andrew Watt committed to capturing that comprehensive immediacy in a recording process that was completed in a matter of weeks (albeit with a year between sessions).[1] The band was encouraged to come without demos, without instruments, and feed off each other's energy. It captures the feeling of solidarity, of five becoming one, of transcendent possibility, that is the hallmark of a live experience. The sense of connection that defines a Pearl Jam concert is embedded within the music itself, and it offers an immediate and intentional response to the tension between a fear of loss, a desire for continuity, and the necessity of change at the heart of each song.

Dark Matter is a remarkable record, full of life because it is haunted by death, made up of individual moments given coherence by their totality. It is afraid of endings even as it embraces the beginnings that follow. It understands that human connections are as strong as iron and as insubstantial as memory. It creates fresh scars to heal old wounds. It is the start of a closing chapter that has yet to be written and cannot be completed alone. It is an album that reaches for immortality and finds it in continuity. It hopes and mourns and searches for meaning and significance, but, above all, it dreams of love.

"SCARED OF FEAR"

Lyrics:	Eddie Vedder
Music:	Eddie Vedder, Jeff Ament, Stone Gossard, Mike McCready, Matt Cameron, and Andrew Watt
Additional Musicians:	Pool Cue, Sean Penn
Live Debut:	Rogers Arena in Vancouver, British Columbia, Canada, May 4, 2024
Alternate Versions/ Notable Performances:	Pearl Jam Headquarters in Seattle, Washington, U.S.A., April 22, 2024 (broadcast via *The Howard Stern Show*)

"Scared of Fear" begins with an ambient introduction modeled after "Master/ Slave," and while it does not reprise itself after "Setting Sun," Jeff constructed the intro off the three-chord melody that closes out the record.[2] It gives *Dark Matter* a sense of cyclical timelessness appropriate for a record looking to create a future out of its past.

"Scared of Fear" recalls the sturdy "Who Ever Said," with a classic Pearl Jam riff that feels immediately familiar without being repetitive. The band barrels forward with an infectious energy that becomes increasingly apprehensive as the song progresses. Eddie slides right into a vocal pocket that wears his years as a strength, and his grasp of melody on "Scared of Fear" (and the whole record) is effortless without being flashy.

"Scared of Fear" explores the costs of broken communication. The lyrics grapple with the fear of confrontation ("In my weakness did I somehow get too loud?") despite knowing full well the terrible cost of avoidance and silence. They interrogate the past in search of the resolve needed to break the cycles that threaten the future. *Dark Matter* is a record about creating and strengthening connections, and the fears referenced in the title are the fear of losing what you have, the fear of taking risks to preserve it, and the fear of being alone.

This transitions each time into a two-part chorus that unpacks the ease with which we trap ourselves in self-destructive cycles of blame, anger, silence, and guilt, and it is the first appearance of slight but transformative variations in lyrical construction that Eddie will use to significant effect throughout the record. "I think you're hurting yourself just to hurt me ... I think you're hurting yourself 'cause you hurt me." The pattern is understood, but there is a co-dependent fear of confrontation for fear of breaking a fraying connection. "Your secret is well and safe with me."

And there are consequences, chronicled in the evolving bitter litany of the chorus:

> We used to laugh
> We used to sing
> We used to dance
> We used to crash
> We used to drink
> We had our own scene
> We were our own scene
> We used to believe

The past tense is quietly devastating. This world is gone, a casualty of our silence. And we are charged to save what is left in the haunted and mournful bridge "Hear the voices calling..." We will have to answer, despite our fear.

The music ramps up the emotional weight and stakes as Eddie raises *Dark Matter*'s most important question: "Is this what we've become? One last setting sun?" Resolve starts to build "I'll give but I can't give up" alongside one final fear "I'll live, not long enough." There is so much to set right, and we are running out of time.

"Scared of Fear" is a hyper present song about loss and memory. And it is impossible not to read the song as part recrimination, part reflection on the self-destructive wreckage of the musical community that Pearl Jam was a part of. What obligations follow from being that final setting sun, and what happens when its light is gone? *Dark Matter* spends the rest of its runtime giving shape to an answer.

"React, Respond"

Lyrics:	Eddie Vedder
Music:	Eddie Vedder, Jeff Ament, Stone Gossard, Mike McCready, Matt Cameron, and Andrew Watt
Live Debut:	Rogers Arena in Vancouver, British Columbia, Canada, May 4, 2024

"React, Respond" fully embraces the punk/new wave fusion Pearl Jam usually edges around. The music is full of a clawing, sneering energy that tries to find healthier, more intentional ways to process anger and bitterness, guilt and fear—a frustrated and impatient song about the value of grace and patience. The pre-chorus build is surprisingly atmospheric with its plinking guitar and Eddie's haunting moan. Eddie's rap adjacent vocals are a reminder that the band shares some history with the Red Hot Chili Peppers, and the ferocious ending includes the most unhinged Eddie growl-scream since "Do the Evolution."

The lyrics initially feel political, and "You are innocent until proven innocent. You are hurting and it's so magnificent" feels like commentary on Donald Trump's post-presidential legal struggles. Yet there is little specificity, and the advice and critique offered by "React, Respond" aims at something more universal. It argues that the evils in our world stem from division, and division stems from self-doubt, self-hate, and fear. These enervating, self-inflicted wounds metastasize into anger that we instinctively inflict upon each other as a form of self-protection.

"React, Respond" challenges us to channel our pain, our frustration, and our rage into something positive in those moments "when what you get is what you don't want." Something that shares and therefore builds upon our need and our power, amplifying it into something transformative and self-sustaining. If we can "turn this anger into nuclear fission" then "the light gets brighter as it grows" and "the darkness, it recedes."

This is not easy. It takes intentionality and will, an ability to carefully respond instead of instinctively react. And it requires vulnerability and a leap of faith, but the payoff justifies the risk.

"Wreckage"

Lyrics:	Eddie Vedder
Music:	Eddie Vedder, Jeff Ament, Stone Gossard, Mike McCready, Matt Cameron, and Andrew Watt
Single Release Date:	April 17, 2024
Peak U.S. Chart Position:	1 (*Billboard* Hot Hard Rock)
Live Debut:	Rogers Arena in Vancouver, British Columbia, Canada, May 4, 2024

The gently tumbling "Wreckage" creates an autumnal backdrop for its bittersweet musings, a welcome respite after *Dark Matter*'s stormy beginnings. The music moves forward while standing still, trapped in regret as life passes by. "Wreckage" has some of the most forlorn lyrics on the record, but the performances manifest an insistence to learn from "the mistakes we all make and perfectly repeat" reminding us failure is a precondition of deep and lasting growth.

"Wreckage" is a song about life after loss, and the patterns in our lives that lead us there. There is a sense of inevitability that runs through "Wreckage," as thoughts in darkened days spool out into darkened weeks and beyond. There is a palpable sense of longing for something we cannot get back, the understated beauty of its gliding melody masking some of the more quietly apocalyptic lyrics on *Dark Matter*:

Combing through the wreckage
Pouring through the sand
Surrounded by the remnants
What we could and couldn't have
Raking through the ashes
Falling through my hands
Charcoal on the faces in the
Burned up photographs

Eddie also leans into familiar water imagery as something destructive, uncontrollable, unknowable. "How you are like the sun hiding somewhere beyond the rain … rivers overflowing, drowning all our yesterdays." And in the final regretful moments before the first chorus, he pines "I've only ever wanted for it not to be this way, but you're now like the water and the water will find its way."

There is loss in the performance, and remorse, but not grief. It would be easy to lean into that feeling, especially as the singer is shouldering responsibility for the loss, but "Wreckage" is focused on what comes next, "holding out, holding on," and learning one of *Dark Matter*'s central lessons:

Visited by thoughts
And not just in the night
That I no longer give a fuck
Who is wrong and who's right
This game of winner takes all
And all means nothing left
Spoils go the victor
And the other left for dead

Within any conflict, especially between those we love or need, there is a point at which the cost of winning is so high, the damage so catastrophic, it is indistinguishable from losing. The word "wreckage" is significant. This is a song of loss, but not absence. Absence would be easier and cleaner, but not better. Absence is a break in continuity. Wreckage lingers. It remains. It occupies space. You cannot passively forget. You must actively clear it away or fold it into what comes next. *Dark Matter* insists that there are opportunities in the mistakes we have made if we are brave enough to interrogate them. And as "Wreckage" reaches its climax it commits to finding them, "combing through the wreckage."

"DARK MATTER"

Lyrics:	Eddie Vedder
Music:	Jeff Ament, Stone Gossard, Eddie Vedder, Mike McCready, Matt Cameron, and Andrew Watt
Single Release Date:	February 13, 2024
Peak U.S. Chart Position:	1 (*Billboard* Hot Hard Rock)
Live Debut:	Rogers Arena in Vancouver, British Columbia, Canada, May 4, 2024
Alternate Versions/ Notable Performances:	Dark Matter (Instrumental): B-side of single

"Dark Matter" is a pulsing earthquake of a song, its music all shimmery tremors and seismic shocks. Within the percussive drama (featuring one of the most visceral solos on the album), it continues to explore the costs of running from and refusing to take responsibility for relationships. Its dark matter is the baggage (social, interpersonal, internal, political, structural) that prevents us from seeing each other ("steal the light from your eyes") or empathizing with each other ("drain the blood from our hearts"). It is the disassociated experience of dividing ourselves into tribes that leaves no one feeling satisfied, safe, or whole. We are left "eroding away" and "pulling apart," and Eddie's voice is rich with a resigned, weary sadness—unable to stop it. Just bear witness.

"Dark Matter" builds masterfully in its pre-chorus as Eddie's voice takes on a pleading edge and he calls for us to see through the dark matter into the messy, interdependent consequences of our division and distance, a world in which no one takes responsibility (or accountability) for anyone else, leaving us all to suffer as a result. "It's strange these days when everyone else pays for someone else's mistake." Power is not equal. Responsibility is not equal. But we all own the consequences, and to a lesser extent, the cause.

The longer "Dark Matter" goes on the less measured it becomes. There is a rising intensity as the music and lyrics begin to feel extractive. A blunt drill powered by brute, wrenching force. Painful, destructive, outrageous. The performance captures the experience of living in a world not designed for living well. This is not presented as a revelation. It plays instead like a confirmation of known grievances that must nevertheless be named. The central dark matter image makes sense in this context—the hidden substance that makes up our world is our profound alienation from each other. Oppositional and totalizing, but only so long as it remains invisible.

"WON'T TELL"

Lyrics:	Eddie Vedder
Music:	Eddie Vedder, Jeff Ament, Stone Gossard, Mike McCready, Matt Cameron, and Andrew Watt
Live Debut:	Rogers Arena in Vancouver, British Columbia, Canada, May 4, 2024

"Won't Tell" is the fullest expression of the pop sensibilities embedded throughout *Dark Matter*, a song that evokes U2 in both its aspirations and its chiming, climactic guitars. Beautiful, sly, seductive, bombastic, it possesses moments that feel genuinely glorious as they reveal romantic impulses hiding in plain sight.

"Won't Tell" is based on a dream of Jeff's that Eddie reworked into a dream of his own.[3] Although there is a tangible immediacy to the music, it evokes an ethereal longing that reaches beyond what is in front of it—stretching out into dreams with confidence it can bring something back capable of unlocking "the chains in my heart." Some secret truth that makes the world understandable, that restores what was taken or creates what was never there. Something to make us finally whole, and finally free. A perfect and enduring human connection in an imperfect and transient world.

It is just a dream. Our lives will never be without loss and absence. But "Won't Tell" embraces the beauty of desires we cannot fully name, cannot completely describe, and cannot hold for long, yet feel achingly real in the fleeting moments we can grasp them:

> As she smiled and played a minor chord
> In a key I never heard before
> One song and it was done.

The song fades, but we can try to carry its clarity with us. The key that unlocks our heart, that opens it to change, is the recognition that our hopes and needs will never be fully satisfied, and that this is okay. Perfection is impossible, but when we "allow for a bit of grace" we can finally embrace the beautiful, restorative purity of an imperfectly realized dream. It is a generative fire that burns safely, always:

> For in my dream you told
> Me to let the longing go
> And the promise I still hold
> Won't tell a soul

If we hold onto that dream, there will always be something waiting for us. Secret, secure, and forever ours and ours alone.

"UPPER HAND"

Lyrics:	Eddie Vedder
Music:	Eddie Vedder, Jeff Ament, Stone Gossard, Mike McCready, Matt Cameron, and Andrew Watt
Live Debut:	Rogers Arena in Vancouver, British Columbia, Canada, May 4, 2024

The atmospheric "Upper Hand" is a song of movements. Its opening build rises and decays in equal measure, a self-contained musical evocation of what it means to live. It transitions seamlessly into the most stately and assured performance on *Dark Matter*, a composition that feels like Pink Floyd covering "Yellow Ledbetter." And it is unapologetically swept away in a third act whose joyful climax seeks to define the end in its own terms, answerable to nothing but the love that conjured it into being.

"Upper Hand" begins with the devastatingly unadorned realization that "the distance to the end is closer now than it's ever been." And from there it grapples with the inevitability of that end. That its timing will forever be beyond our control. Time belongs to the gods and the circumstances of our endings are theirs to decide. A reality we happily avoid for as long as possible, but one that cannot be put off forever:

> I apologize, so sorry 'bout the timing
> But you know, something that I never had
> Was the upper hand

The end is coming, "the lines, once defined, getting blurry now." But what matters is whether our life was lived well ("no room left on the pages"), and on our own terms ("though the book, it may never be read by anyone, by anyone but me").

While "Upper Hand" is contemplative, it never gives into melancholy. We try our best, and do not always succeed. What matters is that we tried. And rather than surrender its spirit, it looks for ways to pass it on. To find someone who will read our story and fold it into their own. Someone who will carry our work forward and hold the memory of our love. We cannot forestall the end, but we can assign its meaning. We cannot live forever, but we do not have to fade away.

"Waiting for Stevie"

Lyrics:	Eddie Vedder
Music:	Eddie Vedder, Jeff Ament, Stone Gossard, Mike McCready, Matt Cameron, and Andrew Watt
Live Debut:	Moda Center in Portland, Oregon, USA, May 10, 2024

A small cohort of Pearl Jam songs serve as mission statements. Songs that, within the span of their runtime, encapsulate the essence of what Pearl Jam is. Not their sound, but their purpose, their transformative potential. "Alive." "Breath." "Rearviewmirror." "Corduroy." "Given to Fly." And twenty-six years after "Given to Fly," we have "Waiting for Stevie," a song that revisits the ache and longing at the heart of *Ten* with a lifetime of perspective, validating those feelings and pointing the way forward.

"Waiting for Stevie" was conceived by Andrew Watt and Eddie while waiting for (an extremely late) Stevie Wonder to record a part for Eddie's 2022 solo record *Earthlings*. It is a massive song, featuring a riff that swallows the sky, a soaring vocal that carries its message across vast expanses of time and distance, and a band performance that provides the necessary lift. Every element of the composition plays less like a song than a reclamation of some long-forgotten truth. There is a loose frame story, but like "Alive" it is important for what it evokes rather than its actual narrative. There is a young girl at a concert, plagued by anxiety, self-doubt, and uncertainty, who loses herself in the music, and in doing so finds herself. But really, it is about legitimating your fears. Understanding that even if you experience them alone, the experience of them is shared, and you are not alone. You have value. You have worth. You have power and voice. And you will, in time, discover them. Just hold on.

"Waiting for Stevie" begins with a perfect encapsulation of adolescence and one of the most powerful opening lyrics in the entire catalog: "You can be loved by everyone, and not feel, not feel loved." But this fear stays with us, always. This uncertainty is not an adolescent experience. It is a human one: "You can be told by everyone, and not hear a word from above." The same doubt. The same imposter syndrome. The truths we cannot feel, and the powerlessness that follows. This is who we are. All of us.

We look for a source of meaning to validate and empower us. To help us feel, for just a fleeting moment, like the people we wish we were or could become. The people we cannot see that we truly are. And we find this in the music we share with each other:

Swallowed up by the sound
Cutting holes in the clouds
Finds herself in the song
Hears her own voice rising

Music is something celestial, descending so that we might elevate ourselves. It is empowerment. It is connection. It is the ascendance achieved through the experience of music, and the people who made it, and the community that forms around it. As each person lifts their own voice they carry others with them. A collective act of self-creation whose power is infinite.

"Waiting for Stevie" addresses the self-defeating, cyclical fear that you are less than. That you are diminished. That the best part of yourself is a lie, rather than the core of who you are. "You can relate, but still can't stop or conquer the fear you are what you're not." Other lyrics explore similar dynamics. The fear that you are less than your potential, your value, your worth. The need to love, to trust, the need to have something to give and to know that it will matter.

The song structure is unconventional, featuring a hybrid verse/chorus construction and the ghost of a bridge before resetting for a second half overtaken by a roaring solo that punctuates an already overloaded emotional experience. And all the while Eddie's mantra embeds itself underneath the music: "You can be loved. You can be love." You are not alone, and what you can give means more than you can know.

Dark Matter feels like a live album, and "Waiting for Stevie" is a perfect distillation of the communal transcendence of Pearl Jam's live experience. It is the first time you pumped your fist during an "Alive" solo. It is the first time you closed your eyes as Eddie sang the opening notes of "Release." Your first "Better Man" sing along. Your first "hallelujah" during "Do the Evolution." The first time you joined the climax of "Black." A lived experience. A shared experience. A perfect experience. And while it does not last, you carry the echoes with you, a memory of strength to call upon in times of weakness and doubt.

The heart of "Waiting for Stevie" is the heart of Pearl Jam. The elemental reciprocity of love.

There is a beautiful interlude that follows "Waiting for Stevie." A badly needed moment to take a breath as Eddie sings "Be mighty. Be humble. Be mighty humble." A reflection on the power, privilege, and responsibility of having a voice and the opportunity to share it.

"Running"

Lyrics:	Eddie Vedder
Music:	Eddie Vedder, Jeff Ament, Stone Gossard, Mike McCready, Matt Cameron, and Andrew Watt
Additional Musicians:	Backing vocals, Jeff Ament, Andrew Watt, and Mark Smith
Single Release Date:	March 22, 2024
Peak U.S. Chart Position:	9 (*Billboard* Hot Hard Rock)
Live Debut:	Rogers Arena in Vancouver, British Columbia, Canada, May 4, 2024
Alternate Versions/ Notable Performances:	Pearl Jam Headquarters in Seattle, Washington, U.S.A., April 22, 2024 (broadcast via *The Howard Stern Show*)

The hyper kinetic transition from the meditative ending of "Waiting for Stevie" into "Running" should not work and somehow does. "Running" needs to lower the stakes after an emotionally intense run of songs. Here the late album cooldown track is truly needed. But "Running" does not sacrifice its energy in the process. Jeff's bassline is propulsive, and the familiar punk chords are colored in by drilling guitar fills. The melody is surprisingly agile, and the gang vocals are inclusive. The bridge interjects some welcome drama, and there is a completely reckless and chaotic outro. Everyone is having a grand time, and the song knows exactly what it is.

There is a "burn it down" shrug to lyrics like "lost in the tunnel and the tunnel's getting funneled like the sewage in the plumbing 'cause we left the fucking water running" but its winking sincerity ensures it never devolves into nihilism. "Running" does not abandon the lessons on shared accountability learned in "Dark Matter." The bridge interjects some weight when Eddie fears he is "living in the shadows, crossing my fingers, a date with the gallows and a reprieve not looking lightly." Themes exploring frustration, uncertainty, the finality of endings, and the fear they will come before we are ready ensure that "Running" stays grounded and relevant despite a superficial lightness. It is frustrated and tired, but never exhausted. Movement has always been one of Eddie's primary metaphors for change and possibility, and "Running" refuses to stop. If it does, nothing changes, and we all lose.

"Something Special"

Lyrics:	Eddie Vedder
Music:	Eddie Vedder, Jeff Ament, Stone Gossard, Mike McCready, Matt Cameron, Josh Klinghoffer, and Andrew Watt
Live Debut:	Rogers Arena in Vancouver, British Columbia, Canada, May 4, 2024

"Something Special" is country-tinged, playful, and relentlessly catchy. The musicianship is lovely, and everyone completely commits to their performance, lending "Something Special" a legitimacy, if not gravitas, it might not otherwise have.

Eddie is singing to his daughters, offering a loving father's affirmation of their worth and value. The sunny presentation takes on extra resonance in the context of Eddie's familial journey—the trauma of "Alive," the longing of "Release," the anxiety cutting across *Lightning Bolt*. He explores his hopes and dreams for his children, but they are nested within a subtle bed of his fears. Underneath a sunny exterior "Something Special" is quite a bittersweet song. His birds are flying from their nest, and he is anxious to cram in every bit of advice he can before they are gone. Because the next time they need to discover strength in themselves he may not be there to help them find it.

The final lyric "we've done all we can do" is delivered with a sigh, and not of relief. Of finality. Whatever happens next is beyond his control. In a very real way, this is where he says goodbye. The care never ends. The fear never ends. The love never ends. But life is for them to manage now. He can only hope he has done enough, knowing it never can be.

"Got to Give"

Lyrics:	Eddie Vedder
Music:	Eddie Vedder, Jeff Ament, Stone Gossard, Mike McCready, Matt Cameron, and Andrew Watt
Live Debut:	Rogers Arena in Vancouver, British Columbia, Canada, May 6, 2024

"Got to Give" is an open-hearted and optimistically gritty homage to Springsteen and The Who, sharing DNA with Pearl Jam's other songs that use driving as a metaphor for renewal. There are echoes of the same fears as in "Scared of Fear," but with better communication. It embraces necessary conflict, seeing through the "cheap disguise" that masks the challenge of imperfect people trying to share a life. Where "Scared of Fear" floated along on anxious energy, "Got to Give" is running on both stubborn optimism and open acceptance that a life in process will always be messy and frustrating. "Whoever said love is a compromise knew you." It commits to lean into, rather than fight this:

And here I am just picking up the parts
A broken engine busted lifted up on blocks
Should have made the turn when the road got rough
But who knew?

The chorus is a series of commitments, informed by lessons learned throughout the record: "I'll be the last one standing. I'll be the first to forgive." To be vulnerable, and to care less about winning or balancing the ledger than about being together: "Give it away, empty handed. Breaks in my heart 'til something gives." "Got to Give" holds onto our fraying human connections until we are finally ready to receive core experiential truths:

> Let's get to the point
> We are all heard and seen
> Let's get to the point, we can
> We can believe
> That we are better
> Together, you and me
> Can take on anyone
> Anyone
> If you can see
> Something's got to give

There is real last stand energy to the final moments of the song that echo "Force of Nature"—a recognition that, for all its simplicity, and all its power, love is an impossibly fragile miracle. The struggle to protect it, to keep it safe and strong, is both the all-consuming work of a lifetime, and the only work worth doing.

"Setting Sun"

Lyrics:	Eddie Vedder
Music:	Eddie Vedder, Jeff Ament, Stone Gossard, Mike McCready, Matt Cameron, and Andrew Watt
Live Debut:	Rogers Arena in Vancouver, British Columbia, Canada, May 4, 2024

Pearl Jam writes three types of album closers. Some are triumphant or defiant. Some are quiet and meditative. Some are anxious and uncertain. "Setting Sun" is in the rarefied company that lives in all three spaces, at once familiar and new, like an improvisation on an old theme.

There is initially a tropical beach feel to the music of "Setting Sun," the sound of a life that has known real joy, juxtaposed against lyrics that cannot escape the existential fear of it falling apart at the end. Before the work is done. While the need remains. Even paradise cannot disconnect our perfect moments from the decay of time. And if "River Cross" was a prayer for more time, "Setting Sun" is a plea to make the most of it. The impossible longing for forever.

"Setting Sun" initially makes a quiet commitment to keep moving forward in the face of endings. It is grounded in the need for intimacy and powered by an enduring faith it can be found, if we strive to be worthy of it:

Keep knocking the door
Cause I know someone's there
I wait on the porch
Hoping someday I'll be let in
They say in the end
Everything will be okay
If it's not okay
Well then, it ain't the end

The sentiment is not dissimilar from "All or None," though it comes more from a place of hope than muscle memory. It is elevated in a chorus that ties together themes running through the record—the longing for connection, the desire to stretch the moments we share out into forever. And the recognition that forever ends, one moment at a time, until we are once again alone:

Had dreams to you I would belong
Had the dream you would stay with me 'til Kingdom Come
Turns out forever has come and gone
Am I the only one hanging on?

"Setting Sun" explores what it means to be left behind, and to be the one leaving. The lyrics and music unite in beautiful mourning over the recognition that, one way or another, we will someday lose the love we have. As the music hits its sustained peak, Eddie clings to his invocation: "If you could see what I see now, you'd find a way to stay somehow," as if willing forever into existence. For all of us. "May our days be long until Kingdom Come."

"Setting Sun" makes the impossible wish to linger on within the spaces carved out by our love. For as long as we can, for as long as we need, but not, ultimately, forever. Lives change, loves change, we change. Our lives and loves change us. And someday they must end. As the music reaches its crescendo and *Dark Matter* closes, we come to our final and most important choice. How will it end? "We could become one last setting sun" and watch our light fade. Or we can "be the sun at the break of dawn" and find a way to live on. If not in ourselves, then in the lives we touched and the love we shared. The connections we made, and the people who navigate their own paths by the light we created.

And when understood that way, it turns out there is no choice after all.

"Let us not fade."

Our shared humanity is the dark matter between us. And what we fear is its power. It forges the chains that bind us. It anchors our love. It imagines the impossible. It conquers death. It guides us through the wreckage of our world.

We just need to see it. To feel it. To be guided to it. Thirty-three years ago, Pearl Jam promised to try. Thirty-three years later, against all odds, they have kept that promise. To keep shouting until we hear. To keep shouting until we believe. Until their voice is no longer needed because we have joined in.

You are not alone.

You are loved.

Don't give up.

B-sides, Outtakes, and Non-Album Tracks

Through soundtracks, B-sides, fan club singles, and compilations, Pearl Jam has released an enormous wealth of additional material, to say nothing of their vast collection of live improvisations and cover songs. We have discussed some, but by no means all, of the most significant songs within other chapters. What follows is a comprehensive list of every original Pearl Jam song to ever receive a formal release outside of a concert album.

"Acoustic #1"
Appears on *Pearl Jam Twenty: Original Motion Picture Soundtrack*
Lyrics: Eddie Vedder
Music: Stone Gossard
Recorded date: September 1991
Release date: September 19, 2011

"All Night"
Appears on the *Lost Dogs* compilation album
Lyrics: Eddie Vedder
Music: Jack Irons, Jeff Ament, Stone Gossard,
                     Mike McCready, and Eddie Vedder
Recorded date: 1995/1996
Release date: November 11, 2003

"Alone"
Appears on the "Go" single and the *Lost Dogs* compilation album with alternative vocals (2003)
Lyrics: Eddie Vedder
Music: Dave Abbruzzese, Jeff Ament, Stone Gossard,
                     Mike McCready, and Eddie Vedder

Recorded date: March 1993
Release date: October 25, 1993

"Angel"
Appears on the 1993 Fan Club/Holiday Single
Lyrics: Eddie Vedder
Music: Dave Abbruzzese
Recorded date: September 1991
Release date: Christmas 1993

"Be Like Wind"
Appears on *Pearl Jam Twenty: Original Motion Picture Soundtrack*
Music: Mike McCready
Recorded date: 2010
Release date: September 19, 2011

"Bee Girl"
Appears on the *Lost Dogs* compilation album
Lyrics: Eddie Vedder
Music: Jeff Ament
Recorded date: October 18, 1993
Release date: October 18, 1993

"Black Red Yellow"
Appears on the *Hail, Hail* single and an alternate take appears on the *Lost Dogs*
compilation album
Lyrics: Eddie Vedder
Music: Eddie Vedder
Recorded date: 1995/1996
Release date: October 21, 1996

"Brother"
Appears on the *Lost Dogs* compilation album (instrumental) and the 2009
reissue of *Ten*
Lyrics: Eddie Vedder
Music: Stone Gossard
Recorded date: April 26, 1991
Release date: November 11, 2003 (instrumental)
                      March 24, 2009 (full song)

"Can't Deny Me"
Released digitally via *PearlJam.com*

Lyrics: Eddie Vedder
Music: Mike McCready
Recorded date: February 2018
Release date: March 10, 2018

"Chinese"
Available as bootleg recordings from the 2011 debut on SiriusXM
Lyrics: Eddie Vedder
Music: Stone Gossard
Recorded date: September 1991
Release date: December 28, 2011

"Cready Stomp"
Appears on the 2011 reissue of *Vs.*
Music: Mike McCready
Recorded date: February–May 1993
Release date: March 28, 2011

"Dead Man"
Appears on the "Off He Goes" single, the Legacy Edition of the *Dead Man Walking: Original Motion Picture Soundtrack* (as an Eddie Vedder solo track, engineered and mixed by Adam Kasper), and the *Lost Dogs* compilation album
Lyrics: Eddie Vedder
Music: Eddie Vedder
Recorded date: 1995/1996
Release date: January 11, 1997

"Dirty Frank"
Appears on the "Even Flow" single; as a bonus track on European releases of *Ten*; a promotional single for *Alive* (reissued in 2021); and an alternate take appears on the *Lost Dogs* compilation album
Lyrics: Eddie Vedder
Music: Stone Gossard, Jeff Ament, Mike McCready, and Dave Abbruzzese
Recorded date: January 1992
Release date: April 6, 1992

"Don't Gimme No Lip"
Appears on the *Lost Dogs* compilation album
Lyrics: Stone Gossard
Music: Stone Gossard
Additional Musicians: Stone Gossard, vocals

Recorded date: 1995/1996
Release date: November 11, 2003

"Drifting"
Appears on the 1999 Fan Club/Holiday Single and an alternate take appears on
the *Lost Dogs* compilation album
Lyrics: Eddie Vedder
Music: Eddie Vedder
Additional Musicians: Eddie Vedder, harmonica
Recorded date: November 30, 1999
Release date: December 1999

"Education"
Appears on the *Lost Dogs* compilation album
Lyrics: Eddie Vedder
Music: Eddie Vedder
Additional Musicians: Mitchell Froom, keyboard; Mike McCready, piano
Recorded date: 1999/2000
Release date: November 11, 2003

"Evil Little Goat"
Appears on the 2009 reissue of *Ten*.
Lyrics: Eddie Vedder
Music: Stone Gossard, Jeff Ament, Mike McCready,
                        Dave Krusen, and Eddie Vedder
Recorded date: October 20, 1990
Release date: March 24, 2009

"Falling Down"
Appears on the 2010 Fan Club/Holiday Single
Lyrics: Eddie Vedder
Music: Stone Gossard, Jeff Ament, Mike McCready,
                        Jack Irons, and Eddie Vedder
Recorded date: June 20, 1995
Release date: September 23, 2011

"Fatal"
Appears on the *Lost Dogs* compilation album
Lyrics: Stone Gossard
Music: Stone Gossard
Recorded date: 1999/2000
Release date: November 11, 2003

"Foldback"
Appears in the *Touring Band 2000* compilation film
Music:	Jeff Ament
Recorded date:	1999/2000
Release date:	May 1, 2001

"Get It Back"
Appears on the *Good Music to Avert the Collapse of American Democracy, Volume 2* benefit album
Lyrics:	Matt Cameron
Music:	Matt Cameron
Recorded date:	February 2018
Release date:	October 2, 2020

"Happy When I'm Crying"
Appears on the 1997 Fan Club/Holiday Single
Lyrics:	Jack Irons
Music:	Jack Irons
Recorded date:	February–September 1997
Release date:	Christmas 1997

"Harmony"
Appears in the *Touring Band 2000* compilation film
Music:	Stone Gossard
Recorded date:	1999/2000
Release date:	May 1, 2001

"Hitchhiker"
Appears on the *Lost Dogs* compilation album
Lyrics:	Eddie Vedder
Music:	Eddie Vedder
Recorded date:	1999/2000
Release date:	November 11, 2003

"Hold On"
Appears on the *Lost Dogs* compilation album and an acoustic demo appears on the 2011 reissue of *Vs.*
Lyrics:	Eddie Vedder
Music:	Stone Gossard
Recorded date:	March–April 1991
Release date:	November 11, 2003

"In the Moonlight"
Appears on the *Lost Dogs* compilation album
Lyrics: Matt Cameron
Music: Matt Cameron
Recorded date: 1999/2000
Release date: November 11, 2003

"Just a Girl"
Appears on the 2009 reissue of *Ten*
Lyrics: Eddie Vedder
Music: Stone Gossard
Recorded date: October 23, 1990
Release date: March 24, 2009

"Last Soldier"
Appears on the 2001 Fan Club/Holiday Single
Lyrics: Eddie Vedder
Music: Mike McCready
Recorded date: October 21, 2001
Release date: Christmas 2001

"Leatherman"
Appears on the "Given to Fly" single
Lyrics: Eddie Vedder
Music: Eddie Vedder
Recorded date: February–September 1997
Release date: December 22, 1997

"Let Me Sleep (Christmas Time)"
Appears on the first Fan Club/Holiday Single and the *Lost Dogs* compilation
album
Lyrics: Eddie Vedder
Music: Mike McCready
Recorded date: December 1990
Release date: December 30, 1991

"Of the Earth"
Appears on *Pearl Jam: Live at Third Man Records*
Lyrics: Eddie Vedder
Music: Eddie Vedder
Recorded date: June 9, 2016
Release date: July 31, 2016

"Out of My Mind"
Appears on the "Not for You" single
Lyrics: Eddie Vedder
Music: Dave Abbruzzese, Jeff Ament, Stone Gossard,
                          Mike McCready, and Eddie Vedder
Recorded date: April 2, 1994
Release date: March 21, 1995

"Olé"
Released digitally via PearlJam.com
Lyrics: Eddie Vedder
Music: Jeff Ament
Recorded date: May 2011
Release date: September 8, 2011

"Other Side"
Appears on the "Save You" single and the *Lost Dogs* compilation album
Lyrics: Jeff Ament
Music: Jeff Ament
Additional Musicians: Jeff Ament, guitar; Stone Gossard, bass
Recorded date: February–May 2002
Release date: December 9, 2002

"Olympic Platinum"
Appears on the 1996 Fan Club/Holiday Single
Lyrics: Nick DiDia
Music: Nick DiDia
Additional Musicians: Brendan O'Brien, bass; Stone Gossard, drums;
                          Nick DiDia, keyboard; Mike McCready, phone
Recorded date: 1996
Release date: Christmas 1996

"Sad"
Appears on the *Lost Dogs* compilation album
Lyrics: Eddie Vedder
Music: Eddie Vedder
Recorded date: 1999/2000
Release date: November 11, 2003

"Santa Cruz"
Appears on the 2008 Fan Club/Holiday Single
Lyrics: Eddie Vedder

Music: Eddie Vedder
Recorded date: January 2009
Release date: May 9, 2009

"Santa God"
Appears on the 2007 Fan Club/Holiday Single
Lyrics: Eddie Vedder
Music: Eddie Vedder
Additional Musicians: Jeff Ament, Wurlitzer and bells; Eddie Vedder, uketar.
Recorded date: 2007
Release date: December 20, 2007

"Strangest Tribe"
Appears on the 1999 Fan Club/Holiday Single and the *Lost Dogs* compilation album
Lyrics: Stone Gossard
Music: Stone Gossard
Additional Musicians: Stone Gossard, percussion; Eddie Vedder, piano.
Recorded date: November 30, 1999
Release date: Christmas 1999

"Sweet Lew"
Appears on the *Lost Dogs* compilation album
Lyrics: Jeff Ament
Music: Jeff Ament
Additional Musicians: Tchad Blake, Wurlitzer; Jeff Ament, vocals.
Recorded date: 1999/2000
Release date: November 11, 2003

"Thunderclap"
Appears in the *Touring Band 2000* compilation film
Music: Eddie Vedder
Recorded date: 1999
Release date: May 1, 2001

"Turning Mist"
Appears on the 2009 Fan Club/Holiday Single
Lyrics: Mike McCready
Music: Mike McCready, Jeff Ament, Matt Cameron,
                        and Stone Gossard
Additional Musicians: Mike McCready, vocals and piano; Barrett Jones, Hammond B3.
Recorded date: 2009
Release date: June 7, 2010

"U"
Appears on the "Wishlist" single and an alternate take appears on the *Lost Dogs* compilation album

Lyrics:	Eddie Vedder
Music:	Eddie Vedder
Recorded date:	February–September 1997
Release date:	May 5, 1998

"Wash"
Appears on the "Alive" promotional CD and an alternate take appears on the *Lost Dogs* compilation album

Lyrics:	Eddie Vedder
Music:	Stone Gossard, Jeff Ament, Mike McCready, and Dave Krusen
Recorded date:	January 29, 1991
Release date:	July 7, 1991

"Whale Song"
Appears on the *Music for Our Mother Ocean, Volume 3* benefit album and the *Lost Dogs* compilation album

Lyrics:	Jack Irons
Music:	Jack Irons
Additional Musicians:	Jack Irons, guitar and vocals; Eddie Vedder, EBow.
Recorded date:	February–September 1997
Release date:	August 17, 1999

"2,000 Mile Blues"
Appears on the 2009 reissue of *Ten*

Lyrics:	Eddie Vedder
Music:	Jeff Ament, Mike McCready, and Dave Krusen
Recorded date:	April 21, 1991
Release date:	March 24, 2009

"4/20/02"
Uncredited hidden track on the *Lost Dogs* compilation album

Lyrics:	Eddie Vedder
Music:	Eddie Vedder
Recorded date:	April 20, 2002
Released date:	November 11, 2003

Epilogue
Our Fandom

Single Video Theory closes with director Mark Pellington interviewing Eddie, posing the question "What does Pearl Jam mean to you?" Eddie smiles, and the video cuts away, but the absence of an answer is the answer. Anything Eddie says might undercut the legitimacy and authenticity of someone else's experience of Pearl Jam, an outcome anathema to the inclusive ethos at the heart of the band.

We approached *I Am No Guide: Pearl Jam Song by Song* in the same spirit. Every fan is drawn to a different element of Pearl Jam's music. There is a song for every moment, and every moment matters to someone. So, we tried to set aside our own preferences and approach each song on its own terms. But here, at the end of the journey, we want to share a bit of our own relationship and history with Pearl Jam and what their music means to us. Come find us at Red Mosquito (forums.theskyiscrape.com) and share your story. We would love to hear it.

Stip's Pearl Jam Journey

I subscribe to the "why say it in 100 words when you could say it in 1,000" theory of writing, but I will try and be brief. I discovered Pearl Jam through Weird Al Yankovich. It was April 1992, I was fifteen years old, and my musical tastes had not left the 1980s—Prince, Madonna, Michael Jackson, Bon Jovi, Poison. But my heart belonged to Weird Al. I watched the world premiere of his "Smells Like Nirvana" video, and laughed so hard I could barely breathe. I was vaguely aware there was a band called Nirvana, and since "Smells Like Nirvana" was so great, I decided to take a risk and buy *Nevermind* (on cassette) without knowing a single song.

And that was it. Within seconds of pressing play, grunge had killed hair metal. It was not just that I instantly had a new favorite band. Some part of me understood there was no going back. There was the before, and my first glimpse of the after. I played that tape of *Nevermind* for an entire summer. I do not think I listened to anything else.

That fall I got my first job, and with that money I purchased my first CD player. I just needed CDs. I joined Columbia House's record club to start my collection (six CDs for the price of one. What a time to be alive!) I got *Nevermind*, obviously. Madonna and Prince's greatest hits records. Some Weird Al albums. And I got *Ten,* because I heard Pearl Jam was kind of like Nirvana.

It was September 1992, and I was sixteen years old. I was in my room, doing math homework. I put on *Ten* for the first time. "Once" sounded cool—I liked the aggression. And then "Even Flow" begins and that was it. Two times in one year. A before, and an after. While *Nevermind* felt primal, *Ten* felt infinite. This is the band. I will never need another. And while my musical tastes have evolved over time, Pearl Jam has never been dislodged from its position. My all-caps FAVORITE band. The soundtrack to my life.

Pearl Jam's lyrics (the fusion of Eddie's words and voice) drew me in immediately. Because the early album booklets were so withholding it added to the mystery. No one truly knew what Eddie was saying. No one could confidently decipher him. But I knew, just knew, whatever it was, it was important. The wisdom of the ages, or at least the cheat codes a white suburban teenager needed to find his place in the world. I spent hours with headphones, carefully transcribing every muttered word. I typed up my own lyric books and made my poor dad print them at work. I was laughably wrong in some cases. Truth be told, I am still not 100 percent sure about all the words to "Corduroy." At times, I got so attached to what I thought Eddie was saying, it was a letdown to learn the actual lyrics.

I finally saw Pearl Jam live for the first time in 1996. Randall's Island, night one. Getting tickets was a hideous pain in the ass (who among us was not secretly relieved when Pearl Jam ended their Ticketmaster boycott?). Someone offered me $600 for my ticket (in 1996 dollars!), but it was priceless to me. That evening was one of the most intense and transcendent experiences of my life. I spent the night standing in a downpour and did not even notice until it stopped (during "Indifference" of all songs). I have always preferred studio albums to bootlegs, but there is nothing, absolutely nothing, better than that live experience. I have been to just under thirty shows (Uniondale in 2003 remains my favorite), and for those who organize their lives around their tour schedule, I get it. It is not the choice I made. But I absolutely understand.

My fandom has gone through phases. There was my obnoxious, imperial phase that lasted through college where I would argue, without irony, that "Bugs" had better lyrics than any Beatles song. There was the phase when I wanted my Pearl Jam serious and deep, and struggled to make space in my heart for songs like "Who You Are." There were times when I resented when Jeff, Matt, or Stone wrote lyrics, since it meant Eddie did not. In the early 2000s I discovered the Red Mosquito forum and for twenty years that community has kept my fandom activated even during the stretches where nothing is happening. The board transformed private listening into something communal. It made Pearl Jam something I could share and created a space where I could belong. It made this book possible.

There were comparative highs and lows in my love for each album. But every record has been rich in emotional insight and found a way to capture what I knew to be true and could not express myself—the longing and need that I felt and still feel. Pearl Jam has always found a way to elevate and legitimate my lived experience during every phase of my life.

Eventually, I settled into a comfortable relationship with the band's music and learned to appreciate each song as a piece of a larger puzzle, informed by the nearly 200 songs surrounding it. The meanings of these songs, or at least what they mean to me, have evolved and changed as my life has evolved and changed. But at every critical juncture Pearl Jam has been there. Not just to help me process that moment, but to create that continuity between the person I was then, the person I am now, and the person I keep trying to find. To bridge past, present, and future. It is a privilege, really, to open my heart up to a band, and take them with me as a living, breathing, changing thing. It lets me hold onto that youthful sense of possibility without having to sacrifice the wisdom gained from the life I have been privileged to live. Not everyone gets to have that experience. It means everything. It has been everything. And after thirty plus years of fandom, more than anything, what Pearl Jam means to me is gratitude.

Brandon's Pearl Jam Journey

I am sitting here, wanting to tell you how my Pearl Jam story began, and I am struggling to start the story with a mental picture that would not draw complete incredulity from my children. Listen, guys, we used to listen to music on giant boxes that we called shelf systems. I just tried to Google a picture of one, and you cannot even do that. It was a big wooden box. There was a dual tape deck in the middle for making mix tapes. The last one I made was given to my wife while we were dating. There was a CD player somewhere in there. The amplifier and equalizer were all built in. My uncle had a record player on top, but either records were not cool or I was not cool when I got mine. Oh, and did I mention the giant wood-grain speakers on either side. This was a significant piece of furniture. This was no free Spotify account on a phone that fit in your pocket. This was a commitment, and I got my first one for Christmas in 1991.

My parents gave me two CDs. Mariah Carey's *Emotions* and Boyz II Men's *Cooleyhighharmony*. Strap in folks, we've got a ways to go. Here I was (checks Chapter 1), four months after the release of the album that spawned this whole project, and I was absolutely and completely oblivious to it. Stay with me though. I was getting there. Because earlier that year, Bryan (no relation) found a dubbed cassette of Metallica's *Garage Days Re-Revisited* in a field where we were playing tackle football without pads, helmets, or even long pants and we played that tape until it barely played at all. I know, I know, the timelines don't really line up. I am not good with dates. Around this same time, I was the only honors student at my high school to skip out of AP U.S. history to take geography with the baseball coach in the corner basement room near the bathroom with all of the kids in suspension and the athletes desperately clinging to a C- average. Please don't let it worry you that I was the one put in charge of every single date in this book.

By now you're yelling at your book, "Brandon, tell us about Pearl Jam!" To you, I say, "You just read a whole book about Pearl Jam, can't you just chill out for a minute and let the story wash over you? I haven't even flown to Germany yet!" Pearl Jam first played Germany in March 1992. That has nothing to do with my story. I just wanted you to know that it is a date, and I am aware of it. I also want you to be aware that you were just yelling at a book.

OK. I went to Germany in the summer of 1992, and I developed a crush on Carli, a woman that was really far too old for me, and it is embarrassing to commit that story to text which, presumably, will be available to the whole world for a reasonable price at your favorite book store, easily purchased by her or my friend Chris who will laugh at how I changed the name. While we were hanging out in Munich, she introduced me to her musical obsession, Pearl Jam. If you are wondering why I had never heard of Pearl Jam a full year after the release of *Ten*, let me share one more story. I grew up in a fairly religious home and was not allowed to watch MTV when I was in high school. That meant that I had to sneak that channel in after school and late at night after my parents had gone to bed. Well, back then you watched MTV by setting your television to channel 3 and powering up a cable box on top. Our remote had a "Favorite" button, which automatically took you to the most-watched channel. So, when my parents hit that button and got MTV, it was extremely hard to stay on top of popular music because the cable box started going to work with my dad.

Back to Germany, I was there, giving puppy dog eyes at my crush when suddenly, the most amazing thing I ever heard was playing through the headphones of my

Sony DiscMan (still four times heavier than an iPhone). I wish there was less archaic technology in my story, but I can't help that now. I can, however, tell you that this moment was carved into my brain like the Challenger explosion or the 9/11 attacks. She skipped "Once," making the little digital number readout jump from 1 to 2, and dropped "Even Flow" on me out of the gate. No Pearl Jam virgin should have "Even Flow" dropped on them like that. It's irresponsible. It's like uploading the works of Shakespeare directly into the brain of a baby. It's too amazing to process all at once.

I had that CD on repeat for the whole rest of my trip, staying up late with it, missing subway trains because I couldn't hear people calling my name, and being a general pain in the ass as I discovered a sound and a message that I needed so badly at that time of my life. I have lived a wonderful, privileged life, but as a teen, I was struggling to find myself, and it was disheartening. Then, and the decade that followed, was the time when Pearl Jam spoke to me the most. The way *Ten* pushed against the world and everything that came before lined up perfectly with my leaving the nest and hammering out who I was. I wore out multiple CD versions of *Ten*, *Vs.*, and *Vitalogy* before leaving college.

And then came the community. The internet was new and my roommate, majoring in computer science, taught me how to code a rudimentary website. Nothing special, but enough to put pictures and animated gifs of Homer Simpson onto a Geocities site (pre-MySpace, which was pre-Facebook). It was enough to cast my Pearl Jam obsession into the stratosphere, and in the pre-Google days, Pearl Jam fans were able to forge connections along those thin threads, online bulletin boards, trading forums, Song X, and the Concert Chronology on FiveHorizons.com. It helped that this world was populated by the kindest people you could ever hope to know.

Among the Pearl Jam community were angels who would take the best handheld recording device they could afford to concerts, buy beers for the people sitting next to them in exchange for a promise not to scream, and then record the show. They would not just take that show home and listen to it; they would share it. There was a giant community of traders with an online list of shows. If you went a show and wanted a souvenir, or if you were like me and could not make it to a show because your parents wouldn't let you go to a concert that wasn't Christian rock, you could pick a show, send that person blank cassettes, and they would dub the show onto those cassettes (using those giant shelf systems from paragraph one) and mail them back to you. So, in a time when Brian was struggling to find the music venue on Randall's Island, and I was calling some backwater, third-party phone bank to get tickets to the Toledo, Ohio, show only to have the phone lines melt from the call volume, twice, I was still able to drop a cassette into my Walkman and pretend that I was right there on the floor.

When I finally saw Pearl Jam live, it was at Blossom Music Center in 1998, a gorgeous outdoor venue in the middle of what is now Cuyahoga Valley National Park, and it was an experience I wouldn't trade with anyone. "Hail, Hail" still lights me up for no other reason that it is the first song I heard while looking Eddie Vedder in the eyes. Twelve rows back on Mike's side, the best side because you get a two-fer with Jeff, I sang every lyric and never sat down. I had been listening to this band in whatever way I could, albums, cassettes, CD imports from Quonset Hut in Akron, an obscure song downloaded over a phone line probably via Napster, which meant it just ended abruptly about forty-three seconds before the end of the song, and finally, I got to hear them in the way they are meant to be heard, with 23,000 fellow fans screaming, "Hello," to an "Elderly Woman Behind the Counter in a Small Town" and thrusting our hands in the air to sing "Hallelujah" when we sing with our choir.

When I look over my Pearl Jam fandom, the band, to me, is always the thing I am finding at the end of a long search. They were the music I was looking for at the end of a lot of musical experimentation. They were at the apex of a loving, sharing community of wonderful people. They were the live experience that I wanted for years. They were even the rare collectible I was bidding up on eBay. *Riot Act* was that angry voice I wanted to hear all through the Bush Administration. *Lost Dogs* was all those songs that I struggled to find via online forums. Pearl Jam is a never-ending puzzle that brings new surprises and magic every step of the way. The influential band they mentioned in an interview could take you down a months-long path of new albums. That list of books they shared on World Book Day 2017 led to hours of reading. It is how I landed at TheSkyIScrape.com, first a community that loved Pearl Jam like I loved Pearl Jam, then a place to collect and categorize all the amazing ways that I and others have found to love this band.

It even continues for me today. As we work on this last chapter, *Dark Matter* is a slow burn for me. I had my first listen in a movie theater, and maybe the sound was not the best, but I had a hard time connecting. Even now, as the phrase, "best album since *Yield*" rings in my ears, I have not put it that high in my personal rankings, but I keep searching. I keep finding bass lines I missed and lyrics that hit right. My current favorite moment is at the beginning of "Something Special" where the song almost falls apart and does not happen just before Ed starts sing. I have opened myself up to connect to this album, and because this album is actually about connection, it is starting to happen, which makes it the perfect capstone to my Pearl Jam experience—at least until album #13 gets here.

Album Rankings (and Favorite Songs)

Stip	Brandon
1. *Vitalogy* ("Corduroy")	1. *Vs.* ("Indifference")
2. *Ten* ("Alive")	2. *Vitalogy* ("Last Exit")
3. *Vs.* ("Rearviewmirror")	3. *No Code* ("In My Tree")
4. *Dark Matter* ("Waiting for Stevie")	4. *Yield* ("Do the Evolution")
5. *Gigaton* ("Dance of the Clairvoyants")	5. *Ten* ("Porch")
6. *Backspacer* ("Force of Nature")	6. *Pearl Jam* ("Gone")
7. *Yield* ("Do the Evolution")	7. *Gigaton* ("Buckle Up")
8. *Lightning Bolt* ("Mind Your Manners")	8. *Binaural* ("Of the Girl")
9. *Pearl Jam* ("World Wide Suicide")	9. *Lightning Bolt* ("Pendulum")
10. *Riot Act* ("I Am Mine")	10. *Dark Matter* ("Wreckage")
11. *No Code* ("Red Mosquito")	11. *Backspacer* ("Gonna See My Friend")
12. *Binaural* ("Rival")	12. *Riot Act* ("Love Boat Captain")

Endnotes

Chapter 1

1 Givony, R., *Not For You: Pearl Jam and the Present Tense* (Bloomsbury, 2022), p. 89.
2 Neely, K. "Pearl Jam Come Alive," *Rolling Stone,* October 31, 1991.
3 Crow, C., *Pearl Jam Twenty* (Simon & Schuster, 2011), p. 6.
4 Come find Stip and B at forums.theskyiscrape.com/.

Chapter 2

1 A note on pronouns: Unless a character is specifically gendered in a song, *Pearl Jam: Song by Song* will use gender-neutral pronouns. It should be noted that in most cases, characters given a male gender reflect an autobiographical instinct on Eddie's part rather than a gender specific experience.
2 Buchanan, B. "Eddie Vedder Reveals Heartbreaking Real Meaning of 'Even Flow,'" *Alternative Nation,* August 10, 2018 (www.alternativenation.net/eddie-vedder-reveals-heartbreaking-even-flow-real-meaning-of-even-flow).
3 Miller, B., Nevins, A. "Richardson teen-ager kills himself in front of classmates," *The Dallas Morning News, January 9, 1991.*
4 Vedder, E. *I Am Mine,* narrated by Eddie Vedder, (Audible, 2021).
5 Cohen, J. "The Pearl Jam Q&A: *Lost Dogs,*" *Billboard,* 2003 (web.archive.org/web/20050317133911/http:/www.billboard.com/bb/specialreport/pearl_jam/pg1.jsp).
6 Vedder, E., quoted in Crow, C., *op. cit.* p. 280.

Chapter 3

1 Jones, A., *Pearl Jam—The Illustrated Story, A Melody Maker Book* (Hal Leonard Corp, 1995).
2 According to Eddie, the vocals to "W.M.A." were recorded immediately after the experience, Jones, A., cited in Givony, R., *op. cit.* p. 145.

Chapter 4

1 Vedder, E., quoted in Crow, C., *op. cit.* p. 146.
2 Givony, R., *op. cit.* p. 254.
3 Pearl Jam would go on to name a free four-and-a-half-hour radio broadcast on January 8, 1995, *Self Pollution Radio*, featuring live performances from Pearl Jam, Soundgarden, Mudhoney, Mad Season, and songs from David Grohl that would debut on the first Foo Fighters record.
4 The image is admittedly more complex and potentially problematic viewed from a 2022 lens.
5 "My $10 corduroy jacket was going for $400 from Chanel or whoever," Marks, C. "Eddie Vedder Breaks His Silence," *Spin,* January 1995.
6 Vedder, E., quoted in Crow, C., *op. cit.* p. 152.
7 *LA Times,* November 20, 1994.

Chapter 5

1 Weisbard, Eric, *et al.* "Ten Past Ten," *Spin*, August 2001.
2 *Ibid.*

Chapter 6

1 The musical influence of new drummer Jack Irons is readily apparent, who represents a dramatic stylistic departure from Dave Abbruzzese and invited Pearl Jam to experiment and redefine both their sound and identity as something sustainable in the long term.
2 *No Code*'s album cover is a collage of 144 Polaroid photographs. There is no apparent meaning, though images recur. But when the four panel Digipak is unfolded and you step back, a picture of a triangle with an eyeball in the center emerges. According to Eddie, "you have the *No Code* triangle, which means 'Do not resuscitate.' I thought that was symbolic of where we were with the group: If we're dying, let us die. Don't try to save us. We don't want to live as vegetables." Vedder, E., quoted in Crow, C., *op. cit.* p. 188.
3 The lyric comes from Wisconsin-area band The Frogs' percussionist Dennis Flemion, who wrote "I miss you already. I miss you always" in one of Eddie's notebooks. The Frogs opened for Pearl Jam, and Pearl Jam included their cover of "Rearviewmirror" on the single for "Immortality."
4 "Lukin" is a reference to Matt Lukin, a founding member of Seattle bands The Melvins and Mudhoney. When Eddie's stalker problems were at their peak, and he was not comfortable in his own spaces, he would often go to Lukin's house to drink, unwind, and escape.

Chapter 7

1 Moon, T., "Stone Gossard, Calling Off the Crusades," *Philadelphia Inquirer,* February 8, 1998.
2 "Interview with Eddie Vedder," Microsoft MusicCentral, February 1998.

3 Garbarini, V., "All For One: Pearl Jam Yield to the Notion That United They Stand and Divided They Fall," *Guitar World*, March 1998.
4 *Ibid.*
5 Brownlee, C., "Still Alive," *Seattle Sound Magazine*, March 2009.

Chapter 8

1 And, originally, it did, until Mike and Eddie deconstructed the song to make it less uplifting and inspirational. Per Eddie: "We were excited about it for a while, but when we got down to recording it, it was too nice, too right there—it was a little too close to 'Given to Fly'. We changed the tempos, and then one night, Mike and I, after working on it all day and getting frustrated, just flipped it backwards, and in about 35 minutes, it became 'Light Years'."
2 The word "together" is circled in the liner notes just in case the importance of the lyric is missed.
3 Gossard, S., quoted in Crow, C., *op. cit.* p. 234.

Chapter 9

1 Reid, G., "Eddie Vedder: Grunge control," *The New Zealand Herald*, November 9, 2002.
2 Fricke, D., "Eddie Vedder's Combat Rock," *Rolling Stone*, May 29, 2003.
3 From Eddie's introduction to "Thumbing My Way" at the February 13, 2003 show in Sydney, Australia.

Chapter 10

1 Hiatt, B., "The Second Coming of Pearl Jam," *Rolling Stone*, June 16, 2006.
2 Gundersen, E., "Pearl Jam: Life after 'Suicide'," *USA Today*, June 15, 2006.
3 Hiatt, B., *op. cit.* Eddie is referencing Johnny Ramone.
4 Vedder, E., quoted in Crow, C., *op. cit.* p. 314.
5 As Stone said, "we did consider using narration to thematically unify the album, but ultimately a less conceptual structure just felt right." Kerr, D., "Explore and not Explode," *The Skinny*, May 2006.
6 The West Memphis Three were three teenage men convicted in 1994 of the 1993 murder of three boys in West Memphis, Arkansas. Widely believed by many to be wrongfully convicted due to police and jury bias, they were released in 2011. Echols wrote these lyrics while on death row.
7 "He certainly didn't cop out and make it about somebody else, like another writer I know. One way to deal with negative energy and frustration is to kind of look within. If nothing else, effect some change in yourself. If you're in a position of feeling pretty together at that point, then you feel like you can make a contribution to society, as opposed to being a fucking wreck and just adding to the pile of destructive forces you can find yourself surrounded by. And that's exactly, verbatim, what's in the song, really. Like 'shining a human light.' That's all from Mike." Vedder, E., quoted in Crow, C., *op. cit.* p. 313.

Chapter 11

1 2007's *Into the Wild* soundtrack was Eddie's first solo album, the soundtrack for the 2007 Sean Penn film of the same name. The songs feature an open, unadorned sound, with several songs making extensive use of fingerpicking technique, especially "Guaranteed," which won a Golden Globe and nominated for a Grammy award for Best Song Written for a Motion Picture, Television or Other Visual Media. "Rise," another song from that album, received a 2009 Grammy award nomination for Best Rock Vocal Performance, Solo.

Chapter 13

1 Cohen, J., "The Spin Interview: Pearl Jam Dark Matter Producer Andrew Watt," *Spin*, April 15, 2024 (www.spin.com/2024/04/andrew-watt-pearl-jam-interview/).
2 Rose, L., "Pearl Jam's Stone Gossard and Jeff Ament," *Broken Record Podcast*, April 23, 2024.
3 *Ibid.*

Bibliography

Brownlee, C., "Still Alive," *Seattle Sound Magazine*, March 2009

Buchanan, B., "Eddie Vedder Reveals Heartbreaking Real Meaning of 'Even Flow'," *Alternative Nation*, August 10, 2018 (www.alternativenation.net/eddie-vedder-reveals-heartbraking-even-flow-real-meaning-of-even-flow)

Cohen, J., "The Pearl Jam Q&A: *Lost Dogs*," *Billboard*, 2003 (web.archive.org/web/20050317133911/http:/www.billboard.com/bb/specialreport/pearl_jam/pg1.jsp)

Cohen, J "The Spin Interview: Pearl Jam Dark Matter Producer Andrew Watt," *Spin*, April 15, 2024 (www.spin.com/2024/04/andrew-watt-pearl-jam-interview/)

Crow, C., *Pearl Jam Twenty* (Simon & Schuster, 2011), p. 6

Fricke, D., "Eddie Vedder's Combat Rock," *Rolling Stone,* May 29, 2003

Garbarini, V., "All For One: Pearl Jam Yield to the Notion That United They Stand and Divided They Fall," *Guitar World*, March 1998

Givony, R., *Not for You: Pearl Jam and the Present Tense* (Bloomsbury, 2022), p. 89

Gundersen, E., "Pearl Jam: Life after 'Suicide'," *USA Today,* June 15, 2006

Hiatt, B., "The Second Coming of Pearl Jam," *Rolling Stone,* June 16, 2006

"Interview with Eddie Vedder," Microsoft MusicCentral, February 1998

Jones, A., *Pearl Jam—The Illustrated Story, A Melody Maker Book* (Hal Leonard Corp, 1995)

Kerr, D., "Explore and not Explode," *The Skinny,* May 2006

LA Times, November 20, 1994

Marks, C., "Eddie Vedder Breaks His Silence," *Spin,* January 1995

Miller, B., Nevins, A., "Richardson teen-ager kills himself in front of classmates," *The Dallas Morning News*, January 9, 1991

Moon, T., "Stone Gossard, Calling Off the Crusades," *Philadelphia Inquirer*, February 8, 1998

Neely, K., "Pearl Jam Come Alive," *Rolling Stone,* October 31, 1991

Reid, G., "Eddie Vedder: Grunge control," *The New Zealand Heraldm* November 9, 2002

Rose, L., "Pearl Jam's Stone Gossard and Jeff Ament," *Broken Record Podcast*, April 23, 2024

Vedder, E., *I Am Mine,* narrated by Eddie Vedder (Audible, 2021)

Weisbard, E., *et al.*, "Ten Past Ten," *Spin*, August 2001